D0053301

VOICES FROM THE WORLD OF

Jane Austen

For Miranda

VOICES FROM THE WORLD OF

Jane Austen

MALCOLM DAY

D&C

David and Charles

31143007736961
823.7 Day
Day, Malcolm.
Voices from the world of
Jane Austen

A DAVID & CHARLES BOOK
Copyright © David & Charles Limited 2006

David & Charles is an F+W Publications Inc. company
4700 East Galbraith Road
Cincinnati, OH 45236

First published in the UK in 2006
Text copyright © Malcolm Day 2006

Malcolm Day has asserted his right to be identified as author of this
work in accordance with the Copyright, Designs and Patents Act, 1988.
All rights reserved. No part of this publication may be reproduced, stored
in a retrieval system, or transmitted, in any form or by any means, electronic
or mechanical, by photocopying, recording or otherwise, without prior
permission in writing from the publisher.

The publisher has endeavoured to contact all contributors of text and/or
pictures for permission to reproduce.

A catalogue record for this book is available from the British Library.

ISBN-13: 978-0-7153-2379-3 hardback
ISBN-10: 0-7153-2379-2 hardback

Printed in Great Britain by CPI Bath Press
for David & Charles
Brunel House   Newton Abbot   Devon

Commissioning Editor   Ruth Binney
Editor   Ame Verso
Copy Editor   Val Porter
Head of Design   Prudence Rogers
Designer   Sarah Clark
Design Assistant   Eleanor Stafford
Production Controller   Kelly Smith

Visit our website at www.davidandcharles.co.uk

David & Charles books are available from all good bookshops; alternatively
you can contact our Orderline on 0870 9908222 or write to us at FREEPOST
EX2 110, D&C Direct, Newton Abbot, TQ12 4ZZ (no stamp required UK only);
US customers call 800-289-0963 and Canadian customers call 800-840-5220.

Contents

Introduction

The first question anyone might ask about this book is: what was Jane Austen's world? The author of such famous works as *Pride and Prejudice* and *Emma* lived for most of her life shut away in the depths of rural Hampshire. Yet her novels give us tantalizing glimpses of a wider world and assume a knowledge of its classes, customs and habits which, though taken for granted by her contemporary readers, sometimes puzzle us today. Though she chose not to depict scenes of war, her country was actually at war for most of her life and three of her brothers saw active service; though she depicted no mob violence, her period was one of great civil unrest; and though she chose not to portray rural poverty, she was acutely aware of its depredations nearby.

The margins of Jane's world were broad. Drawing a definitive line between what is a part of her 'world' and what is not has to be discretionary, and I apologize in advance for omissions, deliberate or not, that readers feel should be included. By way of example, I would say that Lord Nelson's victory at Trafalgar in 1805 falls within Jane Austen's orbit in so far as she had two brothers in the navy, one of whom sailed in Nelson's fleet and wrote of his experiences. On the other hand, Napoleon's retreat from Moscow seven years later – though no less momentous in European history – has no 'voice' in connection with her life in Hampshire and so is not represented.

The second question one might ask of this title is: what precisely *were* the voices? The answer is that they are heard in the writings, personal or otherwise, of the people living during her lifetime, 1775 to 1817: diaries, letters, essays, travelogues, sermons, treatises, newspaper and magazine articles and notices. Letter writing was the only way of keeping in touch with loved ones who might live several days' journey away. Jane herself corresponded with her many siblings, especially Cassandra, and her relatives, some of whom lived abroad, in Paris, Bengal and the West Indies. The famous and the infamous have their say, from king and parliament to protesters clamouring for reform in a time of widespread prejudice and injustice. Voices of invention vie with those of traditionalists in every sphere of activity: in the arts, in science, medicine, industry and in the daily turn of society. Etiquette, fashion, education and religious belief were all subjects of comment and each had their champions.

And, of course, this was all grist to the author's mill. Some of the 'voices' are taken from the mouths of Jane's characters. Her novels, though works of fiction, carry such a tone of authenticity that they make a valuable contribution as examples of what was said and done in her day. Indeed, so accurate were her portrayals that a damning review of her fiction in a literary journal, *The British Critic*, in 1818 considered her work to be so true to life that it lacked imagination:

Not only her stories are utterly and entirely devoid of invention, but her characters, her incidents, her sentiments, are obviously all drawn exclusively from experience ... She seems to have no other object in view, than simply to paint some of those scenes which she has herself seen, and which every one, indeed, may witness daily.

Her heroes and heroines make love and are married, just as her readers make love, and were or will, be married ... She seems to be describing such people as meet together every night, in every respectable house ... and to relate such incidents as have probably happened, one time or other, to half the families in the United Kingdom.

She makes her *dramatis personae* talk; and the sentiments which she places in their mouths, the little phrases which she makes them use, strike so familiarly upon our memory as soon as we hear them repeated, that we instantly recognize among some of our acquaintance, the sort of persons who she intends to signify, as accurately as if we had heard their voices ... Her merit consists altogether in her remarkable talent for observation; no ridiculous phrase, no affected sentiment, no foolish pretension seems to escape her notice.

I hope that the collection of quotations presented in this book will enrich the reader's appreciation of Jane Austen's novels and provide a thrilling insight into the world in which she lived.

A Note on Style

Writing style differed from that of today in certain minor respects. Nouns would very often be capitalized in mid-sentence; some writers, especially Jane Austen, would abbreviate words and use superscript endings, thus Even^g for Evening, Apoth^y for Apothecary, G^s for Gardens. Diarists and even professional writers did not all have perfect spelling and some words were habitually misspelled (again, Jane Austen was a culprit). Other words were spelled in ways that are now old-fashioned, for example, 'beleive', 'chuse', 'rosted' (roasted). Some punctuation might also seem strange: commas were plentiful and full stops were frequently followed by a dash.

Monetary Values

Inflation since the 18th century means that £1 then would buy what £50 (or about US$87) will buy today. Parson Woodforde paid 0.2.6 (2 shillings and 6 pence) to have a tooth pulled out, roughly equivalent to £6.25 in today's money. The currency was imperial and coins were minted in basic denominations of pounds, shillings and pence, where 12 pennies (d) equalled a shilling (s) and 20 shillings equalled a pound sterling (£). Other denominations were the guinea, worth 21 shillings, and the crown, worth 5 shillings.

Malcolm Day

Austen Family Tree

WILLIAM AUSTEN
(1701–1737)
Surgeon of Tonbridge

REV. THOMAS LEIGH
(d. 1764)
Rector of Harpsden

THOMAS LEIGH
(1747–1821)
mentally
handicapped

JAMES LEIGH
(1735–1817)
(later called James
Leigh-Perrot,);
m.
Jane Cholmeley,
tried for grand
larceny in 1800,
d. 1836

JANE LEIGH
(1736–83)
m.
Dr Edward Cooper,
and bore Edward
and Jane

CASSANDRA LEIGH
(1739–1827)
=

REV. GEORGE
AUSTEN
(1731–1805)
Rector of Steventon
and Deane

PHILADELPHIA AUSTEN
(1730–1792)
m.
Tysoe Saul Hancock
(1711–75)

LEONORA AUSTEN
(1732–?)

ELIZA HANCOCK
(1761–1813)
m.
(1) Jean Capot de Feuillide
in 1781
(guillotined in 1794) and bore
Hastings
(1786–1801)
(2) Henry Austen, and bore
no more children

REV. JAMES
AUSTEN
(1765–1819)
Rector of Steventon
m.
(1) Anne Matthew in 1792,
and bore Anna;
(2) Mary Lloyd in 1797,
and bore James Edward and
Caroline Mary Craven

GEORGE
AUSTEN
(1766–1838)
mentally
handicapped

EDWARD
AUSTEN
(1767–1852)
known as
Edward Knight
after 1812
m.
Elizabeth Bridges in 1791,
and bore eleven children,
of whom the eldest was
Fanny-Catherine (b. 1793)

REV. HENRY-
THOMAS AUSTEN
(1771–1850)
Banker and later
curate of Chawton
m.
Eliza Hancock
(see above)

CASSANDRA-
ELIZABETH
AUSTEN
(1773–1845)

FRANCIS-
WILLIAM
AUSTEN
(Frank)
(1774–1865)
Naval officer
m.
(1) Mary Gibson in 1806,
and bore eleven children;
(2) Martha Lloyd in 1828,
and bore no children

JANE
AUSTEN
(1775–1817)

CHARLES-JOHN
AUSTEN
(1779–1852)
Naval officer
m.
(1) Frances Palmer in 1807,
and bore four children;
(2) Harriet Palmer in 1820
(Frances's sister), and bore
four more children

Marriage, Wealth and Breeding

It is a truth universally acknowledged, that a single man in possession of a good fortune must be in want of a wife. However little known the feelings or views of such a man may be on his first entering a neighbourhood, this truth is so well fixed in the minds of the surrounding families, that he is considered as the rightful property of some one or other of their daughters.

So begins one of the best-known books in the canon of English literature. Of all Jane Austen's novels probably no sentence says more than this one (which opens *Pride and Prejudice*) about the author's single most obsessive concern: marriage. This venerated institution formed the very heart of Georgian England, the key to a strong and stable society. Its binding laws safeguarded the nation's network of privileged landownership and ensured that ancestral estates passed undiminished from one generation to the next. The eldest son, heir and possessor of good fortune, to which Jane Austen refers, naturally became the coveted prize every respectable female dreamed of winning.

With the man came pride, high status, and much else besides. The principle of primogeniture spawned all manner of complexities and anxieties about inheritance and the plight of family relations who did not have the luck to be a first-born male. Marriage was the concern, therefore, of not just the matrimonial couple but of all members of the two families involved, especially unmarried sisters and yet-to-be-widowed mothers who might, with certainty, come to depend on such a liaison for financial security.

Pride and Prejudice accurately portrays a world beset with anxiety about securing suitable marriage partners. The story is set in Hertfordshire in the mid-1790s and revolves around the Bennets, a family of five daughters. Their concerns, and the dilemmas they face, would have been typical of the time.

There being no son as heir, the property is due to pass to the next nearest male descendant of the ancestor. In the Bennets' case this is a distant cousin. The manor has about a thousand acres and produces a modest income, which could all disappear into the hands of Mr Bennet's cousin should Mr Bennet die. His wife's nervousness about the future – a state no doubt common to the women on whom her character is modelled – takes a fresh turn when she hears of an interesting new tenant at grand Netherfield Park. She raises the subject with her somewhat apathetic husband:

> 'Mrs. Long says that Netherfield is taken by a young man of large fortune from the north of England; that he came down on Monday in a chaise and four to see the place, and was so much delighted with it that he agreed with Mr. Morris immediately; that he is to take possession before Michaelmas, and some of his servants are to be in the house by the end of next week.'
>
> 'What is his name?'
>
> 'Bingley.'
>
> 'Is he married or single?'
>
> 'Oh! single, my dear, to be sure! A single man of large fortune; four or five thousand a year. What a fine thing for our girls!'
>
> 'How so? How can it affect them?'
>
> 'My dear Mr. Bennet,' replied his wife, 'how can you be so tiresome! You must know that I am thinking of his marrying one of them.'
>
> 'Is that his design in settling here?'
>
> 'Design! nonsense, how can you talk so! But it is very likely that he *may* fall in love with one of them, and therefore you must visit him as soon as he comes.'
>
> ... [Mrs. Bennet] was a woman of mean understanding ... The business of her life was to get her daughters married; its solace was visiting and news.

Marriage certainly was a business. Mr Bingley's income of £4,000 a year derives from the interest on his inheritance of £100,000. These sums would have been typical for a man of high status and large landholding, though in Mr Bingley's case the wealth has accrued from his father's successful trade (we know not what) in the north of England. Compared with the Bennet girls, who would each have a dowry of just £1,000 to take away with them after their mother's death, Mr Bingley's income must have seemed highly attractive. However, he is not the only big fish in the sea. A friend of the Bingley family by the name of Fitzwilliam Darcy comes down to one of the balls held in the local assembly rooms and turns out to be even better endowed, being in possession of a large ancestral estate:

> **Mr. Darcy soon drew the attention of the room by his fine, tall person, handsome features, noble mien; and the report which was in general circulation, within five minutes after his entrance, of his having ten thousand a year. The gentlemen pronounced him to be a fine figure of a man, the ladies declared he was much handsomer than Mr. Bingley.**

Traditionally, both in the real world and in the world of Jane Austen's fiction, aristocratic families did not leave to chance such important matters as whom their sons and daughters would marry. It was important for families within the same social stratum to maintain connections with each other, and parents felt it their duty to facilitate a union of social equals. Not to do so, and to allow into their circle a person from a lower background, would be a betrayal of their own. It might even jeopardize their own jealously guarded position in society and, by opening the door to an unknowable quantity, could also threaten the very fabric of their privileged world. Hence Darcy's outrage (expressed to Elizabeth) when he later finds himself in love with her, a mere Bennet girl:

> **Could you expect me to rejoice in the inferiority of your connections? To congratulate myself on the hope of relations, whose condition in life is so decidedly beneath my own?**

Match-Making

It was commonplace in the 18th century for marriages to be arranged by the parents of aristocratic families. Even as late as the 1780s the tradition was still in evidence. This was what Harriet Spencer, daughter of Lord Spencer, had to say when she became engaged to the son and heir of the Earl of Bessborough:

> **I had not the least guess about it till the day papa told me. I wish I could have known him a little better first, but my dear papa and mama say that it will make them the happiest of creatures, and what would I**

**not do to see them happy ... I have a better chance of being reasonably
happy with him than with most people I know.**

Many daughters married simply to please their parents. It happened in Jane
Austen's own family early in the 1780s, when she herself was a young girl.
Her cousin Eliza Hancock met a dashing young Frenchman, reputedly one
of the finest officers in France, rich, and a count into the bargain. Before long
they were married. In Eliza's words:

**It was a step I took much less from my own judgement than that
of those whose councils & opinions I am the most bound to follow,
I trust I shall never have any reason to repent it.**

The counsels and opinions were those of her mother (her father having
died), who found the prospect of hooking up to the French aristocracy
irresistible and did everything she could to expedite the union. This included
persuading the trustees (one of whom was Jane's father, George Austen)
of a trust fund set up for Eliza by her godfather, the colonial administrator
Warren Hastings, to release the proceeds early and 'pay them over into the
French Funds', for the Comte de Feuillide was expected to inherit a good
fortune, 'but at present but little'. Smelling a rat, the trustees baulked at such
recklessness and rushed letters off to Warren Hastings alerting him:

**Mr Austen [Jane's father] is much concerned at the connection
which he says is giving up all their friends, their country, & he
fears their religion ...
I wrote Mrs Hancock ... who is in France where I believe she
intends to end her days, having married her daughter there to a
gentleman of that country, I am afraid not very advantageously,
although she says it is entirely to her satisfaction, the gentleman
having great connections & expectations. Her uncle Mr Austen,
and Brother don't approve of the match. The latter is much concerned
at it; they seem already desirous of draining the mother of every
shilling she has.**

The circumstances were made complicated by the various relationships of
Warren Hastings. George Austen had known him as a friend when a young
man and it was to George, in the capacity of a tutor, that Hastings sent his

infant son to receive an English education. When Hastings' wife died in childbirth, his friendship in India with George's sister Philadelphia Hancock grew into something more serious, and it is thought likely that Eliza was their love child, though officially acknowledged as his goddaughter.

While Eliza's mother boasted to her Parisian friends of the young couple's wealth and must have frequently dined out on her connection with Lord Hastings, who was by then Governor-General of India, Eliza eventually confided in her cousin Phylly Walter that her match with the Comte was not one made in heaven. Phylly noted:

The Countess has many amiable qualities, such as the highest duty, love and respect for her mother: for her husband she professes a large share of respect, esteem and the highest opinion of his merits, but confesses that Love is not of the number on her side.

Eventually political circumstances would decide Eliza's fate. Her aristocratic husband became a victim of the French Revolution and was guillotined in 1794. Eliza returned to England a released woman, happy to indulge once again in the pleasures of London society, an environment as likely as not to produce a new husband.

Throughout the 18th century a series of institutions had been set up to facilitate courting. Every county town had its assembly rooms where balls were staged regularly during a season for the specific purpose of matching couples. At the same time a sea-change in attitudes to marriage was occurring. Greater prominence was being given to that radical new idea, 'freedom of choice'. Parental authority was no longer the primary force in determining who the spouse should be. Even financial and political considerations, though they were important, might not always override a daughter's will.

Many parents felt unsure of what exactly their priorities should be. Their daughter's happiness was their first consideration but they certainly were not going to abandon her to a whim. If the practice of formally arranging marriages was becoming less commonplace, it was being replaced by a rise in the more subtle art of match-making, though the degree of subtlety varied considerably. The problem of ambitious parents overplaying their hand in the process was identified by society magazines of the time. A spoof letter appeared in *The Lady's Monthly Museum* in 1798 expressing a young lady's dismay at the whole sorry business:

Now as my papa and mamma have been trying for the last three years to match me, and have for that purpose carried me from our country seat to London, from London to Brighton, from Brighton to Bath, and from Bath to Cheltenham, where I now am, backwards and forwards, till the family carriage is almost worn out, without my having more than a nibble, for I have never yet been able to hook my fish, I begin to be afraid that there is something wrong in their manner of baiting for a husband, or in mine of laying in the line to catch him.

O! how my heart did beat with joy when my mamma first acquainted me with the thought I ought no longer to be buried in the country, where there was scarcely a chance of my ever having an offer beyond a fox-hunting squire or a card-playing parson; and that I might, like other young ladies of my birth and station, pick up a man of rank and fortune!

... to confess the truth, dear Goody, I was tired of lawns and trees, fish ponds and walled gardens, horses and hounds, and all the rusticities of life; and I wished to escape from them. But though I have, by the indulgence of my parents, seen all that is to be seen of the beau monde, and have never acted the prude, but at every proper advance have looked as much as to say, Come on, if you dare; no one has ever offered me any thing beyond a fashionable compliment. I rather suspect that my parents are the real and genuine cause of my disappointment; for no sooner had we taken up our residence in town, than my mamma hinted to all our female married acquaintances the object of our journey; and no sooner did a man to their mind pay me the least attention, than, in their over-anxiety to engage him, they gave such broad hints, as left him nothing to fear as to their approbation, and therefore made him more indifferent about mine. They wished me to win hearts, and yet they never allowed any of my supposed admirers time enough to disclose their sentiments, before they shifted the scene; for, according to their maxim, love is improved by distance, and the effect of a first impression is heightened by difficulty of access.— Several gentlemen, indeed, who were put to this test, pursued the route we took, and a kind of acquaintance was renewed; but this was never suffered to arrive at any maturity; for if a lord only smiled at me, I was cautioned to avoid inferior persons, and throw out all my lines to catch him. This conduct probably defeated its own purpose, as I lost the respect of my equals, and was

not likely, when the motive was so obvious, to gain the affection
of my superiors. If this season at Cheltenham proves untoward I
have reason to apprehend I shall be doomed to Rusty Hall for life;
unless some kind, worthy creature of a man will deign to come and
look after me, instead of my looking after him. As my heart is still
disengaged, I think, at the age of twenty three, I could love any man
who had pretensions to my regard, and who was neither old, ugly,
nor ill-natured.

   Your friend and admirer
    Biddy, Willing

Added to the anxiety of finding Mr Right was the perception (and
reality) that eligible bachelors were thin on the ground. The high cost of
maintaining a wife and household put a lot of men off the idea of marriage.
This, coupled with an increasing surplus of females over males as the century
drew to a close, partly the result of war and partly because of a higher infant
mortality among males, created near-hysteria. In Jane's social milieu, match-
making had become almost a profession among some women who had little
else to think about, as the author highlights in *Sense and Sensibility*:

Mrs Jennings was a widow with an ample jointure. She had only two
daughters, both of whom she had lived to see respectably married,
and she had now therefore nothing to do but to marry all the rest of
the world. In the promotion of this object she was zealously active,
as far as her ability reached; and missed no opportunity of projecting
weddings among all the young people of her acquaintance. She was
remarkably quick in the discovery of attachments, and had enjoyed
the advantage of raising the blushes and the vanity of many a young
lady by insinuations of her power over such a young man ...

Society magazines condemned the antics of over-eager mothers and
fathers, saying that such avid manhunts were reprehensible and that they
contributed to a decline in the popularity of marriage, especially among men
living in London, as *The Lady's Monthly Museum* commented:

Railing at matrimony is become so fashionable a topick that one
can scarcely step into a Coffee-house or a Tavern but one hears
declamations against being clogged with a wife and family, and a fixed

resolution of living a life of liberty, gallantry, and pleasure as it is called; the consequence of this must prove injurious.

When a young man accidentally falls into the company of a girl whose temper, beauty, and circumstances are really calculated to attract his regard, and finds her father and mother striving with mutual art to cajole him into a connection with her; when he sees them exerting all the grimace and cant of an auctioneer to engage purchasers, by puffing the lot, and expatiating upon qualities, which every lover is fond of discovering with his own eyes, he begins to suspect that there is some latent deception in character, disposition, or fortune; and, as is common in ordinary affairs, shrinks back from the purchase, which is offered too cheap to be good.

Not all parents, of course, involved themselves so counterproductively in their daughters' fortunes. Some, with a nod to progressive thinking, left the whole thing up to the individuals. Jane's own parents make an interesting case. Her mother, Cassandra Leigh, came from an aristocratic family. One ancestor, Sir Thomas Leigh, was Lord Mayor of London at the time of Queen Elizabeth I's coronation, a later Sir Thomas Leigh had sheltered Charles I during the Civil War, and Cassandra's grandmother, Mary Brydges, was sister to the Duke of Chandos. Jane's father George Austen, on the other hand, was an orphaned boy whose own grandmother had been a lowly school housekeeper. Though the match on paper looked one-sided, George had attributes in his favour. He was tall, handsome and intelligent. At the age of 16 he went up to St John's College, Oxford, performed well, and could easily have chosen a comfortable career as an academic (Cassandra's father was also at Oxford). But the life of an Oxford don was not for him. A mid-century rhyme by Tom Wharton may have summed up his feelings:

These fellowships are pretty things,
We live indeed like petty kings:
But who can bear to waste his whole age
Amid the dullness of a college,
Debarr'd the common joys of life,
And that prime bliss – a loving wife.

Dons not being allowed to marry, George certainly did not wish to be deprived of the joys of marital bliss. The sticking point was always going to be the money. He had become ordained as a minister of the Church of England, and as such his prospects were indeterminable. George tried to hide his impoverished state behind an air of genteel prosperity, courting her in the elegant squares of Bath and college gardens of Oxford. But Cassandra was no fool and, while she dearly loved this man, she was going to find out exactly what was in store for her as a future parson's wife.

George inherited the parish rectory at Steventon in Hampshire. However, far from being a rural idyll, it was a pokey little dwelling set in an unlovely landscape. As Jane's nephew James Edward Austen-Leigh recollected:

One cannot be surprised that, when Jane's mother, a little before her marriage, was shown the scenery of her future home, she should have thought it unattractive, compared with the broad river, the rich valley, and the noble hills which she had been accustomed to behold at her native home near Henley-upon-Thames.

Furthermore, the house was in a fairly dilapidated state, very damp and altogether uninviting. Not wishing to reveal to the lovely Cassandra the full squalor of the place he was proposing to be their marital home, George hit on the idea of renting the nearby Deane Parsonage for a modest sum, and escorted his prospective fiancée to a viewing. However, on inspection, the couple were horrified to discover that conditions there were even worse than at Steventon.

The deceit and humiliation might have been too much for either of them to bear had it not been for the death soon afterwards of Cassandra's father. This changed her circumstances at a stroke. The need to stop prevaricating and decide once and for all whether to bite the bullet and marry George Austen became paramount. The dowry due to her would be modest. Some leasehold properties in Oxford and just £1,000 when her mother died were all it amounted to. On the other side, George's clerical income was estimated to be about £100 a year, together with whatever the farmland produced. There was the prospect of gaining the livings of the two neighbouring parishes to Steventon, Ashe and Deane, which had been bought on George's behalf by his wealthy uncle Frank, though their vacancy depended on the demise of the existing incumbents.

So, from a financial point of view, things looked precarious. Certainly George Austen would not have been considered an ideal match for Cassandra in her parents' eyes, but in every other respect he was all

Cassandra wished for in a man. His character, intelligence and warmth made him a perfect companion. There was also the not inconsiderable question of her age. She was now 25 and had to take a hard look at her options. Other men in the running sometimes found it alarming that a woman should express opinions, and her humour (what she called her 'sprack wit') might also be a source of irritation, but to George these traits were sources of interest and joy. Married they would be, perhaps flying in the face of prudence; but this was something Jane Austen took as a springboard for characterizing her novels. The marriage would also be an example to Jane in years to come when considering such a venture herself.

The Dowry

The question of how much money was enough to get married, of how much constituted 'wealth' anyway, and what the pay-off was between wealth and happiness, were matters that vexed many a real woman. It certainly greatly concerns the Dashwood sisters, Marianne and Elinor, in *Sense and Sensibility*. Marianne tells her sister:

'You have no ambition, I well know. Your wishes are all moderate.'

'As moderate as those of the rest of the world, I believe. I wish, as well as every body else, to be perfectly happy; but, like every body else, it must be in my own way. Greatness will not make me so.'

'Strange that it would!' cried Marianne. 'What have wealth or grandeur to do with happiness?'

'Grandeur has but little,' said Elinor, 'but wealth has much to do with it.'

'Elinor, for shame!' said Marianne, 'money can only give happiness where there is nothing else to give it. Beyond a competence, it can afford no real satisfaction, as far as mere self is concerned.'

'Perhaps,' said Elinor, smiling, 'we may come to the same point. Your competence and my wealth are very much alike, I dare say; and without them, as the world goes now, we shall both agree that every kind of external comfort must be wanting. Your ideas are more noble than mine. Come, what is your competence?'

'About eighteen hundred or two thousand a year; not more than that.'

Elinor laughed. 'Two thousand a year! One is my wealth! I guessed how it would end.'

What was a typical dowry? As marriage was a financial partnership, the bride's parents were expected to contribute to the couple's future by offering, through a dowry, a sum to cover the upbringing of the children and the running of the matrimonial home. Usually the mother divided her dowry among the daughters and the father added to this sum from his savings. The question of how much might be enough therefore depended on the number of children and size of the house, the servants required and so on. Characteristically, Marianne and Elinor Dashwood have different ideas of sufficiency, or 'competence' as Marianne puts it. Elinor's declaration that £1,000 would mean wealth to her contrasts greatly with Marianne's minimum requirement of double that sum.

Jane Austen paints a similarly typical scene in *Pride and Prejudice*, where Mr Bennet has promised Elizabeth and Jane £1,000 each, which is considered meagre and, what's more, will only become available on their mother's death. Luckily they both marry rich men. Even luckier is Fanny Price in *Mansfield Park*, who has no dowry at all but has the opportunity of marrying Henry Crawford with an income of £4,000 a year. Higher up the scale is Fanny's aunt Lady Bertram, who had £7,000 as her dowry, which Jane Austen wryly remarks was considered to be at least £3,000 less than the going rate to be a baronet's wife.

Once married, a woman's property belonged to her husband. But a legal contract, the marriage settlement, could be drawn up to guarantee that the bride had a certain amount of money 'settled' on her. This entitled her to receive the interest from that money during her lifetime and the money could be passed on to her children in her will; the dowry was also intended to make provision for widowhood. But after Jane Austen's father died in 1805, his family, including Jane, were forced to take small rented premises until her brother Edward housed them comfortably at Chawton Cottage in Hampshire at his own expense. Even marrying well, financially speaking, was no passport to a life of ease forever more.

Marriage for Security

The lengths to which women would go to achieve financial security through matrimony were well known to Jane Austen. Eliza Hancock's marriage to the French count bore some resemblance to the experience of her own mother, Jane's aunt Philadelphia Hancock, which she divulged to Jane: Philadelphia had been obliged to travel to India to marry a man for whom she had little or no affection. The union was a simple agreement in which she offered her friendship and her body in return for his money. Jane was so struck by her predicament that she used it in *Catherine, or the Bower*, a minor novel written a few months after her aunt's death in 1792:

> **The eldest daughter had been obliged to accept the offer of one of her cousins to equip her for the East Indies, and tho' infinitely against her inclinations had been necessitated to embrace the only possibility that was offered to her, of a Maintenance; Yet it was *one*, so opposite to all her ideas of Propriety, so contrary to her Wishes, so repugnant to her feelings, that she would almost have preferred Servitude to it, had Choice been allowed her—. Her personal Attractions had gained her a husband as soon as she had arrived at Bengal, and she had now been married nearly a twelvemonth. Splendidly, yet unhappily married. United to a Man of double her own age, whose disposition was not amiable, and whose Manners were unpleasing, though his Character was respectable. Kitty had heard twice from her friend since her marriage, but her Letters were always unsatisfactory, and though she did not openly avow her feelings, yet every line proved her to be Unhappy.**

Romantic Love

As well as the uncertainty parents felt about their priorities in the quest for suitable spouses for their daughters, there was a tricky new motive to be considered, that of romantic love. One of the causes for this vogue, which overtook the propertied classes in the last quarter of the 18th century, was the rise of the romantic novel, especially novels written by women such as Ann Radcliffe, Fanny Burney and Mary Barker. From 1770 to 1790 the number of novels published by women increased fourfold.

It was not the existence of romantic love, which was nothing new, that posed the threat but the acceptance of it among men and women of marriageable age – and their parents – as a worthy reason for tying the knot. A fictitious mother's letter to *The Lady's Monthly Museum* in 1799 complained of a daughter's obsession with the vogue for romantic fiction:

> She teazes me almost to death:—'Now, my dear mamma!' she will cry, 'here is something so elegantly sentimental, so bewitchingly sweet, so

fascinatingly charming, that you must listen to it ...' In consequence
of this endearing solicitation I am compelled to attend to some
whining, love-sick nonsense, which, perhaps, thirty or forty years
ago, might have pleased me, had it come from the lips of a handsome
young man. I do not wish to suppress tenderness; but ... infusing false
and romantic notions, [seems] to injure, rather than to improve, the
natural feelings of sensibility.

Many a drawing room stirred in rage at such giddy notions. What is more,
since the Marriage Act of Parliament in 1754 had decreed that all couples
in England under the age of 21 needed the consent of their parents in order
to marry, defiant under-age romantics had been forced to flee over the
border to Scotland for a ceremony conducted in secrecy. *The Universal
Magazine* declared:

Of all the arrows which Cupid has shot at youthful hearts, [the
modern novel] is the keenest. There is no resisting it. It is the literary
opium that lulls every sense into delicious rapture ... In contempt of
the Marriage Act post-chaises and young couples run smoothly on the
North Road.

At Gretna Green, situated just a few miles inside Scotland, a local
blacksmith hit upon the idea in the 1750s of offering wedding services.
All that Scottish law required were two witnesses and a minimum age of 16.
According to Pennant's *Tour in Scotland*, published in 1772, it was not long
before the business turned into a lucrative earner:

Here the young pair may be instantly united by a fisherman, a joiner,
or a blacksmith, who marry from two guineas a job to a dram of
whisky. But the price is generally adjusted by the information of the
postillions [coach drivers] from Carlisle, who are in the pay of one or
other of the above worthies; but even the drivers, in case of necessity,
have been known to undertake the sacerdotal office.

And it was not only the young who eloped. In a letter to her sister Cassandra
in 1808, Jane Austen referred to a former neighbour who had become a
subject of gossip when the newspaper revealed she had secretly fled from her
husband with another man:

> This is a sad story about Mrs Powlett. I should not have suspected
> her of such a thing.—She staid the Sacrament I remember, the last
> time that you & I did.—A hint of it, with Initials, was in yesterday's
> Courier; & Mr Moore guessed it to be Lord Sackville, beleiving there
> was no other Viscount S. in the peerage.

But not all turned out badly for the cuckolded Colonel Powlett, who
managed to win £3,000 in compensation for the adultery.

The turmoil caused by love was an evergreen source of entertainment for
the Austens and their friends. Indeed Jane found herself to be the subject
of attention on one occasion. Shortly after her 20th birthday, during the
New Year social whirl of 1796, an excited Jane reported to Cassandra on
an evening spent at Deane House in a neighbouring village:

> We had an exceeding good ball last night ... I danced twice with
> Warren, and once with Mr Charles Watkins, and, to my inexpressible
> astonishment, I entirely escaped John Lyford. I was forced to fight
> hard for it, however. We had a very good supper, and the greenhouse
> was illuminated in a very elegant manner ... I wish Charles [their
> brother] had been at Manydown, because he would have given you
> some description of my friend, and I think you must be impatient to
> hear something about him.

The friend in question was an Irishman, Tom Lefroy, a bright, handsome
20-year-old studying law at Trinity College, Dublin. He was spending a
holiday with his uncle and aunt-in-law at the rectory of Ashe, a village
near Jane's family home at Steventon. Jane had a close relationship with
Cassandra, who was just two years her elder and was then engaged to be
married. Jane must have felt even better able than usual to confide in her
sister about romantic feelings, knowing she was in love herself:

> You scold me so much in the nice long letter which I have this
> moment received from you, that I am almost afraid to tell you how
> my Irish friend and I behaved. Imagine to yourself everything most
> profligate and shocking in the way of dancing and sitting down
> together. I *can* expose myself, however, only *once more*, because
> he leaves the country soon after next Friday, on which day we
> *are* to have a dance at Ashe after all. He is a very gentlemanlike,

good-looking, pleasant young man, I assure you. But as to our having
ever met, except at the three last balls, I cannot say much; for he
is so excessively laughed at about me at Ashe, that he is ashamed of
coming to Steventon, and ran away when we called on Mrs Lefroy a
few days ago.

Tom Lefroy, normally shy and quiet, was teased about the fling he was having
with Jane, though he was so taken by her charm that he felt compelled
to pay her a visit the following morning. If the heart strings hadn't been
fluttering before, they certainly were now. In a few days' time the promised
dance at the Ashe ball would be upon them and Jane was in high spirits:

Our party to Ashe to-morrow night will consist of Edward Cooper,
James [Jane's brother] (for a Ball is nothing without *him*), Buller, who
is now staying with us, & I—I look forward with great impatience to
it, as I rather expect to receive an offer from my friend in the course
of the evening. I shall refuse him, however, unless he promises to give
away his white Coat ...

With affected nonchalance Jane endeavoured to protect her pride in case
she received no such 'offer' of marriage by stating in advance how little this
dashing Irishman meant to her. He had turned up at her house in a white
overcoat, which Jane playfully dismissed as vulgar, but the signs are clear that
she was hopeful. Furthermore, the same jocular tone continued when she
said she wished to dispense with all other suitors:

Tell Mary [her friend Mary Lloyd] that I make over Mr Heartley & all
his Estate to her for her sole use and Benefit in future, & not only him,
but all my other Admirers into the bargain wherever she can find them,
even the kiss which C. Powlett wanted to give me, as I mean to confine
myself in future to Mr Tom Lefroy, for whom I do not care sixpence ...
   Friday.—At length the Day is come on which I am to flirt my last
with Tom Lefroy, & when you receive this it will be over—My tears
flow as I write, at the melancholy idea.

Despite the characteristic tone of jovial optimism, it seems her inner feelings
betrayed a measure of realism, if not despair, at the notion that all would
come to nought. After this letter there is a silence about what happened

next. Presumably Tom Lefroy did not propose. The next we hear about him is two years later when he was staying again at Ashe, without seeing Jane. His aunt-in-law Mrs Lefroy came to Steventon and Jane was able to catch up on the news, as she wrote in a letter to Cassandra:

> **I was enough alone to hear all that was interesting ... of her nephew she said nothing ... She did not once mention the name of [Tom] to me, and I was too proud to make any enquiries; but on my father's afterwards asking where he was, I learnt that he was gone back to London in his way to Ireland, where he is called to the Bar and means to practise.**

However, behind the scenes Mr and Mrs Lefroy, as acting hosts to their nephew and therefore responsible for him in the absence of his parents, were alarmed at the proceedings unfolding before their eyes. Underneath the playful ribbing dealt out to Tom, his guardians were anxious about the possibility that this penniless youth might, in a rush of blood, propose to a girl who herself had no dowry to speak of. When his parents discovered what had been going on, they severely reprimanded their son for leading Jane on when he was in no position to propose marriage, having no prospect of an income for some time to come. Tom was packed off to London to live under the roof of his great-uncle while studying law at Lincoln's Inn. In time he did become a successful barrister, his long career culminating in the position of Lord Chief Justice of Ireland. He married happily but never forgot Jane, for whom he admitted he had had a 'boyish love'.

Guidance to Young Men and Women

The scale of misery wrought by unhappy attachments prompted writers of the time to offer their counsel to both men and women. Lord Chesterfield, statesman and wit, had a good deal of advice to give his illegitimate son and godson on such long-term commitments. Though once described by Samuel Johnson as teaching 'the morals of a whore and the manners of a dancing master', he nevertheless had a down-to-earth understanding of marriage:

> **Do not be in haste to marry, but look about you first, for the affair is important. There are but two objects in marriage, love or money. If you marry for love, you will certainly have some very happy days,**

and probably many very uneasy ones; if for money, you will have
no happy days and probably no uneasy ones; in this latter case let
the woman at least be such a one that you can live decently and
amicably with, otherwise it is a robbery; in either case, let her be
of an unblemished and unsuspected character, and of a rank not
indecently below your own.

The farmer and radical politician William Cobbett summed up his advice
in the form of a list of attributes for young men to look for:

The things which you ought to desire in a wife are chastity; sobriety;
industry; frugality; cleanliness; knowledge of domestic affairs; good
temper and beauty—in that order.

A letter to *The Spectator* endorsed his priorities, by condemning:

Ladies who are too nicely bent on the sordid principles of gain,
interest and ambition, without one serious thought or reflection
on their future state and tranquillity.

One of the period's most influential writers, Mary Wollstonecraft, whose
work Jane Austen would have known, tried to cut through the vanities of the
opposite sex and help women and men make better judgments of potential
partners. Her treatise, *A Vindication of the Rights of Woman*, was standard
reading for progressive thinkers, and on the subject of love and marriage
her advice found favour with young and old:

But one grand truth women have yet to learn. In the choice of a
husband, they should not be led astray by the qualities of a lover –
for a lover the husband, even supposing him to be wise and virtuous,
cannot long remain.
    Were women more rationally educated, could they take a more
comprehensive view of things, they would be contented to love but
once in their lives; and after marriage calmly let passion subside into
friendship – into that tender intimacy, which is the best refuge from
care; yet is built on such pure, still affections, that idle jealousies
would not be allowed to disturb the discharge of the sober duties of
life, or to engross the thoughts that ought to be otherwise employed.

This is a state in which many men live; but few, very few women.

... Men of wit and fancy are often rakes; and fancy is the food of love. Such men will inspire passion. Half the sex, in its present infantine state, would pine for a Lovelace [the dashing poet-soldier and prototype Cavalier]; a man so witty, so graceful, and so valiant; and can they *deserve* blame for acting according to principles so constantly inculcated? They want a lover, and protector; and behold him kneeling before them – bravery prostrate to beauty! The virtues of a husband are thus thrown by love into the background, and gay hopes, or lively emotions, banish reflection till the day of reckoning come; and come it surely will, to turn the sprightly lover into a surly suspicious tyrant, who contemptuously insults the very weakness he fostered.

... In a great degree, love and friendship cannot subsist in the same bosom; even when inspired by different objects they weaken or destroy each other, and for the same object can only be felt in succession. The vain fears and fond jealousies – the winds which fan the flame of love – when judiciously or artfully tempered, are both incompatible with the tender confidence and sincere respect of friendship.

On a similar theme, one of Jane Austen's favourite poets, George Crabbe, encapsulated the abiding strength of love in a single verse, 'His Late Wife's Wedding-Ring':

The ring so worn, as you behold,
So thin, so pale, is yet of gold:
The passion such it was to prove;
Worn with life's cares, love yet was love.

As far as the libido was concerned, there was plenty of advice on that subject too. If the sexual urge waned, society magazines warned, the marriage was in serious jeopardy. Physical attraction alone might be inadequate as a basis for marriage, but it was still an essential ingredient, to be neglected at one's peril. *The Lady's Magazine* of the 1770s carried a letter of brotherly advice to a sister who had recently married:

Give me leave as the tie of blood between us may in some measure authorize the freedom and the friendship we have always had for each other, to mix with the unfeigned joy of congratulation the unrestrainable tenderness of a brother, and concern of a friend, in giving my advice to you in this scene of happiness.

... The observation of some inferior excellencies ... are as essentially necessary to preserve a husband's desires as the more respectable duties of a wife.

It is not enough that a woman should be a domestic friend; she should daily study to invest herself with a hundred little enchanting graces, suitable to the disposition of the man she marries, if she would still retain those unspeakable charms, conceived only by lovers, with which she originally captivated his heart. This grand secret ... my dear sister, lies in this short precept: *Never lose the mistress in the wife*: a text of bullion sense.

For Convenience

With so much conflicting advice flying about, it is a wonder that anyone knew how to decide on such all-important matters. What was unchanging, though, were the harsh economic facts facing a middle-class woman who did not marry. If she did not wish to be a burden to her family, and her home circumstances dictated that she find employment, her respectable options in this unemancipated world were extremely limited: she could become a governess or a lady's companion, neither of which could promise a comfortable living.

If love did not come by her door, fear of a life of poverty and loneliness might start a woman thinking about another option, should it present itself: namely the 'marriage of convenience'. As Jane Austen perceptively notes in *Pride and Prejudice* when Charlotte Lucas receives a marriage proposal from Mr Collins, about whom she has no illusions:

Without thinking highly either of men or of matrimony, marriage had always been her object; it was the only honourable provision for well-educated young women of small fortune, and however uncertain of giving happiness, must be their pleasantest preservative from want. This preservative she had now obtained; and at the age of twenty-seven, without having ever been handsome, she felt all the good luck of it.

Sense and Sensibility expresses the same coolly accepted reality:

'A woman of seven and twenty,' said Marianne, after pausing a moment, 'can never hope to feel or inspire affection again, and if her home be uncomfortable, or her fortune small, I can suppose that she might bring herself to submit to the offices of a nurse, for the sake of the provision and security of a wife. In his marrying such a woman therefore there would be nothing unsuitable. It would be a compact of convenience, and the world would be satisfied. In my eyes it would be no marriage at all, but that would be nothing. To me it would seem only a commercial exchange, in which each wished to be benefited at the expense of the other.'

It is clear from her novels that Jane Austen, like many of her peers, wished most of all for a home of her own. But at what price? Curiously it was at the age of 27 that she received a marriage proposal from her neighbour Harris Bigg-Wither, with whose family the Austens had been friends for many years. Though six years her junior, he was heir to his family home, Manydown, a handsome house and estate, which would become theirs on marriage. Jane got on well with his sisters, who would probably continue living there. The match would also afford some security for her mother and Cassandra in the future. How tempting the offer must have seemed! Would it not be a disservice to her family and his to refuse him? No contemporary records survive to establish exactly what Jane felt about the man. What does remain is a letter written much later by Jane's niece, Caroline Austen, relating what she had learnt:

Mr Wither was very plain in person—awkward, & even uncouth in manner—nothing but his size to recommend him—he was a fine big man—but one need not look about for secret reason to account for a young lady's *not* loving him—a great many would have taken him *without* love ...

He had sense in plenty & went through life very respectably, as a country gentleman—I *conjecture* that the advantages he could offer, & her gratitude for his love, & her long friendship with his family, induced my Aunt to decide that she would marry him *when* he should ask her.

And when that offer did come on the evening of 2 December 1802, while Jane and Cassandra were visiting Manydown, she accepted,

… but that having accepted him she found she was miserable & that
the place & fortune which would certainly be *his*, could not alter the
man—She was staying in his *Father's* house—old Mr. Wither was
then alive—To be sure she should not have said yes—over night—
but I have always respected her for the courage in canceling that
yes—the next morning—All worldly advantages would have been to
her—and she was of an age to know *this* quite well—My Aunts had
very small fortunes & on their Father's death they & their Mother
would be, they were aware, but poorly off—I believe most young
women so circumstanced would have taken Mr. W. & trusted to love
after marriage.

The fallout that came next morning when Jane declared she had changed
her mind must have been dreadful. The sadness and humiliation for Harris,
old man Bigg-Wither's anger, the embarrassment for Jane and Cassandra
– clearly were all too much to bear and the sisters made a speedy departure
from the house. They went to Steventon, where they sought consolation
from their brother James, who was now ensconced there as rector with his
wife Mary, and persuaded him to escort them to Bath so as to be well out
of the area.

Perhaps some of the thinking that went through the novelist's mind that
fateful night is indicated in a letter Jane wrote in 1814 to her niece Fanny
Knight, aged 21, when offering her advice about whether she should marry.
The letter seems like a distillation of all the wisdom Jane had gained over
the years, especially the importance given to love in the equation:

I am perfectly convinced that your present feelings, supposing you
were to marry *now*, would be sufficient for his happiness;—but when
I think how very, very far it is from a Now, & take everything that
may be, into consideration, I dare not say, 'determine to accept him.'
The risk is too great for *you*, unless your own Sentiment prompt
it.—You will think me perverse perhaps; in my last letter I was urging
everything in his favour, & now I am inclining the other way; but
I cannot help it; I am at present more impressed with the possible
Evil that may arise to *You* from engaging yourself to him—in word
or mind—than with anything else.—When I consider how few young
Men you have yet seen much of—how capable you are (yes, I do
still think you *very* capable) of being really in love—and how full of

temptation the next 6 or 7 years of your Life will probably be—(it is the very period of Life for the *strongest* attachments to be formed)— I cannot wish you with your present very cool feelings to devote yourself in honour to him. It is very true that you never may attach another Man, his equal altogether, but if that other Man has the power of attaching you *more*, he will be in your eyes the most perfect ... nothing can be compared to the misery of being bound *without* Love, bound to one, & preferring another. *That* is a Punishment which you do *not* deserve.

Adultery and Divorce

Georgian society was ambivalent towards relationships outside marriage. A blind eye was often turned towards men having affairs. In smart London society it was quite common to see a gentleman – even a public figure – walking about with a mistress on his arm. But for a woman to indulge thus was usually unacceptable.

The notorious Philadelphia Hancock, who had an affair with Warren Hastings in India, the suspected father of her daughter Eliza, drew a good deal of opprobrium in some quarters. A censorious letter of 1765 from Sir Robert Clive (Clive of India) to his wife, Lady Margaret, demanded nothing short of ostracism for the woman:

> In no circumstances whatever keep company with Mrs Hancock for it is beyond a doubt that she abandoned herself to Mr Hastings, indeed, I would rather you had no acquaintance with the ladies who have been in India, they stand in such little esteem in England that their company cannot be of credit to Lady Clive.

But in the normal run of 18th-century life the reason behind such indignation had less to do with moral compunction about a lady's propriety than with the economic risks involved in such affairs. As Samuel Johnson said in 1785:

> Consider, of what importance to society the chastity of women is. Upon that all the property in the world depends. We hang a thief for stealing a sheep; but the unchastity of a woman transfers sheep, and farm and all, from the right owner.

And he reiterated his view:

> Between a man and his wife, a husband's infidelity is nothing ... Wise
> married women don't trouble themselves about infidelity in their
> husbands ... The man imposes no bastards upon his wife.

In other words, the prospect of a woman producing, out of wedlock, a son
who might lay claim to a squire's inherited wealth was the basis of the
gentry's fear, and the law of the land did everything in its power to protect
that inheritance. For instance, a wife's adultery was sufficient ground for her
husband to obtain a divorce, but a husband's was no ground for his wife to
obtain one. Divorces, in any case, were rare since they required a private
Act of Parliament.

In some circles, especially among the upper classes, extramarital
relations were tolerated and bastardy, though considered unfortunate,
carried no stigma. Even figures representing the highest levels of the moral
establishment were found to be 'men of the world'. Horace Walpole, in his
memoirs, wrote of Archbishop Blackburne:

> I often dined with him – his mistress, Mrs Cruwys, sat at the head of
> the table, and Hayter, his natural son by another woman, and very
> much like him, at the bottom ... I have heard, but do not affirm it,
> that Mrs Blackburne, before she died, complained of Mrs Cruwys
> being brought under the same roof.
>
> One story I recollect, which showed how much he was a man of
> the world, and which the Queen herself repeated to my father. On
> the King's last journey to Hanover, the Archbishop being with Her
> Majesty said to her: 'Madam, I have been with your minister Walpole,
> and he tells me that you are a wise woman, and so do not mind your
> husband's having a mistress.

Jane Austen also found these peccadilloes amusing, as she remarked to
Cassandra:

> Eliza has seen Lord Craven at Barton ... She found his manners very
> pleasing indeed.—The little flaw of having a Mistress now living with
> him at Ashdown Park, seems to be the only unpleasing circumstance
> about him.

Bachelors and Spinsters

In 1773 *The Lady's Magazine* complained:

The men marry with reluctance, sometimes very late, and a great many are never married at all.

In the last quarter of the 18th century, about one in five of the younger sons of the nobility and gentry never married. The median age for a man to marry was 28, similar to the figure for the 21st century. The explanation given for such reluctance was the cost. For a younger son (who was denied any slice of the inheritance by the custom of primogeniture), early marriage was likely to increase his expenditure so much as to make him significantly less well off. His best chance of maintaining the social and economic circumstances in which he grew up was to marry an heiress or the daughter of an affluent man who could promise a good dowry. Otherwise, bachelorhood was the most prudent course to take. His emotional and physical needs could be satisfied cheaply with a mistress (or paid for with a prostitute). If he was lucky enough to make his fortune, he might later in life look for a bride from the same class into which he had been born.

Spinsterhood, however, was a worse, if not totally dire, prospect. Jane gave the following advice (some of her last) in a letter to Fanny Knight in 1817:

Single women have a dreadful propensity for being poor—which is one very strong argument in favour of Matrimony.

And it was borne out by the facts. Owing to the shortage of males and a disinclination among younger sons to marry, the spinster or old maid who never married became a common phenomenon in the 18th century.

Nearly a quarter of upper-class girls fell into this category. Because of their social background they were not expected to get a job. If they did not obtain a position in another household as, say, a companion or governess, they had no financial independence. Many remained dependent on their family and were likely to be regarded as useless spongers. In 1785, William Hayley thus commented in *A Philosophical, Historical and Moral Essay on Old Maids*:

If she had received a polite education ... it is probable that after having passed the sprightly years of youth ... [she would be] lodging

in a country town, attended by a single female servant, and with difficulty living on the interest of two or three thousand pounds, reluctantly and perhaps irregularly paid to her by an avaricious or extravagant brother ... Such is the condition in which the unmarried daughters of English gentlemen are too frequently found.

Some might have found an outlet in religious devotion or charity work in the village. It seems that Jane did various jobs, such as sewing and teaching, to help out locally after her father died in 1805. With no pension for the widows and children of clergymen, the Austen family was thrown back on its own resources. Mrs Austen and Cassandra had a small income but Jane had nothing. Something of the bitterness she no doubt felt about impoverished spinsterhood is expressed by her heroine Emma Woodhouse in *Emma*:

Never mind, Harriet, I shall not be a poor old maid; and it is poverty only which makes celibacy contemptible to a generous public! A single old woman, with a very narrow income, must be a ridiculous, disagreeable old maid! The proper sport of boys and girls, but a single woman, of good fortune, is always respectable, and may be as sensible and pleasant as any body else.

Work and
Social Rank

In Jane Austen's day, the job you did was closely allied to your social position. An army officer held a higher status than a naval officer, whose status was, in turn, greater than a doctor or a banker. A finely tuned pecking order existed so that people knew their station in life, right down to the shoe-black and the scullery maid.

But those who did no work at all were held in the highest esteem. A member of the gentry was one of a privileged class, so well off, by virtue of the income generated through his estate and perhaps other property, that he had no need of a job. He simply had to manage the estate, and that was probably mostly done for him by a bailiff. Furthermore, almost everyone accepted this hierarchical system. It had, after all, evolved over a long period stretching back to feudal times. The novelist and journalist Daniel Defoe (1660–1731) made a rough-and-ready division into seven social groups:

The great, who live profusely
The rich, who live plentifully
The middle sort, who live well
The working trades, who labour hard, but feel no want
The country people, farmers, etc. who fare indifferently
The poor, who fare hard
The miserable, that really pinch and suffer want.

Within these categories, it has to be said, there was a multitude of fine differentiations. Distinctions between a lady's maid and a kitchen maid, or between a doctor and a surgeon, or a woman addressed as Madam as opposed to Mrs, were jealously upheld, just as much as were the ranks within the aristocracy. The graded descent from duke to marquis to earl to viscount to baron all fell within the category of hereditary peers of the realm, and all were entitled to sit in the House of Lords, the upper chamber of Parliament. In a tier below them came the baronets, with their hereditary titles but no peerage, hence no entitlement to seats in the Lords. Then came the knights, who had earned their honour, which therefore could not be inherited. Below them came the broad mass of untitled landed gentry, with widely varying levels of wealth.

Jane Austen belonged to another sector of the country gentry: those without land, a class that Walpole described as the 'middling sort' who lay somewhere between wealth and poverty. Jane restricted her characterization to her own experience and never portrayed a figure of higher rank than Darcy, the grandson of an earl. But within her field of observation she was acutely aware of the subtle distinctions of social rank that played such an important role in society, as she illustrates in *Persuasion* when appraising Lady Russell's relationship with the baronet Sir Walter Elliott:

> **She [Lady Russell] was of strict integrity herself, with a delicate sense of honour … as aristocratic in her ideas of what was due to them [the Elliott family], as anybody of sense and honesty could well be … She had a cultivated mind, and was, generally speaking, rational and consistent; but she had prejudices on the side of ancestry; she had a value for rank and consequence, which blinded her a little to the faults of those who possessed them. Herself the widow of only a knight, she gave the dignity of a baronet all its due; and Sir Walter, independent of his claims as an old acquaintance … was, as being Sir Walter, in her apprehension, entitled to a great deal of compassion and consideration under his present difficulties.**

Many of the leading male characters in Jane Austen's novels come from the landowning gentry, and would have inherited their father's entire estate. A second son might, if he came from a wealthy family, inherit some property from his mother or a family relation. Otherwise the second and younger sons would be expected to take up one of the professions, of which the most respectable traditionally were the church, the army and the law. Choosing which was the most suitable was not always an easy task, especially for those who rather begrudged having to work at all. In *Sense and Sensibility* Edward Ferrars (himself a second son but one who behaves like the heir) bemoans the lot of a young man of genteel birth who is forced to take up a career:

It has been, and is, and probably will always be a heavy misfortune to me, that I have had no necessary business to engage me, no profession to give me employment, or afford me anything like independence. But unfortunately my own nicety, and the nicety of my friends, have made me what I am, an idle, helpless being. We never could agree in our choice of profession. I always preferred the church, and still do. But that was not smart enough for my family. They recommended the army. That was a great deal too smart for me. The law was allowed to be genteel enough; many young men, who had chambers in the Temple, made a very good appearance in the first circles, and drove about town in very knowing gigs [smart, light, two-wheeled carriages]. But I had no inclination for the law, even in this less obtruse study of it, which my family approved. As for the navy it had fashion on its side, but I was too old when the subject was first started to enter it – and, at length, as there was no necessity for my having any profession at all, as I might be as dashing and expensive without a red coat on my back as with one, idleness was pronounced on the whole to be the most advantageous and honourable.

The Clergyman's Lot

The steadiest profession to choose was the church. As a rector in a rural parish you would be a respected member of society. You did not need to be especially devout to be ordained as a minister of the Church of England. If you had enough money and connections behind you, you would receive a large house and a job for life.

As with many of the professions, patronage was the key to obtaining a 'living', as it was called. There were a number of routes to securing a benefice, and all depended on who you knew. If you were related to a bishop or dean, you might walk straight into one after being ordained. Others might have to wait 10 or 20 years – it was commonly referred to as 'the gamble'. One stage on the path to becoming a rector was securing a position as curate, the lowliest clergyman, who carried out the day-to-day duties required in a church in the absence of the rector, who might not himself reside in the parish, or otherwise was unwilling to do the work.

Some livings were endowed by public schools and Oxford or Cambridge universities. The only qualification required of a minister was a degree from one of these two universities (no others existed in England in Jane

Austen's time). Again, admittance depended on connections or the award of a scholarship. There were no examinations or rigorous interviews to be passed, as there are today. Once you became a member of a university college you had to wait for a living to become vacant and then present yourself at an election. This was the method by which James Woodforde, attending New College, Oxford, became rector of a parish in 1784. As he implied in his diary, any debating skills would have to be supplemented by other inducements to win over the voters:

> **Dec 15: We had a meeting of the whole House in the Hall at 12 o'clock, to present a Person to the Living of Western Longeville ... Hooke and myself were the two candidates proposed. Many learned and warm arguments started and disputed, and after 2 hours debate the House divided and it was put to the Vote, when there appeared for me 21 votes, and for Mr Hooke 15 only, on which I was declared and presented with the Presentation of the Rectory. The chief speakers for me were the Warden, Mr Holmes, Mr Webber, Mr Gauntlett, and Dr Wall ... I treated the Senr Common Room with Wine and Fruit in the afternoon and in the evening with Arrac Punch [a Scandinavian liqueur based on spirit distilled from palm or rice] and Wine. I treated the Junr Common Room with one dozen of Wine afternoon and in the evening with Arrac Punch and Wine. I gave the Chaplains half a dozen of Wine, the clerks 2 bottles and the Steward one bottle.**

Nepotism and favouritism were taken for granted in the 18th century. Jane Austen saw nothing wrong in her relations providing livings for their own. Many cousins on her father's side had been found parsonages through family connections. Her own father George Austen, who was ordained in 1760, was granted the living of Steventon, near Basingstoke in Hampshire, by his wealthy cousin and landowner Thomas Knight. To this benefice was added the neighbouring living of Deane by a kind uncle. Thus George Austen was set up with a modest endowment with which to get married to Cassandra Leigh in 1764 and he remained rector of Steventon for 40 years.

Wherever there was networking potential, it must have provided quite a temptation for a young man in need of a career. One might speculate that the system was open to abuse, that the motive for taking holy orders was sometimes driven not by any sense of religious conviction but by opportunism. Several characters in Jane's novels are clergymen, and this moral dilemma was sometimes aired in conversation. In *Mansfield Park*, Fanny Price questions the motive of Edmund Bertram, who has the distinct advantage of having the influential Sir Thomas Bertram as a father. Edmund defends himself in a conversation with Fanny:

> 'My taking orders, I assure you, is quite ... voluntary.'
> 'It is fortunate that your inclination and your father's convenience should accord so well. There is a very good living kept for you, I understand, hereabouts.'
> 'Which you suppose has biassed me?'
> 'But *that* I am sure it has not,' cried Fanny.
> '... The knowing that there was such a provision for me probably did bias me. Nor can I think it wrong that it should. There was no natural disinclination to be overcome, and I see no reason why a man should make a worse clergyman for knowing that he will have a competence early in life. I was in safe hands. I hope I should not have been influenced myself in a wrong way, and I am sure my father was too conscientious to have allowed it. I have no doubt that I was biased, but I think it was blamelessly.'

Though many parsons in Jane Austen's environment might have been devoted to their flock, the church did have something of a reputation for idleness. Even vicars who started out in their chosen profession with every intention of carrying out their duties conscientiously might be found guilty of self-indulgence. The evangelical reformer William Wilberforce thought most clergymen unsuited to the task of tackling the present lack of zeal in the church, describing the average vicar as an 'educated, polished, old, beneficed, nobleman's and gentleman's house-frequenting, literary and chess-playing divine'. In another scene in *Mansfield Park* Mary Crawford leaves Sir Thomas Bertram in no doubt as to her feelings about clergymen in general:

> Oh! No doubt he is very sincere in preferring an income ready made, to the trouble of working for one; and has the best intentions of doing nothing all the rest of his days but eat, drink and grow fat. It is indolence, Mr. Bertram, indeed. Indolence and love of ease; a want of all laudable ambition, of taste for good company, or of inclination to take the trouble of being agreeable, which make men clergymen. A clergyman has nothing to do but be slovenly and selfish—read the

newspaper, watch the weather, and quarrel with his wife. His curate does all the work, and the business of his own life is to dine.

In spite of favouritism endemic in the system of clerical patronage, a living, once it did become vacant, did not usually amount to much. George Austen's was quite typical in bringing in only about £100 a year. The usual business plan was to accumulate livings, and live off the proceeds from the land (the 'glebe') that came with the parsonage. The formal duties required of a parson were light, in many cases demanding no more than a single weekly visit. As Sir Thomas Bertram says of his son who has taken on the living of Thornton Lacey, eight miles from his home:

Edmund might, in the common phrase, do the duty of Thornton, that is, he might read prayers and preach, without giving up Mansfield Park; he might ride over, every Sunday, to a house nominally inhabited, and go through divine service; he might be the clergyman of Thornton Lacey every seventh day, for three or four hours, if that would content him.

If the vicar had several livings local enough he might endeavour to serve them all without resorting to the help of a curate, and could be seen racing from one to the next on a Sunday to take successive services. Such frantic figures were called 'gallopers', and became notorious for their bad time-keeping. Bell-ringers were known to wait until they could see the parson approaching on horseback before summoning the parish faithful. That was on a good day – if the weather was bad, the service would probably be cancelled altogether.

Curates fared even worse. Many bemoaned a miserable life, probably having to get by on as little as £50 a year. James, eldest son of George Austen, had his first curacy near Steventon. In a satirical magazine, *The Loiterer*, which he published in Oxford, the dull poverty of his circumstances prompted him to place a spoof advertisement in one issue of 1789:

Wanted—A Curacy in a good sporting country, near a pack of fox-hounds, and in a sociable neighbourhood; it must have a good house and stables, and a few acres of meadow ground would be very agreeable—To prevent trouble, the stipend must not be less than 80 l. [£80]—The Advertiser has no objection to undertaking three,

four or five Churches of a Sunday, but will not engage where there
is any weekly duty. Whoever has such a one to dispose of, may
suit themselves by sending a line, directed to be left at the *Turf
Coffee House.*

As it happens, his wish was soon granted in the form of the curacy of
Overton, situated near Steventon. From there, the best way forward was to
inveigle one's way into the good books of local squires. James was well aware
of how social manoeuvring could advance one's cause faster than any other
expedient. In another article in his magazine he offered the following advice
to inexperienced clergymen on how to get ahead as an impoverished curate:

If the pointers and the spaniels do not more than pay for their keep,
he must be a bad manager, or a bad shot. The pony may live in the
church yard; and as to the hunter, though it be true that hay and
corn are dear commodities; yet if all the good acquaintance and good
dinners, which a man gets by his attendance in the field be fairly
estimated, I know not whether he would not be a gainer at the end
of the year ... And the early lucrative pieces of preferment, which
are obtained by young men who have rendered themselves eminent,
prove beyond all controversy, that our country gentlemen are very
acute distinguishers of genius, and very liberal rewarders of merit.
For nothing is more certain, than a good shot has often brought
down a comfortable vicarage, and many a bold rider leaped into a
snug rectory ... there are numberless ways and means, by which,
in a smaller degree, he [the squire of the parish] may testify his
approbation of the clergyman's conduct. He will not only give him
unlimited leave to sport over his manor ... there shall be a knife
and fork always laid for him at his table ... I must think it a most
fortunate circumstance that every curate has it so much in his own
power to obtain [advantages].

It worked for James. Thanks to some goodwill on the part of his mother's
connections, within a few years he had acquired two additional livings in
Warwickshire. As they were located beyond reasonable travelling distance,
he did not visit them but simply drew the income from their tithes. The
usual terms of a living were possession of a vicarage rent free, together
with some farmland entitling the incumbent to receive tithes from his

parishioners. Tithing was a complex issue. Based on a practice originating in the Old Testament, the tithe in its simplest form was a ten per cent tax on agricultural produce, traditionally taken in kind. This meant that the clergy were obliged to become farmers, a fact that one Member of Parliament speaking in the House of Commons in 1802 regarded as most advantageous:

> **In this country the parish priest is, by the very constitution of his office, in some degree an agriculturist; he is *ex officio* a farmer. He is to take care, undoubtedly, that the ecclesiastic shall not merge in the farmer ... but the moderated and subordinate practice of farming supplies many means of cheap subsistence for the clergyman and his family; many means of easy kindness and hospitality to his poorer parishioners; and many motives of pleasing attachment to the place which furnishes the healthy and amusing occupation of his vacant hours.**

The reality was in many cases a good deal harder than is suggested here. Historically the clergyman had to gather in the tithes himself and store the produce in a tithe barn. This practice was still maintained in a dozen or so counties across southern England, including Hampshire, into the 19th century. The parson would have to visit farms regularly to assess the amount of produce due to him. The practical alternative was to come to some agreement with the farmer about what the monetary value (known as 'compounded' value) of his tithe would be, based on the expected yield that year. The parson would then have to act as an accounts' clerk to keep track of all the payments (and non-payments). The records of John Law, vicar of Brotherton, in 1770 indicate the complex nature of the business:

> **Turnips are paid for according to their value, or as they are let. Potatoes are paid in kind if not compounded for. The tythe of Orchards, Pigs and Geese are also paid in kind, if not compounded for. Rape and all new species of vicarial tythes are to be paid in kind unless compounded for, but Hemp and Flax must be paid according to Statute ... The new Shelling Mill built last year in the quarry Holes is also titheable ... N.B. If Clover and Saint Foin stand for seed the Tythe thereof belongs to the vicar, but if it is cut or made use of for Hay, the Tythe belongs to the Appropriators, or Lessee of the Dean and Chapter.**

Of course, getting their hands on the money was not always easy either. It was in the vicar's best interest to maintain good relations all round. Even the most pleasant demeanour in the world could not prevent some parishioners treating him like an evil tax collector. From his journals John Skinner, a rector in Somerset from 1803 to 1834, clearly had a hard time of it:

On going for letters I met Farmer Bush at the bottom of Radstock Hill, and said to him I wished to have some conversation respecting the tithe of the ground he bought off Charles Dando, as he had not settled the price. I told him on an average the people of Cridlingcot paid me 4s. 9d. an acre; that I supposed he would have no objection to pay that sum. He answered, indeed he never would; that what he had was not worth 3s. nor would he give me more. I felt hurt at his violent manner, and said the best way then of settling the business was by taking it up [going to court]. He replied I might do as I chose, he knew me, and had heard a good deal of me; that the people around knew me well enough. He said he would give me 2s. in the £. I told him, after his unprovoked insolence I would not waste any time by speaking to him: that respecting his tithe he should hear further on a future occasion. On leaving him he called out, *he* was not afraid of parsons.

It is hardly surprising that some vicars did not care to collect all their dues, but if they weren't careful they would be storing up repercussions for successive generations who tried to claim what was rightfully theirs. In the case of George Austen, the sort of scholarly man who might not be expected to take to farming, financial pressure sharpened his business wits. With a growing household to feed and children to educate (by 1775 Jane was the seventh of eight children born), he needed to get the most from his lands. The original glebe at Steventon was only about three acres, but in addition Thomas Knight leased him a nearby pig farm of some 200 acres. Although Mr Austen employed a steward to carry out most of the routine work, he kept abreast of fluctuations in the market.

As the 18th century drew to a close it was not unusual to find clergymen with a greater commercial awareness. Mr Austen had a vested interest in maximizing the revenue from his glebe since he would be nominating James as his curate on retirement. His son would be expected to collect the tithe and forward the proceeds on which the Austens and their unmarried offspring depended. Jane kept a keen eye on progress in this department and relayed the information to Cassandra:

> My father is doing all in his power to increase his Income by raising his Tythes &c, & I do not despair of getting very nearly six hundred a year.

The Army for Gentlemen

The system of primogeniture kept estates intact, but it put pressure on the younger sons to choose a career. The only way the system could survive was if it found opportunities for them in the numerous areas under government patronage: the army, navy, civil service, imperial administration and the higher ranks of the church and the law. The patronage system stayed firmly entrenched well into the 19th century, as illustrated in correspondence complaining about the privileged cream of society, known as the Upper Ten Thousand. The following quote from Matthew Higgins' 'A Letter on Administrative Reform' (1855) is an exaggeration of the truth, but could equally well have applied to England in the 18th century:

> The Upper Ten Thousand hitherto monopolized every post of honour, trust and emolument under the Crown, from the highest to the lowest. They have taken what they wanted for themselves; they have distributed what they did not want among their relations, connexions, and dependents. They have in turn paid their debts of friendship and gratitude, they have provided for their younger sons and their worn-out servants with appointments in the public service.

The problem of having insufficient jobs to occupy the younger sons was alleviated temporarily when England went to war with Revolutionary France in 1793 (the year Louis XVI and his queen, Marie Antoinette, were guillotined). On and off until the Battle of Waterloo 22 years later, the army regularly needed new recruits to swell its ranks of officers. Even at the onset of war, however, to become an officer of the regular army required money, and how much depended on the rank you intended to purchase. Commissions were bought and sold on the open market, often through advertisements in the press, such as this one in an issue of the *Morning Post* for an ensigncy, the lowest ranking officer's commission:

An Ensigncy in an Old Regiment returned from Egypt and now at Malta to be sold, £60 under the regulated price. There are several vacancies in that regiment which makes it an eligible purchase.

The going rate for an ensigncy in the latter part of the 18th century was about £500; a lieutenant-colonelcy could cost as much as £4,000. Payments did not stop there either. Once you had bought your way in, promotion was usually down to patronage rather than ability. If you had the wherewithal, the army was a popular choice – as was the navy – and certainly more glamorous than the clergy. In *Mansfield Park*, Mary Crawford extols the virtues of an officer in the armed forces:

The profession, either navy or army … has everything in its favour: heroism, danger, bustle, fashion. Soldiers and sailors are always acceptable in society. Nobody can wonder that men are soldiers and sailors.

At the outbreak of war regiments from all over the country gathered at Brighton, which offered the shortest overland route from the English Channel to London and was therefore an expected landing ground for a French invasion. There on the pebbled beach the orderly phalanxes of soldiers practised their manoeuvres and drills. It was a source of great pride to onlookers, and in some eyes – including those of Lydia Bennet in *Pride and Prejudice* – nothing could beat a soldier dressed in uniform:

In Lydia's imagination, a visit to Brighton comprised every possibility of earthly happiness. She saw, with the creative eye of fancy, the streets of that gay bathing-place covered with officers. She saw herself the object to tens and to scores of them at present unknown. She saw all the glories of the camp—its tents stretched forth in beauteous uniformity of lines, crowded with the young and the gay, and dazzling with scarlet; and, to complete the view, she saw herself seated beneath a tent, tenderly flirting with at least six officers at once.

The army was a fashionable calling for the aristocracy as well as for gentlemen. The Prince of Wales (the future King George IV) belonged to the 10th Light Dragoons, and Jane Austen's character Frederick, son of General

Tilney of Northanger Abbey, Gloucestershire, belonged to the 12th Light Dragoons, a genuine regiment. Both the heir to the British throne and Jane's fictitious character were dilettantes. As well as offering the opportunity for heroics on the battlefield, the army was attractive to those who regarded the officers' mess as a gentlemen's club, fit for unrestrained gambling, drinking and womanizing. The Prince of Wales was a notorious exponent of these arts (as described in Chapter 7) and no doubt Jane's stationing of Captain Frederick Tilney in a regiment so close to that of the prince was no coincidence.

For those who could not afford a commission in the regular army there was another, cheaper branch, called the militia, which was trained for domestic duty only. The original idea had been to have a corps trained as a home front in order to free up the regulars to fight overseas. In fact the threat of invasion from France was so great at this time that the regulars were replacing the militia for defence duty. The militia operated only in wartime, whereas in times of peace regular soldiers (in the absence of a police force) would be put on to civil duties, such as quelling riots and handling criminals.

Like the regular army, the militia offered its members a good time when off duty. Soldiers were billeted in towns and officers dined with the local families. In *Pride and Prejudice* (composed three or four years into the war with France), Jane Austen portrays the militaristic aspect of society that she must have experienced during this protracted wartime period. Lieutenant George Wickham, stationed with a regiment (unnamed as 'the —shire' as the author cannot give a genuine name) at Meryton in Hertfordshire, has a distinct fondness for his elevated status thanks to the war:

> **Mr. Wickham began to speak on more general topics, Meryton, the neighbourhood, the society, appearing highly pleased with all that he had yet seen, and speaking of the latter especially, with gentle but very intelligible gallantry.**
>
> **'It was the prospect of constant society, and good society,' he added, 'which was my chief inducement to enter the —shire. I knew it to be a most respectable, agreeable corps, and my friend Denny tempted me farther by his account of their present quarters, and the very great attentions and excellent acquaintance Meryton had procured them.'**

Jane's brother Henry joined the Oxford Militia (though he had been expected to take up a career in the church), as he explained in a letter to the bishop of Winchester,

... not being old enough for ordination, and the political circumstances of the time 1793 calling on every one not otherwise employ'd to offer his services in the general defence of the Country.

Although he took a commission as a lieutenant, Henry clearly felt he belonged to an inferior branch of the army. In a letter to Cassandra, in January 1796, Jane outlined his ambitions:

Henry is still hankering after the Regulars, and as his project of purchasing the adjutancy of the Oxfordshire is now over [later revived], he has got a scheme in his head about getting a lieutenancy and adjutancy in the 86th, a new-raised regiment, which he fancies will be ordered to the Cape of Good Hope.

The 86th Regiment was set up for overseas service and was stationed at Portsmouth. It embarked for the Cape in June of that year, alas without Henry, who had to resign himself to stay with the Oxfordshires until he left the army in 1800. He did, however, gain promotion and by all accounts enjoyed the social life of his regiment, stationed for much of the time in East Anglia, and from 1797 conducted with a wife on his arm – his cousin Eliza, widow to the Comte de Feuillide.

Upwardly Mobile in the Navy

The navy was a less aristocratic organization than the army because commissions did not have to be expensively purchased. Though, like the army, it was open to patronage, it offered an ambitious but unmoneyed young recruit greater opportunity to progress through the ranks by his own merits. After the clergy, the navy was Jane Austen's favourite profession for a man (two of her brothers, Francis and Charles, had distinguished careers in the navy). This modern idea of meritocracy that the navy embraced did not sit well with the old-world order of heredity and privilege. In *Persuasion* the arch-representative of the old system is Sir Walter Elliott. In the following scene he is discussing with his daughter Anne and his butler Mr Shepherd the possibility of renting accommodation to men of the navy on their return from service, a prospect which, though to Sir Walter's financial advantage, is causing him, and his like in Jane Austen's day, a good deal of consternation:

Here Anne spoke,—

'The navy, I think, who have done so much for us, have at least an equal claim with any other set of men, for all the comforts and all the privileges which any home can give. Sailors work hard enough for their comforts, we must all allow.'

'Very true, very true. What Miss Anne says, is very true,' was Mr. Shepherd's rejoinder, and 'Oh! certainly,' was his daughter's; but Sir Walter's remark was, soon afterwards—

'The profession has its utility, but I should be sorry to see any friend of mine belonging to it.'

'Indeed!' was the reply, and with a look of surprise.

'Yes; it is in two points offensive to me; I have two strong grounds of objection to it. First, as being the means of bringing persons of obscure birth into undue distinction, and raising men to honours which their fathers and grandfathers never dreamt of; and secondly, as it cuts up a man's youth and vigour most horribly; a sailor grows old sooner than any other man; I have observed it all my life ...

'I was in company with ... a certain Admiral Baldwin, the most deplorable looking personage you can imagine, his face the colour of mahogany, rough and rugged to the last degree, all lines and wrinkles, nine grey hairs of a side, and nothing but a dab of powder at top.—"In the name of heaven, who is that old fellow?" said I, to a friend of mine who was standing near. "Old fellow!" cried Sir Basil, "it is Admiral Baldwin. What do you take his age to be?" "Sixty," said I, "or perhaps sixty-two." "Forty," replied Sir Basil, "forty, and no more." Picture to yourselves my amazement; I shall not easily forget Admiral Baldwin. I never saw quite so wretched an example of what a sea-faring life can do; but to a degree, I know it is the same with them all: they are all knocked about, and exposed to every climate, and every weather, till they are not fit to be seen. It is a pity they are not knocked on the head at once, before they reach Admiral Baldwin's age.'

To an aristocrat's mind, these naval fellows would never suit the salons of good taste frequented by army officers. Apart from ill appearance and the open-door approach that gave a chance to every Tom, Dick and Harry, there was a third objection to the navy: the ill-gotten gains made from plundering vessels on the high seas, where the navy was a law unto itself. One astute observer of his countrymen of the early 1800s was the poet Robert Southey, who had this to say about such practices among the navy:

> The English sailor feels that he is master of the seas. Whatever he sees is to do him homage. He is always on the look-out, not with the fear of an enemy before his eyes, but like a strong pirate with the hope of gain; and when going into action, with an equal or even a superior force, he calculates his profits as certainly as if the enemy were already taken.—'There,' said the master of a frigate, when the captain did not choose to engage a superior French force because he had a convoy in charge— 'There,' said he with a groan, 'there's seven hundred pounds lost to me for ever.'—As for fear, it is not in their nature.

War provided the opportunity to get rich by obtaining 'prize money', the pickings from captured enemy vessels, which were divided among the captain and his crew (the state received nothing). Jane's brother Charles gave each of his two sisters a topaz cross out of prize money, while his elder brother Francis made enough to get married on the proceeds. In *Persuasion* the gallant Captain Wentworth accumulates a sum over the course of eight years amounting to £25,000, turning himself into what would be termed today a self-made man.

Even so, rising up the ranks was always helped by a good word in the right ear – 'interest', as it was known. The following conversation between Captain Wentworth and Admiral Croft indicates the level of competition among eligible naval officers for desirable vacancies. The conversation also covers the danger inherent in boarding a British naval vessel, which was generally inferior in design and seaworthiness to its French and Spanish counterparts. The term 'Gravesend Voyages' was coined after the frequency with which warships went down.

> [Said one of the Miss Musgroves:] 'Your first was the *Asp*, I remember.'
> '... Quite worn out and broken up. I [Wentworth] was the last man who commanded her. Hardly fit for service then. Reported fit for home service for a year or two, and so I was sent off to the West Indies.'
> The girls looked all amazement.
> 'The Admiralty,' he continued, 'entertain themselves now and

then, with sending a few hundred men to sea, in a ship not fit
to be employed. But they have a great many to provide for; and
among the thousands that may just as well go to the bottom as
not, it is impossible for them to distinguish the very set who may
be least missed.'

'Phoo! phoo!' cried the Admiral, 'what stuff these young fellows
talk! Never was a better sloop than the *Asp* in her day. For an old
built sloop, you would not see her equal. Lucky fellow to get her! He
knows there must have been twenty better men than himself applying
for her at the same time. Lucky fellow to get anything so soon, with
no more interest than his.'

'I felt my luck, Admiral, I assure you,' replied Captain Wentworth,
seriously. 'I was as well satisfied with my appointment as you can
desire. It was a great object with me at that time to be at sea; a very
great object, I wanted to be doing something.'

Jane Austen's niece Caroline recalled in her diary the sinking of one of
Charles Austen's ships:

1816, Feb 20: Captain Charles Austen's ship the *Phoenix* was lost.
She went down—all the crew saved. The place is not noted; I do not
remember where it was. The pilot was on board. The *Phoenix* had
been a lucky ship, Admiral Halsted having made his fortune in her,
but her luck had now run out; perhaps she was not as sea-worthy as
she had been, tho' I do not recollect that this was ever said. No blame
fell on the Captain, yet such a misfortune is always a disparagement;
and the war being over, he knew he was likely to wait long for
another ship.

There was no doubting that the navy offered an exciting and romantic lifestyle in an age when there seemed to be no stopping Britannia from ruling
the waves. The stories brought back of adventure and rich spoils and the cult
of Admiral Nelson must have fired the imagination of many a young boy.

And young they were when they joined up. Boys from 12 to 15 years of age
would be admitted to a naval college and trained, normally for three years.
Both Francis and Charles Austen entered the Royal Naval Academy at
Portsmouth at this stage of their lives. Aged just 14, Francis (known to Jane
as Frank) set sail for the East Indies as a lowly midshipman and before the

outbreak of war with France was made a lieutenant, the most junior of the commissioned officers. There would be several lieutenants on board a man-of-war. A mix of good and bad luck in battle would see a series of promotions up to first lieutenant; then came commander, captain, and ultimately admiral of the fleet.

At the age of 31, Francis was appointed flag-captain to Rear Admiral Louis, who was second in command to Lord Nelson. In those momentous times Francis was right at the heart of history-making in the decisive year of 1805. In March of that year Nelson commended his fine seamanship:

> I hope to see [Captain Austen] alongside a French 80-gun ship, and he cannot be better placed than in the *Canopus*, which was once a French Admiral's ship, and struck to me. Captain Austen I knew a little of before; he is an excellent young man.

He sailed with Nelson's fleet chasing the French Admiral Villeneuve to the West Indies and back; he spent September blockading Cadiz; and his ship *Canopus* was fifth in line for the Battle of Trafalgar. At the last minute he was ordered to divert to Gibraltar for water supplies and it was a race to get back in time to face the enemy. In a letter he began writing to his first wife Mary (née Gibson) on 15 October, Frank said:

> I do not profess to like fighting for its own sake, but if there has been an action with the combined fleets I shall ever consider the day on which I sailed from the squadron as the most inauspicious one of my life.

The letter continued on 27 October:

> Alas! My dearest Mary, all my fears are but too fully justified. The fleets have met, and, after a very severe contest, a most decisive victory has been gained by the English twenty-seven over the enemy's thirty-three. Seventeen of the ships are taken and one is burnt; but I am truly sorry to add that this splendid affair has cost us many lives, and amongst them the most invaluable one to the nation, that of our gallant, and ever-to-be-regretted, Commander-in-Chief, Lord Nelson, who was mortally wounded by a musket shot, and only lived long enough to know his fleet successful ... there is not an Admiral

on the list so eminently calculated for the command of a fleet as he
was. I never heard of his equal, nor do I expect again to see such a
man ... he possessed in a superior degree the happy talent of making
every class of persons pleased with their situation and eager to exert
themselves in forwarding the public service ... I cannot help feeling
how very unfortunate we have been to be away at such a moment and
... to lose all share in the glory of a day which surpasses all which
ever went before ... but, as I cannot write upon that subject without
complaining, I will drop it for the present, till time and reflection
reconcile me a little more to what I know is now inevitable.

Though he was bitterly disappointed to have missed Trafalgar, compensation
came the following February with his involvement in the victorious Battle of
St Domingo. Frank was eventually made Admiral of the Fleet in 1863, two
years before his death at the rare old age of 91. His brother Charles rose to
the rank of Rear Admiral.

The New Middle Classes

'The middle classes', as a descriptive term, came into usage at the end of the
18th century to apply to an increasing number of groups in society that had
gained a certain respectability by virtue of belonging to minor professions.
These included bankers, doctors, apothecaries, teachers, attorneys and some
tradesmen. 'Trade' was something of a dirty word among the gentry, who felt
threatened by the new money being made in business. Jane Austen did not
share this snobbish prejudice against trade but had a keen eye on how the
successful ones – the *nouveaux riches* – were worming their way into gentility.
She classifies them socially as 'half-gentlemen' in *Emma*. They tended to be
educated but had no 'breeding' and would always struggle in society for want
of good connections. As Chesterfield put it, they were 'straining to imitate
their betters'. A typical example of a family on the rise is vignetted in *Emma*:

The Coles had been settled some years in Highbury, and were very
good sort of people—friendly, liberal, and unpretending; but, on the
other hand, they were of low origin, in trade, and only moderately
genteel. On their first coming into the country, they had lived in
proportion to their income, quietly, keeping little company, and that
little unexpensively; but the last year or two had brought them a

considerable increase of means—the house in town had yielded greater profits, and fortune in general had smiled on them. With their wealth, their views increased; their want of a larger house, their inclination for more company. They added to their house, to their number of servants, to their expenses of every sort; and by this time were, in fortune and style of living, second only to the family at Hartfield. Their love of society, and their new dining-room, prepared every body for their keeping dinner-company; and a few parties, chiefly among the single men, had already taken place ... The Coles were very respectable in their way, but they ought to be taught that it was not for them to arrange the terms on which the superior families would visit them.

Within the broad gambit of the middle classes some chartered professions had been established. Only doctors licensed by the Royal College of Physicians, for instance, could practise as physicians, though for lowly surgeons and apothecaries, almost anyone could try their hand. There was nothing legally in place to stop someone being a jack of all trades. One man from Ilchester in Somerset advertised himself as 'Apothecary, Surgeon, Coal dealer, Brick and Tile Maker, &c'. Most 'white-collar' workers did not care for corporate professionalism. They regarded themselves as men of business rather than public servants. Attorneys (the equivalent of modern solicitors) involved themselves in various activities, including mortgage broking and banking as well as litigation, and were often called on to be arbitrators in disputes. By a degree of entrepreneurship attorneys could build up quite a large fortune.

Making money was not frowned upon within the middle classes. As the Industrial Revolution gathered pace, businessmen everywhere endeavoured to get their hands on a slice of the cake. Manufacturers, wholesalers, shopkeepers, speculators and investors all cashed in on an economy that was burgeoning with imperial trade. Many a noble had built his fortune on trade, so there was an ambivalent attitude to it in Georgian England. As Daniel Defoe commented:

Our tradesmen are not as in other countries the meanest of our people. Some of the greatest and best and most flourishing families, among not the gentry only but even the nobility have been raised from trade.

The Austens themselves hailed from ancestral clothiers of the Weald in Kent, where they had held some considerable power in the past at the height of the wool trade. Jane's nephew James Edward Austen-Leigh recalled the background in his memoir of his aunt:

> **The clothing business was exercised by persons who possessed most of the landed property in the Weald, insomuch that almost all the ancient families of these parts, now of large estates and genteel rank in life, and some of them ennobled by titles, are sprung from ancestors who have used this great staple manufacture ... The Austens were usually called the Gray Coats of Kent; and were a body so numerous and united that at county elections whoever had their vote and interest was almost certain of being elected.**

One of the new professions that was steadily acquiring respectability as the need for finance expanded was banking. When Henry Austen left the army in 1801, he founded a bank in London with two fellow officers. In time he made a name for himself and was invited to a grand ball organized by the White's Club, held at Burlington House in celebration of the peace of June 1814 with Napoleonic France. Present were the Prince Regent, the Emperor of Russia and the King of Prussia. The party on its own was said to have cost £10,000 (the wealthy Mr Darcy's income for a whole year). Jane was flabbergasted:

> **Henry at White's!—Oh! What a Henry.**

But how the mighty fall! Within two years of this proud day for Henry his bank had fallen into serious debt. His niece Caroline Austen recalled the turmoil in her diary:

> **[1816] was a bad year for our family. The most serious misfortune was my Uncle Henry's bankruptcy, announced on 16th March, an entire surprise at our house, and as little foreseen I believe by the rest of the family. But the apprehension of the coming evil had had much to do with his own illness a few months previously. The Bank was in Henrietta Street, Covent Garden – Austen, Maunde & Tilson ...**
>
> **To my uncle it was ruin, and he saw the world before him, to begin again. In about a fortnight he came to Steventon, *apparently* ... in**

unbroken spirits. I believe he had even then decided on taking Orders. He *had* been destined for the Church, but had preferred going into business and had left St John's College early. Now the old learning was to be looked up, and he went to Oxford to see about taking the necessary degree ... and examinations were not overstrict in the year 1816, so that altogether no difficulties opposed his entrance into the profession to which he now turned.

Various members of the Austen family lost their money as a result of the collapse. In order to become the bank's receiver for Oxfordshire when it was set up, Henry had had to persuade a number of his relations to stump up the required investment: his uncle James Leigh-Perrot put up £10,000 and his brother Edward £20,000; his other brothers made sundry benefactions of a few hundreds each. All was lost. Jane herself seems to have escaped lightly, having just £25 7s in her account at Henrietta Street, some of the proceeds from the sale of *Mansfield Park* (the profits from her other novels she wisely invested in Navy five per cent stock).

The Lower Middles

Beneath the broad raft of middle classes came the tenant farmers, artisans and clerks. By 1790 three-quarters of England's agricultural land was cultivated by tenants. Many did well, as Jane Austen depicts in *Emma* through the character of Robert Martin, a 24-year-old tenant farmer on Mr Knightley's estate. He lives with his widowed mother and two younger sisters, all of whom he has to support. He tends his flock of sheep responsibly, dresses neatly and is determined to make the best of his lot by studying agricultural reports and getting the best prices at market for his wool. But he is not educated and is socially awkward. Emma Woodhouse thinks ill of his sort: his aspirations take him too close for her liking to her social milieu. She warns her friend Harriet Smith, who appears to be attracted to Mr Martin:

'A young farmer, whether on horseback or on foot, is the very last sort of person to raise my curiosity. The yeomanry are precisely the order of people with whom I feel I can have nothing to do. A degree or two lower, and a creditable appearance might interest me; I might hope to be useful to their families in some way or other. But a farmer can need none of my help ...

'He [Robert Martin] will be a completely gross, vulgar farmer [when older], totally inattentive to appearances, and thinking of nothing but profit and loss.'

'Will he, indeed? That will be very bad.' [replied Harriet]

'How much his business engrosses him already is very plain from the circumstance of his forgetting to inquire for the book you recommended. He was a great deal too full of the market to think of any thing else—which is just as it should be, for a thriving man. What has he to do with books? And I have no doubt that he will thrive, and be a very rich man in time—and his being illiterate and coarse need not disturb us.'

Similar sentiments were expressed by the agricultural commentator Arthur Young, who wrote extensively on what he observed of farming culture in *A Six Weeks' Tour through the Southern Counties of England and Wales* in 1770:

Sometimes I see a piano forte in a farmer's parlour, which I always wish was burnt; a livery servant is sometimes found, and a post chaise to carry their daughters to assemblies; these ladies are sometimes educated at expensive boarding-schools, and the sons often at the University, to be made parsons. But all these things imply a departure from that line which separates these different orders of being. Let these things, and all the folly, foppery, expense, and anxiety, that belong to them, remain among gentlemen: a wise farmer will not envy them.

As business grew in the Georgian era, so office life was born. A new class of worker, the clerk, became prominent in towns and cities. Many began work aged 14 and might stay put for the rest of their days. Though Jane Austen spent most of her time in the country, she knew from her family and acquaintances something of working life in metropolitan areas. In the following extract from an essay by the poet Charles Lamb, born, like Jane, in 1775, a clerk reflects on his days spent in drudgery in the city of London.

If peradventure, Reader, it has been thy lot to waste the golden years of thy life—thy shining youth—in the irksome confinement of an office; to have thy prison days prolonged through middle age down to decrepitude and silver hairs, without hope of release or respite;

to have lived to forget that there are such things as holidays, or to remember them but as the prerogatives of childhood; then, and then only, will you be able to appreciate my deliverance.

It is now six-and-thirty years since I took my seat at the desk in Mincing Lane. Melancholy was the transition at fourteen from the abundant playtime, and the frequently-intervening vacations of school days, to the eight, nine and sometimes ten hours' a day attendance at the Counting House. But time partially reconciles us to anything. I gradually became content—doggedly contented, as wild animals in cages.

It is true I had my Sundays to myself; but Sundays, admirable as the institution of them is for purposes of worship, are for that very reason the very worst adapted for days of unbending and recreation. In particular, there is a gloom for me attendant upon a city Sunday, a weight in the air. I miss the cheerful cries of London, the music and the ballad-singers—the buzz and stirring murmur of the streets. Those eternal bells depress me. The closed shops repel me. Prints, pictures, all the glittering and endless succession of knacks and gewgaws [trinkets], and ostentatiously displayed wares of tradesmen, which make a weekday saunter through the less busy parts of the metropolis so delightful—are shut out ... Nothing to be seen but unhappy countenances of emancipated 'prentices and little tradesfolks, with here and there a servant-maid that has got leave to go out, who, slaving all the week, with the habit has lost almost the capacity of enjoying a free hour.

But besides Sundays, I had a day at Easter, and a day at Christmas, with a full week in the summer to go and air myself in my native fields of Hertfordshire. This last was a great indulgence; and the prospect of its recurrence, I believe, alone kept me up through the year. But when the week came round, did the glittering phantom of the distance keep touch with me, or rather was it not a series of seven uneasy days, spent in restless pursuit of pleasure, and a wearisome anxiety to find out how to make the most of them? Where was the quiet, where the promised rest? Before I had a taste of it, it was vanished. I was at the desk again, counting upon the fifty-one tedious weeks that must intervene before such another snatch would come.

... I was fifty years of age, and no prospect of emancipation presented itself. I had grown to my desk, as it were; and the wood had entered into my soul.

Work For a Lady

Few women in Georgian Britain chose to remain unmarried. If they had a reasonable inheritance their status as a single woman was respected. Emma Woodhouse, for example, whom Jane Austen depicts as a typical case of a well-to-do woman, has a dowry of £30,000. This money would have been invested in government bonds paying interest at five per cent, so her annual income would have been £1,500. Ladies of the gentry without money or prospects of money being settled on them through inheritance had very few options to make a living. Some, like Jane, earned a little from writing, but professional work was not considered befitting of a gentle lady. For most, the only real possibilities were as a lady's companion, school teacher or governess. The writer Mary Wollstonecraft experienced life as a companion to an affluent but bored married woman and found the job awful, being obliged to:

> **... live with strangers who are so intolerably tyrannical ... It is impossible to enumerate the many hours of anguish such a person must spend. She is alone, shut out from equality and confidence.**

The work of most school teachers was hardly better, according to Mary Wollstonecraft, who described them as a 'kind of upper servant who has more work than the menial ones'.

Towards the end of the 18th century, when home education was fashionable, by far the most common paid occupation for a gentlewoman was that of governess. She would live in the household and was on duty for 12 hours a day, seven days a week. On top of free board and lodging, she might earn just £10 to £30 a year, leaving precious little for retirement. On the other hand a governess who knew French and had all the right graces might earn up to £100 if she found a position with an affluent family. The following advertisement for a governess appeared in the *Bath Chronicle* in 1798:

> **WANTED.**
> **   A GOVERNESS, who can teach FRENCH and ITALIAN grammatically.—MUSIC enough to teach in the absence of a Master. She is expected to rise early, and will not have a maid to attend her. She is to sleep in the room with a Young Lady, and to eat with her when requested. The salary Sixty Guineas a year.—She will not visit**

with the Lady [of the house], as she is wanted to attend entirely to the education of two Young Ladies. A middle-aged person will be preferred, and of the Protestant Religion.

Even a good position might still be dull and repetitive, as one governess writing in the 1830s recalled:

Cooped up in a school room in some remote part of the house, with the same books, desks, stools, back-boards, an indifferent pianoforte, a noisy canary or two, perhaps a pet cat, and a high fender which eclipses the cheerfulness of the fire. This seclusion from society tends to sour the temper and narrow the ideas, but I am happy to observe a considerable improvement in that class, who are now much more enlightened and liberal.

What is more, the spinster governess suffered ignominiously from social stigma. Not treated as an equal by the heads of the house and not inclined to associate with the servants, she was virtually shut away from society like a prisoner. In some cases she became prey to the nastier instincts of those who chose to exploit her social vulnerability. Many, like Ellen Weeton writing in her *Journal of a Governess*, might consider marriage simply to avoid reproachful attitudes:

The finger of contempt, the smile of ridicule … an old maid is a stock for everyone to laugh at. Every article of dress, every word, every movement is satirized. Boys play tricks on them and are applauded. Girls sneer at them and are unreproved.

In her portrait of Jane Fairfax in *Emma* Jane Austen presents the typical dilemma of a girl with no prospects who is resigned to becoming a governess and is not looking forward to it, likening it to the slave trade. Mrs Elton brings up the sore subject:

'My dear child, the time *is* drawing near; here is April, and June … is very near, with such business to accomplish before us … A situation such as you deserve, and your friends would require for you, is no every day occurrence, is not obtained at a moment's notice; indeed, indeed, we must begin inquiring directly.'

'Excuse me, ma'am, but this is by no means my intention … There are places in town, offices, where inquiry would soon produce something—offices for the sale, not quite of human flesh, but of human intellect.'

'Oh! my dear, human flesh! You quite shock me; if you mean a fling at the slave-trade, I assure you Mr. Suckling was always rather a friend to the abolition.'

'I did not mean, I was not thinking of the slave-trade,' replied Jane; 'governess-trade, I assure you, was all that I had in view; widely different certainly, as to the guilt of those who carry it on; but as to the greater misery of the victims, I do not know where it lies …'

'… I [Mrs Elton] know what a modest creature you are; but it will not satisfy your friends to have you taking up with … any inferior, commonplace situation, in a family not moving in a certain circle, or able to command the elegancies of life.'

Not all situations turned out to be as bad as were feared. Some parents placed high value on the skills of a governess in her provision of a worthwhile education for their children. The journals of Agnes Porter, the intelligent and warm-hearted daughter of an Anglican clergyman who devoted much of her time to educating the daughters of the Earl of Ilchester, describe an employer who is a good deal more considerate than most and who evidently held her in high regard. Quite what caused her to hand in her notice is uncertain:

Had a conversation with Lord Ilchester on the subject of my leaving his family—I told him my own particular affairs would require my giving up the honour of my charge in his lordship's family. I proposed six months as notice, asked him if he thought *that* a proper one? He was indeed deeply affected—seemed both surprised and shocked. I made no reflection on any person nor circumstance; said it was probable I might live with a friend, but if I was disappointed and returned to the same line of education, I should trouble his lordship for a recommendation. I then thanked him for *thirteen* years' protection and *several* years of happiness. The *thanks*, he said, were *due to me*—he took me by the hand and said I had *knock'd him up*, he could not say a word then on the subject, but if it was for my happiness he must acquiesce. At night I reflected on this conversation, was satisfied in my own mind, as I had not said a single word more than I had resolved to do. I had not been induced by any little *female resentments* to hazard or compromise the tranquillity of a family I respected, though I looked upon myself as a victim of circumstances, but I thought I should withdraw with a degree even of dignity. I considered that the three charming little girls whom I had received from their dear mother's hand were now grown up, the youngest near nineteen; I had to the utmost of my power completed their education, and had tried to supply to them a mother's love. The two eldest were married, the third to be presented this spring. Towards them I had performed the part assigned me ... In the afternoon Lady Ilchester invited me to tea, and expressed what she was pleased to term her *sorrow* at my intended departure.

Education and Upbringing

Ladies of good breeding in Georgian England were not expected to have much to do with their infants. Being intimately involved in their upbringing was too childish, for one thing; and it was customary for relations between parents and their children to be kept formal, for respect was valued more highly than affection. Contact was limited to certain times of the day. For the rest, the care of children was placed in the hands of others: wet-nurses, nursemaids and, when they were older, governesses and tutors.

Mrs Austen had a clear idea about child-rearing, described in a memoir by Jane's nephew, James Edward Austen-Leigh (born in 1798, the son of her eldest brother James). Notice that the infant is referred to not as 'he' or 'she', but 'it':

Her [Jane's] mother followed a custom, not unusual in those days, though it seems strange to us, of putting out her babies to be nursed in a cottage in the village. The infant was daily visited by one or both of its parents, and frequently brought to them at the parsonage, but the cottage was its home, and must have remained so till it was old enough to run about and talk; for I know that one of them, in after life, used to speak of his foster mother as 'Movie', the name by which he had called her in his infancy. It may be that the contrast between the parsonage house and the best class of cottages was not quite so extreme then as it would be now, that the one was somewhat less luxurious, and the other less squalid. It would certainly seem from the results that it was a wholesome and invigorating system, for the children were all strong and healthy. Jane was probably treated like the rest in this respect.

This procedure of fostering out children is further evidenced in a letter from Mrs Austen, writing in 1773, about her fifth child, Cassandra, then five months old:

I suckled my little girl thro' the first quarter; she has been weaned and settled at a good woman's at Deane just eight weeks; she is very healthy and lively, and puts on her short petticoats to-day.

Mrs Austen's system of weaning her children early and giving them out to a dry-nurse was not necessarily conventional. Throughout the 18th century there were conflicting views on the best course for bringing up infants. Increasingly there was an argument, on medical and moral grounds, that mothers should breast-feed rather than farm out their babies to a wet-nurse, while others claimed that artificial feeding on animal milk was a healthier option. Advice manuals such as *The Ladies Dispensatory* warned that handing over a baby too young to a foster mother might damage the emotional bond between mother and child:

That those Mothers who do, as it were, discharge their Children from them, and thus dispose of them, do at least weaken, if not dissolve the Bond of Love and Tenderness which Nature ties between them.

How much the Austens' method of child-rearing affected their children's emotional lives is a moot point. While Mrs Austen was away in London on one occasion, her husband wrote on this subject to his 'dear sister' (in fact, the wife of his half-brother) Susanna Walter. He was more than a little dismayed that his wife had abandoned her family duties at Steventon to have a gay old time in London:

I don't much like this lonely kind of life; you know I have not been much used to it, and yet I must bear with it about three weeks longer. ... My James [the eldest son] and his brothers are both well, and what will surprise you, bear their mother's absence with great philosophy: as I doubt not they would mine, and turn all their little affections towards those who were about them and good to them; this may not be a pleasing reflection to a fond parent, but is certainly wisely designed by Providence for the happiness of the child.

The Austen children did not miss their mother when she was away probably because they doted on their foster mother 'Movie' (Bessy Littleworth). It was the Austens' belief that boys should spend as little time as possible at home in the earliest years so that they developed a healthy independence in the best aristocratic tradition of the Leigh family. Revd Austen seemed at first to agree with this principle, which he said was God-given, but there was a change of heart when baby Henry came along. At just six months of age, Henry was brought back to the rectory for good. It is thought that his father put his foot down and was determined that Henry should be put in no doubt as to who his real mother was.

Jane had affectionate relationships with most of her brothers, who figure a good deal in her correspondence. One exception was the second son, George, about whom she said not a word. He was mentally handicapped and at the age of six was put into the care of foster parents. This same couple also looked after the boy's handicapped uncle, Thomas Leigh (Mrs Austen's brother). This seems to have been a fairly standard practice of the time.

Another was adoption. Jane's brother Edward was adopted by the wealthy squire Thomas Knight, in circumstances that might seem today to be strange for adoption but were not uncommon in her time. Those among the landed gentry who remained childless and wished to have an heir might look around for a suitable candidate. Thomas Knight was the benefactor of the two parishes given to George Austen and had been a family friend for many years. After several long stays at the Knights' family home, Edward, aged 16, was duly brought to the huge ancestral estate of Godmersham in Kent, which he would one day inherit. (This proved to be of considerable value to Jane, Cassandra and their mother, who were later given Chawton Cottage, inherited by Edward, when they had no home to call their own.) Quite what Jane thought of her brother's adoption is not known, but in *Emma* she portrays a similar situation in which Frank Weston is adopted by his wealthy relatives, the Churchills. Emma Woodhouse declares:

There is something so shocking in a child's being taken away from his parents and natural home.

Home Education

In the early Georgian period it was normal for aristocratic families to send their sons and daughters away to boarding school. But as the 18th century progressed these schools became increasingly populated by the gentry and new middle classes and so became less attractive to the aristocracy, who did not wish their children to mix outside their social class. The result was a rise in demand for tuition at home, usually to be carried out by a governess. As with the tendency in schools, the governess was popular first with aristocratic families and later among the gentry; by the 19th century she was a regular status symbol of the genteel home.

The reality for many families was that the domestic purse did not stretch to a governess and any education there might be was provided by the mother and the odd visiting tutor. In *Pride and Prejudice* Lady Catherine de Bourgh is shocked that the Bennet daughters had no governess, and were left to learn what they could at home. Elizabeth told her:

'We never had any governess.'

'No governess! How was that possible? Five daughters brought up at home without a governess!—I never heard of such a thing. Your mother must have been quite a slave to your education.'

Elizabeth could hardly help smiling, as she assured her that had not been the case.

'Then, who taught you? Who attended to you? Without a governess you must have been neglected.'

'Compared with some families, I believe we were; but such of us as wished to learn, never wanted the means. We were always encouraged to read, and had all the masters [visiting tutors] that were necessary. Those who chose to be idle, certainly might.'

'Aye, no doubt; but that is what a governess will prevent, and if I had known your mother, I should have advised her most strenuously to engage one. I always say that nothing is to be done in education without steady and regular instruction, and nobody but a governess can give it.'

Jane Austen was a great supporter, in principle, of private tutoring. From other people's experiences of school and her own (she was sent to boarding school at the age of seven and retrieved at ten), she felt that little of any value was taught at most schools whereas a good home could provide plenty of opportunities for learning. However, all depended on what the parents considered to be important knowledge.

Traditionally, girls were brought up to be good wives and mothers with an emphasis on acquiring practical skills in needlework, cooking and making up simple medicines. There was nothing wrong with a little reading and studying as long as girls did not try to show it off in company, or to display a greater knowledge than their husbands. Through the Georgian period women read more widely than in previous generations and in turn wished their daughters to be well read. In some households education acquired a degree of snobbery and was carried to absurd lengths. In *Mansfield Park* Jane Austen's tone indicates how we are to view the Miss Bertrams' high opinion of their own extensive general knowledge. The two girls are in conversation with their mother and her sister, Mrs Norris:

> [Said one daughter,] 'Dear mama, only think, my cousin cannot put the map of Europe together—or my cousin cannot tell the principal rivers in Russia—or, she never heard of Asia Minor—or she does not know the difference between water-colours and crayons!—How strange!—Did you ever hear anything so stupid? ... I cannot remember the time when I did not know a great deal that she has not the least notion of yet. How long ago it is, aunt, since we used to repeat the chronological order of the kings of England, with the dates of their accession, and most of the principal events of their reigns!'
>
> 'Yes,' added the other [daughter]; 'and of the Roman emperors as low as Severus; besides a great deal of the heathen mythology, and all the metals, semi-metals, planets, and distinguished philosophers.'

A home education more typical of the gentry is described in *Northanger Abbey*. The heroine Catherine Morland is the young daughter of a clergyman, not unlike the character of Jane's own father. The following scene indicates the type of subjects commonly taught and also the pitfalls encountered when trying to get an eight-year-old to knuckle down to disciplined study:

> Her mother wished her to learn music; and Catherine was sure she should like it, for she was very fond of tinkling the keys of the old forlorn spinet [small harpsichord]; so, at eight years old she began. She learnt a year, and could not bear it; and Mrs. Morland, who did not insist on her daughters being accomplished in spite of incapacity or distaste, allowed her to leave off. The day which dismissed the music-master was one of the happiest of Catherine's life. Her taste for drawing was not superior; though whenever she could obtain the outside of a letter from her mother or seize upon any other odd piece of paper, she did what she could in that way, by drawing houses and trees, hens and chickens, all very much like one another. Writing and

accounts she was taught by her father; French by her mother: her proficiency in either was not remarkable, and she shirked her lessons in both whenever she could ... She had neither a bad heart nor a bad temper, scarcely ever quarrelsome ... she was moreover noisy and wild, hated confinement and cleanliness, and loved nothing so well in the world as rolling down the green slope at the back of the house.

The Austen family was unusual in having a father who was both learned and temperamentally suited to teaching. He taught his sons at home but not his two daughters (the classics were considered too rigorous for female minds). On reaching the right age, Jane and Cassandra were packed off to boarding school. In the meantime, home provided a congenial environment for learning, as Edward Austen-Leigh wrote in his memoir:

In childhood every available opportunity of instruction was made use of. According to the ideas of the time, she [Jane] was well educated, though not highly accomplished, and she certainly enjoyed that important element of mental training, associating at home with persons of cultivated intellect. It cannot be doubted that her early years were bright and happy, living, as she did, with indulgent parents, in a cheerful home, not without agreeable variety of society.

Her father offered tuition to other boys as well as his sons to supplement his income. In 1780 the pupils would pay £35 each for a year's tuition, board and lodging. There were usually about four pupils, whose parents were either acquaintances of Revd Austen or expatriated; one James Nibbs, for instance, was the son of a wealthy plantation owner in the West Indies. The days were spent studying translations of the Greek and Latin classics such as Virgil's *Aeneid*. If spirits flagged, his wife was on hand to chivvy the boys along with comic rhymes – often a more effective measure than Revd Austen's discipline. When Sir William East's son from Berkshire failed to return to the rectory one summer, it was Mrs Austen who sent him a courteous reminder in verse:

Your Steventon Friends
Are at their wits ends
To know what is become of Squire East;

> They very much fear
> He'll never come here
> Having left them nine weeks at the least ...
>
> Then pray thee, dear Sir,
> No longer defer
> Your return to the mansion of learning;
> For we study all day,
> (Except when we play)
> And eke when the candles are burning.

Mrs Austen dreamed up lots of such light-hearted verses and riddles, which no doubt helped to inculcate a fondness for rhyme and songs that all the Austen children shared. Jane was remembered for being particularly adept at telling stories and regaling her nephews and nieces:

> Her charm to children was great sweetness of manner – she seemed to love you, and you loved her naturally in return – *This* as well as I can now recollect and analyse, was what I felt in my earliest days, before I was old enough to be amused by her cleverness – But soon came the delight of her playful talk – *Everything* she could make amusing to a child – Then, as I got older, and when cousins came to share the entertainment, she would tell us the most delightful stories chiefly of Fairyland, and her Fairies had all characters of their own – The tale was invented, I am sure, at the moment, and was sometimes continued for 2 or 3 days, if occasion served.

Choosing whether to educate at home or at school was not always a straightforward decision. One of the most influential writers of the time on education was the philosopher John Locke, who remained an authority on the subject long after his death in 1704. Even he was unsure about what was best for his son:

> What shall I do with my son? If I keep him always at home, he will be in danger to be my young master; and if I send him abroad [to boarding school], how is it possible to keep him from the contagion of rudeness and vice which is everywhere so in fashion? In my house he will perhaps be more innocent, but more ignorant too of the world ...

I confess both sides have their inconveniences. Being abroad, 'tis true, will make him bolder and better able to bustle and shift among boys of his own age; and the emulation of schoolfellows often puts life and industry into young lads. But till you can find a school wherein it is possible for the master to look after the manners of his scholars, and can show as great effects of his care of forming their minds to virtue and their carriage to breeding as of forming their tongues to the learned languages ... you think it worth while to hazard your son's innocence and virtue for a little Greek and Latin.

The difference is great between two or three pupils in the same house and three or four score boys lodged up and down ... it [cannot] be expected that he [the schoolmaster] should instruct them successfully in anything but their books; the forming of their minds and manners requiring a constant attention ... to every single boy.

Schooling Boys

The 18th century saw a huge expansion of public schools (fee-paying private schools) in England. It also saw a decline in some of the country's grammar schools, privately endowed schools established in the Middle Ages for the education of intelligent children from poorer backgrounds. Many of them did not adapt to the times and stuck rigidly to their classical curriculum, ignoring the demand for reform. Parents from the expanding middle classes, especially those in trade, wanted their children to study subjects more 'useful' than Greek and Latin, such as arithmetic, accounts, modern languages and science. One Eliza Fox, writing her memoirs in 1869, remarked:

Boys at grammar school are taught Latin and Greek, despise the simpler paths of learning, and are generally ignorant of really useful matters of fact, about which a girl is much better informed.

The big public schools – Westminster, Eton, Harrow, Rugby, Winchester, Charterhouse – thrived in an age in which snobbery played a strong part. The school tie counted for as much as ever; and traditional methods, including the cane for discipline, prevailed. As well as flogging at the hands of the schoolmasters, junior boys had to contend with the brutality of their seniors, who were virtually a law unto themselves. Outside lessons, masters more or less left the boys to their own devices. The novelist Henry Fielding

said that public schools were 'the nurseries of all vice and immorality'. One
Westminster boy recalled in the 1790s:

**I have been woken many times by the hot points of cigars burning
holes in my face.**

The cruelty was so commonplace that incidences of rebellion were
sometimes reported. At Winchester College in Hampshire, to which several
of Jane Austen's relatives were sent, there was the so-called 'Great Rebellion'
of 1793 during which boys, protesting against their ill treatment, fired pistols
and threw stones down from the school tower. Public school culture was
wild. There was almost no limit to the amount the boys could drink, gamble,
fight and indulge any sexual bent. Each boy picked up his bill at the end
of term and then the matter was between him and his father to settle. At
Eton, boys wore the latest men's fashions until 1798, when their distinctive
tailcoat suit became standard uniform and a trendsetter for boys. The school
became an icon of male sartorial elegance for upper class families, but it was
also notorious for its licentiousness. One contemporary journal stated:

**Before an Eton boy is ready for University, he may have acquired a
confirmed taste for gluttony and drunkenness, an appetite for brutal
sports and a passion for female society of the most degrading kind.**

Nevertheless, the system had many supporters who reckoned it stood
for everything that was peculiarly English (over 70 per cent of Georgian
ministers of state went to public school). The historian Edward Gibbon, who
attended Westminster School in the middle of the century, had nothing but
praise to offer:

**I shall always be ready to joyn in the common opinion, that our public
schools, which have produced so many eminent characters are the
best adapted to the Genius and constitution of the English people. A
boy of spirit may acquire a praevious and practical experience of the
World, and his playfellows may be the future friends of his heart or
his interest. In a free intercourse with his equals the habits of truth,
fortitude and prudence will insensibly be matured ... The mimic scene
of a rebellion has displayed in their true colours the ministers and
patriots of the rising generation.**

Jane's nephew Edward Austen-Leigh was sent to Winchester College, Britain's first public school, founded in 1382 to feed students into New College, Oxford. Though he maintained he was always happy there, she suspected this might be his pride talking and that he kept some of his experiences to himself. When Edward finally left the school in 1816 she couldn't resist having a little tease:

> **One reason for my writing to you now, is that I may have the pleasure of directing to you *Esqre*—I give you Joy of having left Winchester.—Now you may own, how miserable you were there; now, it will gradually all come out—your Crimes & your Miseries— how often you went up by the Mail to London & threw away Fifty Guineas at a Tavern, & how often you were on the point of hanging yourself— restrained only ... by the want of a Tree within some miles of the City.**

Whatever reforms may or may not have been happening in boys' education, a high value was still placed on achieving the finished gentleman, with all the attributes expected of good breeding. A century earlier John Locke had emphasized the importance of educating the whole person rather than just the intellectual faculties:

> **Reading, and Writing, I allow to be necessary, but yet not the chief Business. I imagine you would think him a very foolish Fellow that should not value a Virtuous or a Wise Man infinitely before a great Scholar.**
> **... The Taylor may make his Cloathes Modish, and the Dancing-Master give fashion to his Motions; yet neither of these, though they set off well, make a well-bred Gentleman; No, though he have learning to boot; which, if not well-managed, makes him more impertinent and intolerable in Conversation. Breeding is that which sets a Gloss upon all his other good qualities, and renders them useful to him, in procuring him the Esteem and Good Will of all that he comes near. Without good Breeding his other Accomplishments make him pass but for Proud, Conceited, Vain or Foolish.**

Locke outlined the main themes of his views in *Some Thoughts Concerning Education* (published in 1693), a classic text that had gone into 25 editions by the time Jane Austen was born and was considered standard reading on how to bring up a gentleman:

> That which every Gentleman (that takes any care of his Education) desires for his Son, besides the Estate he leaves him, is contain'd in these four Things, *Virtue, Wisdom, Breeding, and Learning.*
>
> I place Virtue as the first of those Endowments, that belong to a Gentleman … to make him valued and beloved by others, acceptable or tolerable to himself. Without that I think, he will be happy neither in this, nor the other World.
>
> … The next thing to be taken Care of, is to keep him exactly to speaking of Truth, and by all the ways imaginable inclining him to be *good natur'd.* Let him know that Twenty Faults are sooner to be forgiven, than the *straining of Truth,* to cover any one *by an Excuse.* And to teach him to love, and be *good natur'd* to others, is to lay early the true Foundation of an honest Man: All Injustice generally springing from too great Love of our selves, and too little of others.
>
> *Wisdom* I take, in the popular acceptation, for a Man's managing his Business ably, and with fore-sight in this World. This is the product of a good natural Temper, application of Mind, and Experience together, and so above the reach of Children. The greatest Thing that in them can be done towards it is to hinder them from being *Cunning;* which, being the ape of *Wisdom,* is the most distant from it that can be.
>
> … The next good Quality belonging to a Gentleman, is *good Breeding.* There are Two Sorts of *ill Breeding:* The one a *sheepish Bashfulness:* And the other a *mis-becoming Negligence and Disrespect* in our Carriage; Both which are avoided by duly observing this one Rule, *Not to think meanly of our selves, and not to think meanly of others.*

Locke suggested that people needed to keep things in perspective: how important are modes of style and deportment anyway?

> And in good earnest, 'tis no great matter how they put off their Hats, or make Legs. If you can teach them to find ways to express it acceptably to every one, according to the Fashions they have been used to: And as to their Motions and Carriage of their Bodies, a Dancing-Master will teach them what is most becoming.

You will wonder, perhaps, that I put *Learning* last, especially if I tell you I think it the least part. This may seem strange in the mouth of a bookish Man. When I consider what a-do is made about a little *Latin* and *Greek,* how many Years are spent in it, and what a noise and business it makes to no purpose, I can hardly forbear thinking that the Parents of Children still live in fear of the School-master's Rod, which they look on as the only Instrument of Education. How else is it possible that a Child should be chain'd to the Oar, Seven, Eight, or Ten of the best Years of his Life, to get a Language or two, which might be had at a great deal cheaper rate of Pains and Time, and be learn'd almost in playing?

But most important of all was to be yourself, said Lord Chesterfield, whose *Letters to his Son* are as famous in their way as Locke's treatise:

Carefully avoid all affectation either of body or of mind. It is a very true and a very trite observation that no man is ridiculous for being what he really is, but for affecting to be what he is not. No man is awkward by nature, but by affecting to be genteel. I have known many a man of common sense pass generally for a fool, because he affected a degree of wit that God had denied him. A ploughman is by no means awkward in the exercise of his trade, but would be exceedingly ridiculous if he attempted the air and graces of a man of fashion. You learned to dance, but it was to bring your air and motions back to what they would naturally have been, had [they] not been warped in your youth by bad examples, and awkward imitations of other boys.

Fatherly advice to a son was often made formally in writing, especially on such serious matters as business or career. George Austen penned something of a homily to his 14-year-old son Francis (Frank) when he was about to set sail as a midshipman aboard the *Perseverance* on a voyage to the East Indies in 1788. Frank, who would one day sail with Lord Nelson's fleet to Trafalgar, was a young volunteer straight out of the academy. Still wet behind the ears, he had to rub along with the favoured protégés of the ship's captain and had the additional disadvantage of coming from a non-naval background. In his capacity as the boy's father, Revd Austen did what he could to help his son get off to a good start in his chosen career. What follows is an abbreviated form of a letter full of sober advice and affection:

My Dear Francis

... Now you are going from us for so long a time & to such a distance ... I think it necessary to give you my sentiments on such general subjects as I conceive of the greatest importance to you, & must leave your conduct in particular cases to be directed by your own good sense.

... Your behaviour, as a member of society to the Individuals around you *may* be of great importance to your future well-doing ... The little world, of which you are going to become an Inhabitant, will consist of three Orders of Men—All of whom will occasionally have it in their power to contribute no little share to your pleasure or pain; to conciliate their good will, by every honourable method will be the part of a prudent Man.—Your Commander and Officers will be most likely to become your Friends by a respectful behaviour to themselves, & by an active and ready Obedience to Orders.—Good humour, an inclination to oblige, & the carefully avoiding every appearance of Selfishness will infallibly secure you the regards of your own Mess & of all your Equals.—With your Inferiors ... there is a sort of kindness they have a claim on you for, & which, you may believe me, will not be thrown away on them.

Your conduct ... chiefly comprehends Sobriety & Prudence ... She [Prudence] will teach you the proper disposal of your time & the careful management of your Money ... She will teach you that the best chance of rising in life is to make yourself as useful as possible, by carefully studying everything that relates to your Profession, & distinguishing yourself from those of your rank by a superior Proficiency in nautical Acquirements.

After a few more paragraphs of advice, his father signs off fondly:

I have nothing to add but my Blessing & best Prayers for your health & prosperity, & to beg you would never forget you have not upon Earth a more disinterested & warm Friend than
  Your truly Affect:ᵉ Father
  Geo Austen

The letter clearly held a place close to Frank's heart. Seventy-six years later, at the time of his death in 1865, it was found among his belongings, worn and tattered from frequent reading.

Schooling Girls

Opinions varied about the prospects for women on coming of age. Ellen Weeton, in her *Journal of a Governess*, quoted her father, an old sea captain living in the late 18th century, as saying:

> **Unless a father can provide independent fortunes for his daughters, they must either be made mop-squeezers or mantua-makers [dressmakers], whereas sons can easily make their way in the world.**

An alternative view is held by the character Mrs Norris (sister to Lady Bertram) in *Mansfield Park*:

> **Give a girl an education, and introduce her properly into the world, and ten to one but she has the means of settling well, without further expense to anybody.**

Many parents would have agreed with Mrs Norris on the importance of giving daughters a good education but, unlike today when a woman living in the Western world has plenty of career opportunities at her disposal, her Georgian counterpart had precious few. Parents needed to consider carefully before deciding whether to send their girls to boarding school to acquire the appropriate accomplishments. In a letter to his wife in 1770, Dr Tysoe Hancock, who had returned to Calcutta to work for the East India Company, agonized over the education of his own daughter Eliza (or Betsy), Jane Austen's cousin, who remained in England with her mother, Philadelphia:

> **... it occurred to me that there was very little chance of her having a fortune which might entitle her to a station in life suitable to the education we give her, and that therefore it might conduce to her happiness to be educated in such a manner that she might enjoy a more humble lot should she be obliged to submit to it ... After long revolving ... on a subject of such importance, I am resolved that the same plan of education we formerly agreed on shall be pursued. Many reasons might be given why Betsy's studies should not be interrupted. ... It is very certain that neither languages nor exercises can be attained to any degree of perfection but in the earlier years of life; therefore time now lost will be hereafter [lost].**

The learning of French and her visits to France were to stand Eliza in good stead, of course, for her eventual marriage to the French aristocrat Jean Capot de Feuillide. No doubt much of what else she learned was suitable for such a match.

To find a wealthy husband required the services of a good school. The heroine of *Persuasion*, Sir Walter Elliot's daughter Anne, has spent three years at a reputable school in Bath. Jane Austen mentions no name but most likely it would have been Belvedere House in Lansdown Road, then the best school in the city. The following first impressions of the establishment, run by the Lee sisters, come from the memoirs of Susan Sibbald, who was a new girl there around 1795:

> On reaching the School room, all were employed in some sort of needlework—being Summer at 4 o'clock bonnets, spencers [waist-length jackets], or tippets [shoulder coverings], and walking shoes on, and attended by the 3 Teachers, we were paired off two and two, and took a walk in the country. We had to be home by 6, when those that took tea ... descended to the dining room, where only Miss Mangle presided, and made tea for us.
>
> Afterwards lessons were to be learned for the next day, and then the girls amused themselves with filigree and pasteboard trifles, &c., and the little ones with their dolls ... At half past seven all went down to supper—bread, cheese and beer, by far the lesser number preferred bread and milk which I did. At 8 o'clock Miss [Sophia] Lee entered the school room and read prayers, we all kneeling, of course, after which we all went up to our bedrooms, accompanied by the three Teachers, who saw the young ladies into their rooms ... I was to belong to Mam'selle [the French mistress], and to sleep in a small bed in her room—Miss Clarke, and Miss Sanderson [other pupils] in the same room. In the large room opposite there were 8 girls.
>
> The next morning we were called at six. At half past seven Miss Harriet [Lee] came into the School room and read prayers; at 8 Miss [Sophia] Lee opened the door. We all rose from our seats, turned towards her and curtsied. She went down to the dining room one way while we went by our own stairs ... After breakfast ... by and by comes Mr Perks. He was the Writing Master, and also taught Arithmetic. Many a warm plum, and squeezed bit of ginger bread, he has given me out of his pocket.

... Music lessons three times a week, practising every day. Pianos in two Parlours, and one in the Drawing Room, for the Parlour boarders. Monsieur Becker the Drawing Master came on Tuesdays and Fridays. Wednesday was dancing day, Miss Fleming had a sedan chair of her own, and which she always came in. The lady was very tall and stout, rather plain. She taught the Minuetts, and figure dances. Miss Fleming used often to say, 'Now ladies, do credit to Bath.'

The standard of living at these expensive schools was undoubtedly good, as the next memory from Susan Sibbald reveals:

There was no want of good living at Belvedere House, generally roast beef on Mondays; on Tuesdays and Fridays, roast shoulders of Mutton; a round of beef on Wednesdays; Thursdays boiled legs of mutton, and stewed beef with pickled walnuts on Saturdays, which was much liked. Then two days in the week, we had 'choke dogs' dumplings with currants in them, other days rice or other puddings, but after the meat not before, as was the case in some schools. A few of the girls remained a few minutes after the others had gone up to the School room, and had a glass of port wine each (for which an extra charge was made).

Jane Austen was aware of the prevalence in her day of pretentious schooling, run by institutions that prided themselves so much on their pupils' 'accomplishments' that the result was little more than vanity, likely as not to put off many prospective suitors. An account of a journey in a public stage coach undertaken by Agnes Porter, governess to the Earl of Ilchester, in 1789 gives a cross-section of views about the value of female education:

From Wincanton I set out with a young glover, a middle-aged hatter, and an old grocer, with the addition of a Miss from Sherbourne School who, as soon as we were seated, informed us where she had been educated, and assured us that Sherbourne was the very first place in the world for female accomplishments. The hatter said he should then place his own daughter there, for he thought women could never be taught too much, as knowledge would qualify them to be proper companions for their husbands and, at the same time would, by teaching them their duty, make them humble.

'If they want to learn their duty, let them read the bible' said my neighbour the grocer.

'Sir, will the Bible teach us to talk French as well and as fast as English—will it shew us how to sing and play on the harpsichord, or to *walk in the first position*? Though a very good book, yet it can't do all that for us.'

'And no matter for that' said the glover 'provided a woman can make a good pudding, cast an account, and keep her house neat, I think she may make a wife to please any reasonable man ... Miss, as you say you larnt music, suppose we have a song from you?'

The young woman immediately began one—sang it in a very particular style, and when it was over said to me: '*Shinty vue* (*chantez-vous*—do you sing), *Madame?*'

I told her that I should understand her better if she spoke English.

'La, Ma'am, how I pity you! What, not speak French? I would not give up that accomplishment for the world—well, it certainly is your misfortune, Ma'am.'

When the young woman and I were by ourselves I told her in French that, as I supposed our fellow travellers did not understand that language, I thought it better to decline the pleasure of answering her in French. She looked a little serious, and replied in English 'Ma'am, I am not so far in the French phrases'!

On the other hand a high-powered education might also produce young ladies too knowledgeable for the liking of any potential husband. Through the character of Mrs Goddard, a friend of the Woodhouses in *Emma*, Jane puts her case:

Mrs Goddard was the mistress of a School—not of a seminary, or an establishment, or any thing which professed, in long sentences of refined nonsense, to combine liberal acquirements with elegant morality upon new principles and new systems—and where young ladies for enormous pay might be screwed out of health and into vanity—but a real, honest, old-fashioned Boarding-school, where a reasonable quantity of accomplishments were sold at a reasonable price, and where girls might be sent to be out of the way, and scramble themselves into a little education, without any danger of coming back prodigies.

Jane and her sister Cassandra, at the ages of seven and ten, went first to a school in Oxford attended by their cousin, Jane Cooper, whose aunt Mrs Cawley had set up a respectable school. Having been left thus far to her own devices, it was something of a shock for Jane to be sent to boarding school. Although she had her sister and cousin among her classmates and her brother James nearby at the university, the new regime of petty regulations and confinement had a profound effect after the ease of home life. Writing later, at the age of 13, in James's satirical magazine *The Loiterer*, which he published at Oxford, she recalled with loathing her feelings for the place:

> ... I am sure I never wish to go there [Oxford] again in my life.—
> They dragged me through so many dismal chapels, dusty libraries,
> and greasy halls, that it gave me the vapours for two days afterwards.

When Mrs Cawley decided to move her school to Southampton, the two sisters and their cousin followed; however, a series of unfortunate health matters ensued to disrupt their education further. Being situated in a port, exposure to foreign illness brought in on the ships was always a potential hazard. Rumours spread that typhoid fever was in town, though Mrs Cawley denied them as mere scaremongering. Only when Jane Cooper was forced by illness to write home telling of the news did Mrs Cooper and Mrs Austen realize what was happening and come rushing to the rescue. All three girls caught the infection, Jane suffering badly enough to bring her to the brink of death, but luckily all eventually recovered at home. Unluckily, Mrs Cooper then succumbed to the disease and died after a few weeks.

The Austen girls' education continued some six months later at a curious establishment in Reading. The Abbey School was run by Mrs La Tournelle, who promised the full repertoire of subjects: music, dancing, drawing and writing; needlework and spelling were offered as alternatives (Jane being better at the former), and of course, Mrs La Tournelle's own language, French. But little did their parents know of what went on under the turreted roofs of this former Cistercian monastery. This establishment had none of the austere rigours of Mrs Cawley's. Afternoons were spent in idle gossip and laughter in a rambling, ungovernable gothic mansion that even had its own ghost, in the shape of a one-eyed Henry I, to fuel Jane's lively imagination. It later turned out that the eccentric cork-legged headmistress was not all she made herself out to be, as her obituary in the *Gentleman's Magazine* of November 1797 revealed:

OBITUARY OF REMARKABLE PERSONS
   At Henley-on-Thames of a paralytic stroke aged 60 Mrs Sarah La
Tournelle mistress of a respectable board-school. Her family name
was Hackitt and she was born in London but having early in life
been engaged as a French teacher her employers thought it right to
introduce her into the school under a foreign name. She accordingly
took that of La Tournelle and her real name was probably only known
to a few of her numerous friends who esteemed and respected her for
her integrity and abilities in the way of her profession.

Not only was her French not native, it was also far from fluent, and before
long the fraudster was found out. Getting wind of various misdemeanours
midway through the autumn term of 1786, Mr Austen put his foot down,
objecting to the squandering of his hard-earned income to pay termly fees
of £37 19s for the two girls. Cassandra and Jane were removed just before
the latter's 11th birthday and they never went to school again.

Just as there is today, a good deal of debate was held at this time about
the merits of boarding schools and whether parents, especially aristocrats
who tended to favour such schools, were morally right to send their children
away. *The Lady's Magazine* of 1774 had these harsh words to say about
females of the '*Bon Ton*' (ladies of fashion):

What can we think of a mother, who is scarcely delivered of a
child, which she bore perhaps with regret, and sends it ten or twenty
miles from her, commits it successively to different mercenaries,
at the lowest price, till either the boarding school or the university
receives for several years more the dear children, which scarcely
know her?
   Nothing can justify such monstrous indifference! The most noble
employment of a mother is to form the heart and understanding of
her children in their most early years: it is her duty to give them their
first instructions; this first culture decides the fate of those young
plants, and the impression which is made in our tender years, will
never be effaced ...
   To keep up the appearance of maternal tenderness, the ladies of
the *Bon Ton* make use of a thousand pretences. They do but single
out one which could justify them in sending their daughters at a
distance, which is the danger of a bad example. Indeed, when we

examine what kind of education the daughters receive from such mothers, we have every thing to fear for their innocence. What is called a *genteel* education by some, which is very different from a *good* one, can only prepare a young person for an early defeat.

Having laid the groundwork for an onslaught, the daggers were drawn:

It seems as if all the rudiments of the education ... might be resolved to the dangerous art of *pleasing*. A girl is scarcely weaned when they talk to her about her charms and dress. She is put under the care of a dancing master, who teaches her to hold her head up in an affected manner, to pull up her bosom, and to move as if she were made but of one piece ... She is incessantly talked to about the good air, and external charms, which they assure her must determine her rank in society. She never hears a syllable about her understanding, judgment, or mental endowments. What is the consequence? The little pupil soon learns her lessons, holds herself upright, sings, minces her words, becomes a very pretty puppet; but has nought in her understanding but mere *nothings*.

... A mother, who has been occupied all her life only about her personal charms, is content to have a daughter who is like herself; she has no other end than to make her agreeable: and from hence it is that the numerous race of *coquettes* is perpetuated from mother to daughter.

There is no doubt that by the end of the 18th century the idea that a genteel woman had to be equipped with a good bag of 'accomplishments' was widely accepted, as the feminist reformer Maria Edgeworth pointed out in *Practical Education* in 1798:

Accomplishments are now so common that they cannot be considered as the distinguishing characteristic of even a gentlewoman's education.

Another feminist writer, Mary Wollstonecraft, despised the prevailing system of female education and of girls' upbringing. She likened their minds to flowers that are planted in rich soil – 'their strength and usefulness sacrificed to beauty' so that they fade long before reaching maturity:

One cause of this barren blooming I attribute to a false system of education, gathered from the books written on this subject by men who, considering females rather as women than human creatures, have been more anxious to make them alluring mistresses than affectionate wives and rational mothers; and the understanding of the sex has been so bubbled by this specious homage, that the civilized women of the present century, with a few exceptions, are only anxious to inspire love, when they ought to cherish a nobler ambition, and by their abilities and virtues exact respect.

... It is acknowledged that they spend many of the first years of their lives in acquiring a smattering of accomplishments; meanwhile strength of body and mind are sacrificed to ... the desire of establishing themselves—the only way women can rise in the world—by marriage. And this desire making mere animals of them, when they marry they act as such children may be expected to act: they dress; they paint, and nickname God's creatures ... Can they be expected to govern a family with judgement, or take care of the poor babes whom they bring into the world?

Betterment for the Poor

Until the Education Act of 1870, formal education of children in England and Wales was limited to fee-paying private schools. In 1699 the Society for Promoting Christian Knowledge (SPCK) had been founded to provide education for the poor, but its early progress was slow until a newspaper printer, Robert Raikes, opened a Sunday school in Gloucester in 1780 and popularized the idea. The movement grew rapidly with the support of Anglican bishops, and before the end of the century more than a thousand Sunday schools were built across the country, attended by a quarter of a million pupils. Other educational initiatives of the period included the non-Conformists' British and Foreign School Society, founded in 1810 and patronized by the Whig political party, and its Church of England rival, the 'National' or Church Schools, established a year later, which became the most common form of popular education in the English village.

It became fashionable for ladies of leisure to put something into the community by teaching the poorest children, and sometimes adults. Though she would not like to have been described as a 'lady of leisure', Jane Austen herself is said to have taught children in her local village. At Sunday schools children were taught to read and, to a lesser extent, to write, which was considered an unnecessary skill. Scripture was taught, as were piety, drills and a few manual skills. A schedule for Sunday schools located in the Bath area read as follows:

> The children are divided into classes, viz. Letters, spelling, and reading. Also into classes of perfect and imperfect catechists ... Twenty children are as many as one master or mistress can take proper care of ... The different instruction the children receive, with the singing of the psalms, occasions a diversity that makes the time pass without listlessness. To learn to be silent, and to bear confinement, is the foundation on which all instruction must be built ... By being able to repeat the verses of the Psalms they are to sing, many children who cannot read can join in singing. They begin with learning two Psalms, and are now perfect in eight, which is a sufficient number ... Those children who cannot read are ordered when they kneel to hold up their hands in a supplicating posture; it has a very good effect on the children, and has a very decent appearance.

But the key to these schools was the catechism. By inculcating a sense of moral values, teachers hoped to produce honest and hard-working folk who were growing up amid the new Industrial Revolution, and so prevent criminality at the workplace and in society generally. A pioneering spirit behind Sunday schools was the children's writer Sarah Trimmer, who wrote this catechetical dialogue:

> *Instructor:* There is one kind of dishonesty which is often practised without thought by workmen, and that is wasting the time for which they are paid and the materials belonging to the Trade or Manufacture they work at. Of the same nature with this is the crime of many household servants who take every opportunity of being idle and who make no scruple of wasting provisions or giving them away without leave ...
> *Question:* Is it honest for workmen to waste and destroy the materials and implements which they make use of?
> *Answer:* No.
> *Question:* Who do these things belong to?
> *Answer:* Their Master.

Question: Whose eyes see you when your master is not by?
Answer: God's.

By no means did everyone think well of the idea of educating the poor.
Many would have agreed with the following, uttered at the turn of the 19th
century by the MP Davies Giddy, a future president of the Royal Society,
who believed it was actually harmful:

> Giving education to the labouring classes or the poor would be
> prejudicial to their morals and happiness; it would teach them to
> despise their lot in life, instead of making them good servants in
> agriculture and other laborious employment. Instead of teaching
> them subordination, it would render them fractious and refractory.

University and Beyond

On leaving school many young men went to university, of which there were
two in 18th-century England: Oxford and Cambridge. Their colleges were
male only and the dons (tutors) had to be Anglican and celibate. A relaxed
atmosphere of carefree indolence was typical of the time, as Edward Gibbon
described in this vignette of the sybaritic Oxford don:

> The fellows of my time were decent easy men, who supinely enjoyed
> the gifts of the founder; their days were filled by a series of uniform
> employment; the chapel & the hall, the coffeehouse & the common
> room, till they retired weary and well-satisfied, to a long slumber.
> From the toil of reading, or thinking, or writing they had absolved
> their conscience. As a gentleman-commoner, I was admitted to the
> society of the fellows, and fondly expected that some questions
> of literature would be the amusing and instructive topics of their
> discourse. Their conversation stagnated in a round of college business,
> Tory politics, personal anecdotes & private scandal; their dull & deep
> potations excused the brisk intemperance of youth.

Hardly different was the life of the young men of rank and fortune who
could afford to become undergraduates (known as gentleman-commoners
at Oxford and fellow-commoners at Cambridge). The order of the day was
flouncing around in handsome dress, drinking and regaling, with servants at

their beck and call like retainers at a gentlemen's club. George Pryme,
a Cambridge don in the early 19th century, recollected that:

> **Undergraduates dressed regularly for dinner in white waistcoats,
> white stockings, low shoes, and wore their wigs fully combed, curled,
> and powdered.**

The Poet Laureate of the late 1780s, Dr Thomas Wharton, was the Professor
of Poetry at Oxford from 1757 to 1790 and drew the following sketch (in *A
Companion to the Guide and a Guide to the Companion*) of students' recreations
undertaken in the name of study:

> **The prevailing notion is erroneous with regard to the number of our
> libraries. Besides those of Radcliffe, Bodley, and private colleges, there
> have of late years been many libraries founded in our coffee-houses,
> for the benefit of such academics as have neglected or lost their
> Latin and Greek. In these useful repositories grown gentlemen are
> accommodated with the Cyclopaedia. The magazines afford history,
> divinity &c., the Reviews form the complete critic, and enable the
> student to pass his judgment on volumes which he never read ... As
> there are here books suited to every taste, so are there liquors adapted
> to every species of reading. Amorous tales may be perused over arrack
> punch and jellies; politics over coffee; divinity over port; and defence
> of bad generals and bad ministers over whipt syllabubs. In a word we
> may pronounce that learning is no longer a dry pursuit.**

There were also the more serious-minded students, including the future
prime minister William Pitt the Younger, the historian Edward Gibbon, the
reformer William Wilberforce, and the writer Horace Walpole, as well as the
would-be clergymen hoping to secure one of the choice livings in the gift
of their college. Poor applicants could attend only by winning scholarships.
Jane's father won a scholarship from Tonbridge School to St John's, Oxford.
His sons, James and Henry, followed him on bursaries paid under the rule of
'Founder's Kin'. This old custom admitted free entrance to anyone who could
prove he was descended from the original benefactor of a college. In their
case Mrs Austen traced her descent to the founder Sir Thomas White via the
Leigh family's Perrot connections (James Perrot of Northleigh, Oxfordshire,
was her great-grandfather).

However the students spent their time, all were expected to pass an examination before receiving their precious bachelor's degree. But as the Revd Dr Vicesimus Knox, Fellow of St John's College, Oxford, revealed in a series of essays in 1778, the standard of these examinations left much to be desired:

> **Every candidate is obliged to be examined in the whole circle of the sciences by three masters of arts of known choice. The examination is to continue from nine o'clock till eleven. The masters take a most solemn oath that they will examine properly and impartially. Dreadful as all this appears, there is always found to be more of appearance in it than reality, for the greatest dunce usually gets his testimonium signed with as much ease and credit as the finest genius.**

After university, or sometimes instead of it, an exciting venture was the grand tour of Western Europe, visiting sites of cultural interest. Typically a young man would spend one or two years travelling through France, Italy, Germany and the Netherlands, usually under the wing of a tutor, inspecting remains of antiquity, viewing classical paintings and sculptures, and picking up a smattering of foreign languages. Needless to say, the undertaking was an expensive one that only the affluent could afford; it therefore also acquired its own social cachet. Jane's brother Edward, as the heir of Thomas Knight, was given the opportunity to travel round Europe at the age of 21. He stayed with the trendy 'Neufchâtel Set' of English lords in Switzerland and was also received at the court of the Elector of Saxony in Dresden. In Rome he had his portrait painted in the fashionable style of reclining like a dilettante among the classical ruins.

Domestic Life

Jane Austen spent most of her life in Hampshire. Except for five years in Bath and three in Southampton, she lived in comfortable houses among farming communities. The first 25 years of her life were spent at Steventon Rectory. Her nephew Edward Austen-Leigh, who also lived there, recalled the setting:

> Steventon is a small rural village upon the chalk hills of north Hants [Hampshire], situated in a winding valley about seven miles from Basingstoke ... It may be known to some sportsmen, as lying in one of the best portions of the Vine Hunt. It is certainly not a picturesque country ... The surface continually swells and sinks, but the hills are not bold, nor the valleys deep ... Still it has its beauties. The lanes wind along in a natural curve, and lead to pleasant nooks and corners ... Steventon, from the fall of the ground, and the abundance of its timber is certainly one of the prettiest spots.

In 1775, the year of Jane's birth, William Gilpin toured southern England searching for areas of picturesque beauty and found little to recommend the scenery that surrounded Steventon, just as Mrs Austen had discovered to her disappointment when visiting for the first time on George's arm. In his *Observations of the Western Part of England ...* Gilpin said that the road from Winchester to Basingstoke:

> ... passes through a country, with little picturesque beauty on either hand. It becomes by degrees flat and unpleasant, and soon degenerates into common-field land, which, with its striped divisions, is of all kinds of country generally the most unpleasant.

The description of common fields having 'striped divisions' reveals that agricultural enclosure (see page 234) had not yet changed the look of the landscape in these parts. The area had its own charms for those who knew it well, and they did not care that it might not please an artist's eye. The following verse was penned by James Austen, who not only grew up in the parsonage but remained there as its incumbent until his death in 1819:

> True taste is not fastidious, nor rejects,
> Although they may not come within the rule
> Of composition pure and picturesque,
> Unnumbered simple scenes, which fill the leaves
> Of nature's sketch book;

When George Austen retired in 1801 he moved his family to Bath, where they lived in a series of leased premises until his death in 1805. The subsequent period was a difficult time for all, emotionally and financially. A further series of domestic upheavals was finally ended in 1809 when Jane's brother Edward (now surnamed Knight after his adoptive family) gave Mrs Austen and her two daughters a permanent home at Chawton Cottage, near Alton in Hampshire. Her niece Caroline Austen (the daughter of James) recalled the house, which in many ways resembled the rural home of their childhoods in Steventon:

> It had been originally a roadside Inn—and it was well placed for such a purpose—just where the road from Winchester comes into the London and Gosport [Portsmouth] line.
>
> The front door opened on the road, a very narrow enclosure of each side, protected the house from the possible shock of any runaway vehicle—A good sized entrance, and two parlours, called dining and drawing room, made the length of the house; all intended originally to look on the road—but the large drawing room window was blocked-up and turned into a bookcase when Mrs. Austen took possession and another was opened at the side, which gave to view only turf and trees—A high wooden fence shut out the road all the length of the little domain, and trees were planted inside to form a shrubbery walk—and there was a pleasant irregular mixture of hedgerow, and grass, and gravel walk and long grass for mowing, and orchard ... There was besides a good kitchen garden, large court and many

out-buildings, not much occupied—and all this affluence of space
was very delightful to children.

Everything *indoors* and *out* was well kept—the house was
well furnished, and it was altogether a comfortable and ladylike
establishment, tho' I beleive the means which supported it, were
but small—

The house was quite as good as Parsonage houses then—and much
in the same old style—the ceilings low and roughly furnished—*some*
bedrooms very small—*none* very large but in number sufficient to
accommodate the inmates, and several guests.

The Austens, like most upper middle class families, would frequently have
visitors staying over for several days. Travel had become easier as a result
of road and carriage improvement, and a good house was one that catered
for extensive socializing. Caroline Austen went on:

The dining room could not be made to look anywhere *but* on the
road—and *there* my Grandmother often sat for an hour or two in the
morning, with her work or her writing—cheered by its sunny aspect,
and by the stirring scene it afforded her.

I beleive the close vicinity of the road was really no more an evil
to *her* than it was to her grandchildren. Collyer's daily coach with
six horses was a sight to see! and most delightful was it to a child to
have the awful stillness of night so frequently broken by the noise of
passing carriages, which seemed sometimes, even to shake the bed—

Morning Routine

A typical day followed a set pattern. Meals were prepared by servants and
consumed at regular times. Around these stations of the day other activities
of necessity and leisure were undertaken according to the role of each family
member. Jane's niece continued:

Aunt Jane began her day with music—for which I conclude she had
a natural taste; as she thus kept it up—tho' she had no one to teach;
was never induced (as I have heard) to play [piano] in company; and
none of her family cared much for it. I suppose, that she might not
trouble *them*, she chose her practising time before breakfast—when

she could have the room to herself—She practised regularly every morning—She played very pretty tunes, I thought—and I liked to stand by her and listen to them; but the music, (for I knew the books well in after years) would now be thought disgracefully easy—Much that she played from was manuscript, copied out by herself—and so neatly and correctly, that it was as easy to read as print—

In a world devoid of recorded music and with professional performances restricted usually to Bath or London, it was normal for every family to have its provider of music. In this household it was Jane, not Cassandra. The piano was positioned in the sitting room where she would usually practise for an hour before breakfast. Living in an exciting time for music when the Classical age of Mozart was dovetailing with the new Romantic sound of Beethoven, piano playing was a popular accomplishment. All the great composers were male, yet it was women who played the music at home while the men listened and appreciated. Jane's taste in music was not advanced but she was a competent player, having been taught by one of the organists at Winchester Cathedral. He would travel the 14 miles to their home on a regular basis to give Jane lessons, paid for by her father.

Often a few errands were run before breakfast. Jane went shopping before eating while staying in London once and would sometimes write letters at this hour. Gentlemen might take a brisk walk to work up an appetite.

Affluent ladies would engage a housekeeper to manage the household; women of Jane Austen's class would normally run the house and supervise servants themselves. This included the keeping of household accounts in a ledger book and discussions about the day's menu and any preparations that might be needed to receive guests. If there were grown daughters in the home they would each have their set domestic duties. Jane's niece described her aunt's charge:

At 9 o'clock she made breakfast—*that* was *her* part of the household work—The tea and sugar stores were under *her* charge—*and* the wine—Aunt Cassandra did all the rest—for my Grandmother had suffered herself to be superseded by her daughters *before* I can remember.

Tea and sugar in those days were precious commodities, kept under lock and key; the servants were strictly forbidden any access. Unlike today, tea would not have been drunk whenever someone felt like a cup, but only at breakfast and after dinner in the early evening (as coffee might be taken today). Sugar came from British colonial plantations in the West Indies and tea was imported from China (not yet from India). Each of these commodities attracted high excise duties which, until Pitt the Younger reduced the tariffs, encouraged a considerable volume of smuggling. In the mid-1780s Pitt estimated that more than half of Britain's tea was consumed without paying duty. Rather like poaching, smuggling was thought of as a petty crime that added a bit of spice to life, and most households received contraband supplies, whether it was tea, sugar or tobacco. Parson James Woodforde, a respected, if roguish, man of the cloth, recorded in his diary in 1777:

Andrews the smuggler brought me this night about 11 o'clock a bagg of Hyson Tea 6 pound weight. He frightened us a little by whistling under the parlour window just as we were going to bed. I gave him some Geneva [gin] and paid him for the tea at 10/6 per pound.

When tea was first brought to Europe in the 17th century, Chinese bowls were also imported for its drinking. In *Mansfield Park* Mrs Price makes a reference, old-fashioned by Jane Austen's time, to having a 'dish of tea'. The fine quality of bone china prompted manufacturers such as Josiah Wedgwood to reproduce porcelain for the British market, which excited a good deal of snobbery among competing families. Mrs Dashwood in *Sense and Sensibility* finds it galling to discover better china than her own in an inferior setting:

And the set of breakfast china is twice as handsome as what belongs to this house. A great deal too handsome, in my opinion, for any place *they* can ever afford to live in.

Snobbery and fashion for drinking tea were one thing, health and changing customs were another matter, and tea did not go down well in all quarters of society. The polemical writer William Cobbett bemoaned the way that tea had transformed the drinking habits of a nation of traditional beer drinkers. In 1822 he had not a good word to say about the 'poisonous' beverage, especially the effect it had on hard-working labourers:

Only forty years ago, to have a house and not to brew [beer] was a rare thing indeed ... Now there is not a labourer in his parish that

does it, except by chance the malt be given him. The causes of this change have been the lowering of the wages of labour, the enormous tax upon the barley when made into malt, and the increased tax upon hops. These have quite changed the customs of the English people as to their drink.

... The drink which has come to supply the place of beer has, in general, been tea. It is notorious that tea has no useful strength in it ... has badness in it, because it is well known to produce want of sleep in many cases, and in all cases, to shake and weaken the nerves ... Then comes the great article of it all, the time employed in this tea-making affair. It is impossible to make a fire, boil water, make the tea, drink it, wash up the things, sweep up the fire-place, and put all to rights again in less than two hours ... By the time that the clattering tea-tackle is out of the way, the morning is spoiled.

... In a labourer's family, wholesome beer, that has a little life in it, is all that is wanted in general ... Now instead of sitting down to a breakfast upon bread, bacon, and beer, which is to carry him [the labourer] on to the hour of dinner, he has to force his limbs along under the sweat of feebleness. To the wretched tea-kettle he has to return at night, with legs hardly sufficient to maintain him: and thus he makes his miserable progress towards that death which he finds ten or fifteen years sooner than he would have found it had he made his wife brew beer instead of making tea.

In England, coffee was drunk less frequently than tea. Foreign visitors would complain that the English did not know how to make good coffee. One Frenchman concluded:

The English attach no importance to the perfume and flavour of good coffee ... it is always weak and bitter and has completely lost its aromatic flavour.

Coffee seems to have been mainly an upper class drink, requiring even more preparation time than tea, as the beans had to be roasted and ground at home. Jane's brother Edward Knight, who was accustomed to good living at Godmersham, expected to have coffee served at breakfast. A still more luxurious drink was cocoa, or 'chocolate', much loved of Dr Johnson, who used to take it with large quantities of cream, or even melted butter. Both drinks were in evidence when Mrs Austen stayed at her ancestral home of Stoneleigh Abbey in Warwickshire, where she was impressed by the splendid breakfast served:

> At nine in the morning we meet and say our prayers in a handsome Chapel. Then follows breakfast consisting of Chocolate, Coffee and Tea, Plumb Cake, Pound Cake, Hot Rolls, Cold Rolls, Bread and Butter, and *dry toast for me*. The house steward (a fine large respectable looking Man) orders all these matters.

Georgian breakfasts for the middle classes were usually, however, simple meals, consisting of little more than tea and toast. The bread used would not have been like the pure white loaf known today, but a much grainier, unrefined product baked at home. What we take for granted now was unfamiliar to foreigners touring England in the 18th century. Pastor Moritz, a German tourist, remarked:

> The slices of bread and butter given you at tea are thin as poppy leaves, but there is a way of roasting slices of buttered bread before the fire which is incomparable. One slice after another is taken and held to the fire with a fork till the butter soaks through the whole pile of slices. This is called *toast*.

In her domestic role at Chawton, Jane would have been responsible for making the breakfast toast by this method and for boiling up the kettle over the same fire. Not too demanding a task, one might think; nevertheless it was one that could draw a certain amount of pride in its execution, which she has fun with in this satirical dialogue she wrote for her novel *Sanditon*, begun in 1817:

> 'I hope you will eat some of this toast,' said he [Arthur Parker], 'I reckon myself a very good toaster; I never burn my toasts—I never put them too near the fire at first—and yet, you see, there is not a corner but what is well browned.—I hope you like dry toast.'
>
> 'With a reasonable quantity of butter spread over it, very much' said Charlotte—'but not otherwise'.
>
> 'No more do I' said he exceedingly pleased—'We think quite alike there.—So far from dry toast being wholesome, I think it a very bad

thing for the stomach. Without a little butter to soften it, it hurts the coats of the stomach. I am sure it does ... It irritates and acts like a nutmeg grater.'

If Cassandra was away from home Jane would step in to deputize, as it were, and run the house at Chawton. Apparently visitors were always impressed at how tidy and welcoming was the home. The modest cellar stocked mainly home-made wines and spruce beer (a drink produced from the green tips of the coniferous spruce tree). Wines were made from elderberries, gooseberries and currants, and even cowslip flowers, which grew in the garden. Mead and ginger beer were brewed and cherry brandy was kept for special occasions. Other delights regularly enjoyed by Jane's brother Edward Knight at Godmersham were described in a letter she wrote while staying there, apparently in some luxury:

In another week I shall be at home—& then, my having been at Godmersham will seem like a Dream. The Orange Wine will want our Care soon.—But in the meantime for Elegance & Ease & Luxury ... I shall eat Ice & drink French wine, & be above Vulgar Economy ... Luckily the pleasures of friendship, of unreserved Conversation, of similarity of Taste & Opinions, will make good amends for Orange Wine.

After breakfast members of the household attended to the more important domestic tasks. Jane's niece continued:

I don't believe Aunt Jane observed any particular method in parceling out her day but I think she generally sat in the drawing room till luncheon: when visitors were there, chiefly at work—She was fond of work—and she was a great adept at overcast and satin stitch—the peculiar delight of that day—General handiness and neatness were amongst her characteristics.

While gentlemen might go hunting in the morning, a key pastime for ladies living in rural areas was needlework. Women's clothes were not sold ready-made in local shops. Drapers sold material for various purposes, and either a dressmaker was commissioned or, more commonly, ladies and their servants made their own clothes (men would go to local tailors for their needs).

Needlework was therefore an essential handicraft and provided regular occupation for women at home. As well as creating new dresses and bonnets and mending the old, women would make alterations to garments to suit new vogues in style. In 1809 Jane wrote to Cassandra, who was about to visit:

> I can easily suppose that your six weeks here will be fully occupied, were it only in lengthening the waist of your gowns.

On another occasion, when skirt hems were becoming wider and more ornate, Jane implored her sister to keep up with the fashion:

> Miss Chapman had a double flounce to her gown.—You really must get some flounces. Are not some of your large stock of white morn^g gowns just in a happy state for a flounce, too short?

The skill required to make elegant garments was sometimes a cause for despair, especially with impending engagements for which the item was intended, as an exasperated Jane expressed in December 1798:

> I cannot determine what to do about my new Gown; I wish such things were to be bought ready made.—I have some hopes of meeting Martha [Lloyd] at the Christening at Deane next Tuesday, & shall see what she can do for me.—I want to have something suggested which will give me no trouble of thought or direction.

As well as making clothes for her own family, for everyday and special occasions, and other sewing for the household, Jane followed the usual custom of the time and helped the poor by making them baby clothes, simple shifts, and so on.

Some ladies spent their leisure time painting and drawing. Picturesque landscapes were popular in the new Romantic style. Many took the task seriously, others simply dallied with it, as Jane describes in *Emma*:

> Emma wished to go to work directly, and therefore produced the portfolio containing her various attempts at portraits, for not one of them had ever been finished ... Her many beginnings were displayed. Miniatures, half-lengths, whole-lengths, pencil, crayon, and water-colours had been all tried in turn. She had always wanted to do

everything, and had made more progress both in drawing and music
than many might have done with so little labour as she would
ever submit to.

The other main activity of the morning, which would have involved
both men and women, was writing letters. Jane was a keen correspondent,
especially with members of her large family whom she would have seldom
seen. Without telephone or telegraph, but having a national postal system,
the written letter was the standard way of communicating in a world where
travelling even short distances by today's standards would take up too much
time. Caroline Austen recalled Jane's writing desk:

My Aunt must have spent much time in writing—her desk lived in the
drawing room. I often saw her writing letters on it, and I beleive she
wrote much of her Novels in the same way—sitting with her family,
when they were quite alone ... She wrote fully to her Brothers when
they were at sea, and she corresponded with many others of her family
... It was a quiet life according to our ideas but they were readers &
besides the housekeeping our Aunts occupied themselves in working
for the poor & teaching here and there some boy or girl to read &
write. I did not often see my Aunt with a book in her hand but I
beleive ... she read a good deal. I doubt whether she cared very much
for poetry in general; but she was a great admirer of Crabbe ... and
would sometimes say, in jest, that, if she ever married at all, she could
fancy being Mrs. Crabbe.

George Austen had a well-stocked library at Steventon which Jane and
her siblings plundered. She devoured 18th-century authors, novels such as
Henry Fielding's *Tom Jones* and Laurence Sterne's *Tristram Shandy* providing
her with early ideas for characterization. Fanny Burney was influential for
her specifically feminine 'take' on social comedy. Jane liked the works of
Tobias Smollett and Samuel Richardson, especially *Sir Charles Grandison*,
which made such an impression that she dramatized episodes for family
performances at home (see page 173). She also enjoyed some of the Gothic
and sentimental novels of the day. She would have been familiar with
Shakespeare, though preferring contemporary playwrights such as Sheridan
and Goldsmith (also the latter's non-fictional work, *History of England*,
which she parodied in her own version as a 16-year-old); and there was no

bigger fan of Dr Johnson either. Jane would have dipped into collections of sermons, notably *Elegant Extracts* compiled by Vicesimus Knox, Mr Austen's old headmaster at Tonbridge School (she was fond of those by William Sherlock and Hugh Blair). There were also volumes of literary periodicals: *The Spectator*, *The Idler* and *The Rambler*.

The English were remarkably well read in the Georgian period. The classics played a prominent part in the people's civilization, as the German Pastor Moritz observed during his residence in England:

> Certain it is, that the English classical authors are read more generally, beyond all comparison, than the German; which in general are read only by the learned; or at most by the middle class of people. The English national authors are in all hands, and read by all people, of which the innumerable editions they have gone through are a sufficient proof. My landlady, who is only a taylor's widow, reads her Milton; and tells me that her late husband first fell in love with her on this very account; because she read Milton with such proper emphasis. This single instance would prove but little; but I have conversed with several people of the lower class, who all knew their national authors, and who all have read many, if not all of them.

This opinion was backed up by a bookseller, James Lackington, who had noticed a marked increase in his trade by the early 1790s, and not only among the middle classes:

> The sale of books has increased prodigiously within the last twenty years. The poorer sort of farmers, and even the poor country people in general, who before that period spent their evenings in relating stories of witches, ghosts, hobgoblins, etc., now shorten the winter nights by hearing their sons and daughters read tales, romances etc., and on entering their houses you may see *Tom Jones*, *Roderick Random*, and other entertaining books stuck up on their bacon racks.

Afternoons of Leisure

The morning lasted until dinner, the main meal of the day, which was eaten at various times in the afternoon depending on the class of the household. As the century progressed the hour for dinner became later. In 1768 the

16-year-old Fanny Burney described her daily routine at home in her journal:

> We live here, generally speaking, in a very regular way.—we breakfast always at 10, and rise as much before that as we please—we dine precisely at 2, drink tea about 6—and sup exactly at 9.

Generally speaking, the higher the class of person, the later was the hour for dinner. People were aware of a developing snobbery attached to eating late in the afternoon. Writing 30 years later than Miss Burney, Jane admitted to those living in grander style at Godmersham:

> We dine now at half after Three, & have done dinner I suppose before you begin.—We drink tea at half after six.—I am afraid you will despise us.

By 1808 the time for the Austen dinner had advanced to at least five o'clock. At Godmersham it was eaten at 6.30, the more fashionable time by the 19th century. One key factor behind this social pretension was whether the householder could afford candles, by the light of which food could be eaten in the dark winter months. Gas and electricity were still wonders of the future. Candles made of tallow or the more expensive beeswax provided the main source of domestic lighting. Common tallow was a mixture of beef and mutton fat, which when lit gave off an unpleasant smell and dirty smoke. A couple of candles on the table would have given enough light to eat by.

As the gap between breakfast and dinner became ever wider, so there was a need to fill it with an interim snack: luncheon was invented. This usually consisted of cold meats, pickles, hothouse fruit and cakes, consumed informally by anyone who was peckish, and in summer possibly eaten out of doors. In *Sense and Sensibility* Sir John Middleton is popular for his picnics; as the author says, he was 'for ever forming parties to eat cold ham and chicken out of doors'. Just as today there is something of a frenzy among the English to eat outside at the first hint of summer, so there were those in Jane Austen's day who delighted in the opportunity. It was not to everyone's liking, as the author depicts in *Emma* when Mrs Elton tries to persuade Mr Knightley to pick strawberries and have a picnic in his garden:

> 'It is to be a morning scheme, you know, Knightley; quite a simple thing. I shall wear a large bonnet, and bring one of my little baskets

hanging on my arm. Here,—probably this basket with pink ribbon. Nothing can be more simple, you see. And Jane [Fairfax] will have such another. There is to be no form or parade—a sort of gipsy party.—We are to walk about your gardens, and gather the strawberries ourselves, and sit under trees;—and whatever else you may like to provide, it is to be all out of doors—a table spread in the shade, you know. Every thing as natural and simple as possible. Is not that your idea?'

'Not quite. My idea of the simple and the natural will be to have the table spread in the dining-room. The nature and the simplicity of gentlemen and ladies, with their servants and furniture, I think is best observed by meals within doors. When you are tired of eating strawberries in the garden, there shall be cold meat in the house.'

The period after this midday snack was spent, weather permitting, outside, as Caroline Austen described of the time when the Austens lived at Chawton:

After luncheon, my Aunts generally walked out—sometimes they went to Alton for shopping—Often to the Great House—as it was called—to make a visit, or they liked to stroll about the grounds—sometimes to Chawton Park, a noble beech wood—but sometimes, but that was rarely, to call on a neighbour. They had no carriage, and their visitings did not extend far—there were a few families living in the village.

Dinner Time

While living at Steventon Rectory the Austens formed close friendships with the Lloyds, who were one mile away at Deane. In 1789 George Austen let the parsonage to a Welsh widow, Mrs Lloyd, and her two daughters, Martha and Mary. Jane and Cassandra would often walk over to visit them. They borrowed each other's books, and swapped dressmaking patterns and recipes for cooking. Martha would come to form a big part of Jane's domestic life. Of particular note is Martha's collection of recipes, handwritten and bound in a leather book.

There were very few published cookery books at the time. The most widely read were Hannah Glasse's *The Art of Cookery Made Plain and Easy* (1747), Mrs Frazer's *The Practice of Cookery* (1795) and Mrs Rundell's *A New System of Domestic Cookery* (1795).

Martha's book included a section at the back on home remedies (see page 258) and household tips. Among them were instructions on how to make everyday cleaning materials: soaps, shoe polish, varnish for mahogany furniture, as well as finer mixtures such as ink and whiting for silk stockings.

Much of the contents of Martha's book derived from the Austen household. After George Austen and Mrs Lloyd both died in 1805, Martha moved in with the three Austen women and they all lived together in Southampton and at Chawton (Mary Lloyd, who married James Austen in 1792, died three years afterwards). One dinner party held in December at their rented house in Southampton is recalled in a letter to Cassandra from Jane, who enjoyed what she called 'experimental housekeeping', though the party went on too long, finishing after 11pm:

> **The last hour, spent in yawning & shivering in a wide circle round the fire, was dull enough—but the Tray had admirable success. The Widgeon & the preserved Ginger were as delicious as one could wish. But as to our Black Butter, do not decoy anybody to Southampton by such a lure, for it is all gone. The first pot ... proved not all what it ought to be;—it was neither solid, nor entirely sweet ... it had not been boiled enough. Such being the event of the first pot, I would not save the second, & we therefore ate it in unpretending privacy; & tho' not what it ought to be, part of it was very good.**

Owing to Mrs Austen's prudent housekeeping, her family could live reasonably comfortably on the £300 a year her husband earned. Much of their food was home-produced. There was a poultry yard where chickens, bantams, turkeys, geese and ducks were reared. The maids made butter and cheese, baked bread, and cured ham and bacon. There was an extensive vegetable garden and various fruit trees, from which preserves and pickles would be made. Wealthy landowners were able to afford to heat greenhouses and grow oranges, lemons and more exotic fruits such as peaches, grapes and pineapples; the rest of the gentry had to content themselves with eating whatever was in season. The Austen boys were keen game shooters and fresh fish was freely available nearby. While visiting Stoneleigh Abbey in its extensive grounds in 1806, Mrs Austen noted in a letter to her daughter-in-law:

> **The ponds supply excellent fish, the park excellent venison.**

Venison was popular at the time, so was fish. In Hampshire the Austens had a choice of fresh trout, salmon, carp or pike; and in 1801 sardines were introduced into England. While the family was living at Southampton, cod and sole were common dishes, and cod's head was a decorative fancy on the serving dish.

Cooking methods were rudimentary. All was done using an open fire in the kitchen. Meat and poultry were roasted on spits and in pans suspended by chains over the fire; an oven was often built into the wall next to the fireplace. Water would usually be collected from a pump outside. Food storage was a problem in the absence of refrigeration. Some larger estates had an ice house – a circular brick-built pit set deep in the ground and filled with ice from nearby ponds in winter. Most homes would have a basement larder. The task of judging the organic state of game could be tricky: herbs and imported spices could help to disguise the flavour but by and large Georgians simply acquired a taste for high meat and ignored the smell. It was not to everyone's liking, as a conversation in Jane Austen's unfinished novel *The Watsons* (begun in 1804) indicates:

> 'And what had you for dinner, sir?' said his eldest daughter.
> He related the dishes, and told what he had ate himself.
> '… as the partridges were pretty high, Dr. Richards would have them sent away to the other end of the table, that they might not offend Mr. Watson.'

Gluttons there were aplenty in the 18th century. Samuel Johnson, who died when Jane was still a child, was a famous one. Another who lived in her day was Parson Woodforde (1740–1803), who left a daily record of the many dinners eaten at his home in Norfolk. In the summer of 1792 he dined with friends in grand style. One of many now obscure delicacies in those days was calf's head:

> There were six people present and the full menu included boiled tench, Peas soup, a couple of boiled chicken and Pig's face, hashed calf's head, Beans, rosted Rump of Beef with New potatoes etc. 2nd course: rosted Duck and Green Peas, a very fine Leveret rosted, Strawberry cream, Jelly, Puddings etc. Desert—strawberries, cherries and last years nonpareils [apples]. About 7 o'clock coffee and tea.

It may sound like sumptuous fare and there was plenty of it. Presentation tended to be simple and unpretentious, compared with that of the plush Victorians, though the potter Josiah Wedgwood was creating his famous ware at this time; Jane's brother Edward Knight commissioned a fine dinner service from him in 1813 bearing his family crest. Edward Austen-Leigh described a typical dinner table of the Georgian period:

> At that time the dinner table presented a far less splendid appearance than it does now. It was appropriated to solid food, rather than to flowers, fruits, and decorations. Nor was there much glitter of plate upon it; for the early dinner hour rendered candlesticks unnecessary, and silver forks had not come into general use.
>
> The dinners too were more homely ... and the bill of fare in one house would not be so like that in another as it is now, for family receipts were held in high estimation. A grandmother of culinary talent could bequeath to her descendant fame for some particular dish, and might influence the family dinner for many generations. One house would pride itself on ham; another on its game pie, and a third on its superior furmity [frumenty: wheat boiled in milk with spices and sugar], or tansey-pudding [a traditional Easter pudding flavoured with the daisy-like tansy] ... Vegetables were less plentiful and less various. Potatoes were used, but not so abundantly as now; and ... eaten only with roast meat. They were novelties to a tenant's wife who was entertained at Steventon Parsonage; and when Mrs. Austen advised her to plant them in her own garden, she replied, 'No, no; they are very well for you gentry, but they must be terribly *costly* to rear.'

After dinner was a time for leisure. There was no ready-made entertainment, and indoor games were common. Most popular was playing cards, which all the family, but mostly the men, enjoyed. Henry Crawford in *Mansfield Park* is typical of a male who relishes competition, as the author describes:

> He was in high spirits, doing everything with happy ease, and preeminent in all the lively turns, quick resources, and playful impudence that could do honour to the game; and the round table [where card games were played by individuals rather than with partners] was altogether a very comfortable contrast to the steady sobriety and orderly silence of the other.

Often the problem was generating enthusiasm among members of the family who did not share the same mental dexterity for a game, especially when four were required to play it. In some situations cards served a useful purpose in avoiding the need for conversation, in others they were simply a diversion from boredom.

The following conversation from *The Watsons* mentions several games that are still well known today and illustrates a typical evening, with friends visiting the Reverend Watson's family of six children:

'I wish we may be able to have a game of cards tonight,' said Elizabeth to Mrs. Robert, after seeing her father comfortably seated in his arm-chair.

'Not on my account, my dear, I beg. You know I am no card-player. I think a snug chat infinitely better. I always say cards are very well sometimes to break a formal circle, but one never wants them among friends.'

'I was thinking of its being something to amuse my father,' said Elizabeth, 'if it was not disagreeable to you. He says his head won't bear whist, but perhaps if we make a round game he may be tempted to sit down with us.'

'By all means, my dear creature. I am quite at your service; only do not oblige me to choose the game, that's all. Speculation is the only round game at Croydon now, but I can play anything ... Why do you not get him to play at cribbage? Margaret and I have played at cribbage most nights that we have not been engaged.'

... 'Oh, me!' said Tom. 'Whatever you decide on will be a favourite with me. I have had some pleasant hours at speculation in my time, but I have not been in the way of it now for a long while. Vingt-un [twenty-one or pontoon] is the game at Osborne Castle. I have played nothing but vingt-un of late. You would be astonished to hear the noise we make there—the fine old lofty drawing-room rings again. Lady Osborne sometimes declares she cannot hear herself speak.'

Other indoor games that might be played after dinner were billiards (by the men) and backgammon, dominos and chess. Although gambling was outlawed by the middle of the 18th century, playing for money continued in the privacy of the home. Jane Austen once complained of losing three shillings in a single game.

Below Stairs

The Austens were by no means affluent yet they followed the normal practice for households of their size by employing several servants. Without the aid of such modern appliances as washing machines, vacuum cleaners and electric cookers, household chores were labour-intensive. The Austens' household staff usually consisted of a manservant (who doubled as a gardener) and two maids, as well as a washerwoman and a daily help. Staff problems were never far away; they once had to sack their gardener for habitual drunkenness. In the autumn of 1798 Jane detailed the situation at Steventon:

> **Dame Bushell washes for us for only one week more, as Sukey has got a place.—John Stevens' wife undertakes our Purification. She does not look as if anything she touched would ever be clean, but who knows?—We do not seem likely to have any other maidservant at present, but Dame Staples will supply the place of one.**

But by December things had improved:

> **We are very much disposed to like our new maid; she knows nothing of a dairy, to be sure, which, in our family, is rather against her, but she is to be taught it all. In short, we have felt the inconvenience of being without a maid so long, that we are determined to like her, and she will find it a hard matter to displease us. As yet, she seems to cook very well, is uncommonly stout, and says she can work well at her needle.**

Most servants were young and uneducated when first hired, and so it was down to their employers to put time and energy into training their staff. As public transport improved so job mobility improved, and this often meant the training was wasted as new opportunities beckoned and staff endeavoured to better themselves. A scullery maid or chamber maid would aspire to becoming a cook or housekeeper, the two best-paid jobs in the female servant hierarchy.

A list in his diary for 1798 of the wages paid annually by Parson Woodforde shows the differentials between the various post-holders (expressed in pounds, shillings and pence):

To Benj Leggatt, my Farming Man pd. 10.0.0.
To Bretlingham Scurl, my Footman pd. 8.0.0.
To Betty Dade, my House-Maid pd. 5.0.0.
To Sally Gunton, my Cook pd. 5.0.0.
To Barnabas Woodcock, my Yard-boy pd. 2.0.0.

As a result of high staff turnover, it became difficult for servants to find positions where they could get any training, as frustrated employers tended to offer only the bare minimum. One servant, who wrote her autobiography (*Life of a Licensed Victualler's Daughter. Written by Herself*) in 1844, describes her second job, which she obtained at the age of 16 in 1803:

My mistress made me nurse the child, and do everything that was laborious; but all that required any art or knowledge, she not only would not let me do it, but would send me out of the way, with the little boy, while she did it herself. This was done that I should not leave her, or think myself qualified for a better place.

Thus, housemaids earned a reputation for never being any good at anything, being uneducated and untrained. As Samuel Johnson once advised:

Never marry a chamber-maid, for they bring nothing with them but a few old cloaths of their mistresses, and for house-keeping, few of them know anything of it; for they can hardly make a pudding or a pye, neither can they spin, nor knit, nor wash, except it be a few laces to make themselves fine withal.

Keeping hold of good staff depended on providing good terms and good relations between servant and master. There was no stigma attached to servile roles and usually there was a good deal of familiarity between master and man, mistress and maid – something visiting foreigners thought very odd. By all accounts the Austens were conscientious employers and offered reasonable living conditions. But that was not typical of the 18th century, in which servants often had to endure squalid, cramped quarters. In the bigger houses, which might employ up to 15 servants indoors alone, the men – butler, footmen, coachmen, grooms, gardeners, stable boys – slept in the cellars and the females – housekeeper, housemaids, cook, scullery and dairy maids, nurse, nursemaids, governess – slept in the attic. Servants had no recognized right to free time or holidays and were for ever at the beck and call of their master or mistress. The work was hard too. Even in the Austens' household their labourers worked for as long as they could manage, as Jane reported:

John Bond [their labourer] begins to find himself grow old, which John Bonds ought not to do, and unequal to much hard work; a man is therefore hired to supply his place as to labour, and John himself is to have care of the sheep.

Domestic Inventions

While poor labourers depended on peat and turf to heat their cottages, futuristic homes in the latter part of the 18th century were enjoying the latest advances in technology. In the winter of 1784 the inventor James Watt heated a room by steam for the first time and a few years later a bath was run with water heated by steam. In the same decade Josiah Wedgwood, junior, 'warmed different apartments in one building by one stove' – the first instance of central heating.

The cast-iron kitchen range was introduced in 1780, containing an oven on one side and a water heater on the other. All sorts of domestic devices were conceived and made available to the public for the first time. Lucifer matches made lighting candles easier; the first umbrellas went up; clocks had alarms fitted; Pears manufactured their transparent soap; and Mr Schweppes bottled his mineral water. Advances were also made in lavatory design. In 1778 Joseph Bramah patented an improved toilet flushing system using a ball-cock; by the end of the century he had sold several thousand products round the country. It is said that Admiral Nelson had a water closet fitted to each of the dressing rooms adjoining his five bedrooms.

There were those who saw in all this modernization the beginnings of a mass consumer society, which would only increase the gap between the haves and the have-nots. One such voice wishing to alert people to the danger of 'progress' was that of William Cobbett. In 1822 he railed against the passing of good old-fashioned methods, even simple domestic ware:

The plates, dishes, mugs, and things of that kind, should be of pewter, or even of wood. Any thing is better than crockery-ware. Bottles to carry a-field should be of wood. Formerly, nobody but the gipseys and mumpers [beggars], that went a hop-picking in the season, carried glass or earthen bottles. As to *glass* of any sort, I do not know, what business it has in any man's house, unless he be rich enough to live on his means. It pays a tax, in many cases, to the amount of two-thirds of its cost.

Materials in demand were changing as the Industrial Revolution gathered pace. Perhaps the single most important domestic advance of the late 18th century was the Swiss inventor Aimé Argand's oil lamp, patented in England in 1784, which changed the basic design of oil lamps for the first time in thousands of years. The combination of a cylindrical wick, two metal sleeves and a glass chimney that drew the hot air upwards, accelerating the burning, produced ten times the brightness of previous oil lamps with none of their smoke or smell. It became the prototype for the gas burners that would light up Britain in the future, the first street illuminated by gaslight being Pall Mall in 1807. For the first time activities that required visual concentration, such as reading, could be carried on through the dark winter evenings without much strain. The dawn-to-dusk limitation to domestic work could be extended, though not everyone welcomed that particular advance.

Interiors Splendid and Sparse

Jane Austen once spent a week with her mother visiting her grand ancestral home at Stoneleigh Abbey, a place that may well have inspired scenes in her novels involving large medieval mansions such as Donwell Abbey in *Emma* and Northanger Abbey. The Elizabethan house had been built by the Leighs using the foundations and stones of a former Cistercian monastery, knocked down by Henry VIII in the 16th century. In a letter to her granddaughter Mary Austen in the summer of 1806, Jane's mother described her impressions of the house which, it had recently transpired, might be inherited by her brother, James Leigh-Perrot:

Eating Fish Venison and all manner of good things at a late hour, in a noble large Parlour hung round with family Pictures—everything is very Grand & very fine & very large. The house is larger than I could have supposed. Mr. Leigh almost despairs of ever finding his way about ... I have proposed his setting up *directing Posts* at the Angles [corners in passages].

I will now give you some idea of the inside of this vast house, first premising that there are 45 windows in front, 15 in a row. You go up a considerable flight of steps (some offices are under the house) into a large Hall: on the right hand is the dining parlour, within that the Breakfast room, where we generally sit, the only room that looks towards the River [Avon]. On the left hand of the hall is the best drawing room ... these rooms are rather gloomy, Brown wainscoat and dark Crimson furniture; so we never use them but to walk thro' them to the picture gallery. Behind the smaller drawing Room is the estate Bed Chamber, with a high dark crimson Velvet Bed: an *alarming* apartment just fit for a Heroine; the old Gallery opens into it ... There are 26 Bed Chambers in the new part of the house & a great many in the old. There is also a large Billiard Room.

... Poor Lady Saye & Sele [the present occupant] to be sure is rather tormenting, tho' sometimes amusing, and affords Jane many a good laugh.

More modest Georgian homes of the less affluent gentry would still have had good-sized rooms with high ceilings and tall casement windows to let in plenty of light. It was fashionable to polish the wooden floors of the sitting rooms and lay down fine carpets imported from the East. Some carpets were by this time also being made in England – at Axminster and Wilton, for instance.

Furniture, which had traditionally been carved from English oak, now tended to be made of finer mahogany imported from America. It was in common supply both new and second-hand, as Parson Woodforde indicated when he went shopping in 1789:

Bought this day of Willm Hart, Cabinet Maker on Hog Hill Norwich 2 large second hand double-flapped Mohogany Tables, also one second hand Mohogany dressing Table with Drawers, also one new Mohogany Washing-Stand, for all which paid 4. 14. 6. [pounds, shillings and pence] ... I think the whole of it to be very cheap.

This was the age of the great cabinet-makers – Thomas Chippendale (1718–79), George Hepplewhite (d. 1786) and Thomas Sheraton (1751–1806) – whose elegant designs graced the homes of those who could afford them. Alas, the Austens would not have been numbered among them. Jane's nephew Edward Austen-Leigh had no high regard for the furnishings of the Austens' home and gave this insight into their comfort or otherwise:

The furniture of the rooms would appear to us [Victorians] lamentably scanty. There was a general deficiency of carpeting in sitting-rooms, bed-rooms and passages. A pianoforte, or rather a spinnet or harpsichord, was by no means a necessary appendage. It was to be found only where there was a decided taste for music. ... There would often be but one sofa in the house, and that a stiff, angular, uncomfortable article. There were no deep easy-chairs, nor other appliances for lounging; for to lie down, or even to lean back, was a luxury permitted only to old persons or invalids.

Sparse though the interior of the Steventon parsonage generally was, some interesting pieces were to be seen here and there. Jane and Cassandra used their dressing-room as their own private drawing room when they were grown up. Their father's account with a local interior design firm in Basingstoke reveals that the wallpaper was blue, with blue-striped curtains to match. But in 1801 the settled, rarefied life of Steventon came to an end when Jane's father retired. He handed over the property to his son James, while those members of the Austen family then living under one roof – father, mother and two daughters – moved to rented premises in Bath. Removal vehicles had much less capacity than those of today and in many instances it was a cheaper option to leave behind articles, especially fragile pieces, and replace them at the new address. This usually meant auctioning furniture. Beds, a sideboard and some Pembroke tables were all sold, as were Jane's own pianoforte and Mr Austen's library of 500 books (except those that James retained).

Despite some initial shock at being told she would have to move, Jane reconciled herself to the idea of living in reduced circumstances in Bath. Surviving correspondence of hers ends at the time of this move and there is a gap of over three years before her next letter, by which time the Austens had moved again. There is no description of domestic life at No. 4 Sydney Place, Bath, though it was a location Jane is said to have liked, being on the outskirts of the city near open countryside, yet within a short walk of the centre. The house itself faced Sydney Gardens, where concerts and other entertainments were held on gala nights in summer. It would clearly have offered quite a different ambience to what she was used to at Steventon Rectory.

In Public

A small village of Jane Austen's England had little more than a church and a pub to serve its community. Steventon had no more than 30 families, and of those just two ranked above the status of labourer, and it had no shop or inn. The nearest shops for the Austens were at Overton a few miles away. As it happens, Overton was quite a considerable shopping centre, with two butchers, five grocers, four tailors, seven shoemakers, a hairdresser, a clockmaker and various tradesmen such as carpenters and blacksmiths. In larger towns specialist retailers would have included milliners, drapers and haberdashers. Bath was renowned for its wonderful shops, as Mrs Allen enthuses in *Northanger Abbey*:

> **Bath is a charming place, sir; there are so many good shops here.—**
> **We are sadly off in the country; not but what we have very good shops**
> **in Salisbury, but it is so far to go;—eight miles is a long way … and it**
> **is such a fag—I come back tired to death. Now, here one can step out**
> **of doors and get a thing in five minutes.**

The time and effort taken to get to shops made such expeditions tiresome. Most households would provide what they could for themselves – grow their own fruit and vegetables, perhaps keep their own poultry – and buy whatever else they might need direct from local farms. Prices in shops and markets were liable to fluctuate and, in any case, the produce was not always fresh. Milk, particularly in summer, could be hazardous because it was unpasteurized and likely to harbour the bacteria of tuberculosis (known as 'consumption').

By the end of the 18th century every town had a printer and a bookshop. Books were relatively expensive, as they were labour-intensive products made with costly materials. A novel would cost about 7s 6d; some publishers serialized their books to keep down costs for their buyers. As well as books, there were hundreds of magazines, political pamphlets, sermons and volumes of poetry on sale. Just as nowadays, people got to hear of new releases from reviews, lists and the talk of the town. There were numerous book clubs and private subscription libraries sponsored by affluent gentlemen. Those who could not afford to buy their own copies could instead resort to one of the many circulating libraries, mainly run by booksellers and patronized by female readers. A good collection was held in Bath, with which Jane Austen was familiar, and she refers to it in *Persuasion* through her character Lady Russell, an avid reader. An advertisement that appeared in the *Bath Chronicle* in 1784 betrays a proud management:

> **Circulating Library, Cheap Street, Bath,**
> **10s.6d. a Year, 4s. a Quarter,**
> **S. HAZARD most respectfully acquaints his Subscribers and the Company resorting to this City, that, in order to render his Library as agreeable as possible, he has opened a large Room up one Pair of Stairs (fronting the Churchyard) where they may amuse themselves with the NEWSPAPERS and NEW PUBLICATIONS during the Intervals of drinking the Bath Waters, being very near the Pump Room ... He flatters himself it will be found a very comfortable Retreat, as it is covered with a Carpet, and a good Fire will be kept.**
> **Besides a select Collection of near SEVEN THOUSAND VOLUMES, including the most approved modern Publications, NEW BOOKS, Reviews, Votes of the House of Commons, and ... NEWSPAPERS.**

The popularity of these libraries soared in the new age of the Gothic novel: by 1800 there were over 120 in London and more than 250 in the provinces. As well as spine-tingling reads these circulating libraries offered a variety of other delectations, completely unrelated to books. In *Sanditon*, Jane Austen's unfinished novel of 1817 set on the Sussex coast, the library presents itself more like a fashion boutique:

> **Charlotte was to go ... to buy new parasols, new gloves and new brooches for her sisters and herself at the library ... [and tempted though she was by several other items] turned from the Drawers of rings & Brooches, repressed further solicitation & paid for what she bought.**

Church and Parish

The public institution most immediately on hand to the Austen family was the church, structurally a very old building of which Jane must have become fond as she grew up and watched the rites of passage performed for her family and friends in the village. Christenings, weddings and funerals would all have been conducted here by her father, who of course held the living. A description of the church was given by his grandson, Edward Austen-Leigh:

> It must have stood there some seven centuries, and [church historians] would have found beauty in the very narrow early English windows, as well as in the general proportions of its little chancel; while its solitary position, far from the hum of the village, and within sight of no habitation, except a glimpse of the gray manor-house through its circling screen of sycamores, has in it something solemn and appropriate to the last resting-place of the silent dead. Sweet violets, both purple and white, grow in abundance beneath its south wall. One may imagine for how many centuries the ancestors of those little flowers have occupied that undisturbed, sunny nook. Large elms protrude their rough branches; old hawthorns shed their annual blossoms over the graves; and the hollow yew-tree must be at least coeval with [the same age as] the church.

In Jane Austen's England local communities were organized as parishes, served by the church and run by a body of volunteers from the community headed by the parson (elected councils were introduced to oversee local issues in 1894). From early medieval times parishioners had paid tithes to the church for the upkeep of its buildings and to support the community in general. The collection of tithes and dispersal of due monies was the responsibility of the parson and his churchwarden. Since the passing of the Poor Law in 1601 a Poor Rate had been levied on landowners in the parish to support its paupers, though this varied and often did not provide enough.

Clergymen would help out in times of sickness and bad harvest, often keeping their doors open to the poor, especially at festive times such as Christmas, when they would provide dinners. Failing that, parishes had the option of incarcerating the worst cases in workhouses. Only a few hundred of these infamous institutions were founded but their main role was to keep 'undesirables' off the streets and out of sight: they might include the sick and infirm, unemployable rogues, vagrants and village simpletons. Parson Woodforde visited a Norfolk workhouse in 1781:

> **We dined at 3 o'clock and after we had smoked a Pipe etc., we took a ride to the House of Industry about 2 miles West of Dereham, and a very large building at present tho' there wants another Wing. About 380 Poor in it now, but they don't look either healthy or cheerful, a great Number die there, 27 have died since Christmas last.**

Not all clergy were resident in a parish; in fact in the 18th century more than half of Anglican incumbents were non-resident. The system of tithes was open to abuse and in many cases either insufficient sums were raised or clergymen preferred to spend the money improving their own parsonages, while their churches fell into picturesque decay. An angry letter from William Cowper, poet and evangelical reformer, described the miserable conditions to his cousin:

> **The ruinous condition of some of these edifices gave me great offence; and I could not help wishing that the honest vicar, instead of indulging his genius for improvements by enclosing his gooseberry bushes within a Chinese rail, and converting half an acre of his glebeland into a bowling-green, would have applied part of his income to the more laudable purpose of sheltering his parishioners from the weather during their attendance on divine service. It is no uncommon thing to see the parsonage well thatched and in exceeding good repair, while the church has scarce any other roof than the ivy that grows over it. The noise of owls, bats and magpies makes the principal part of the church music; and the walls, like a large map, seem to be portioned out into capes, seas and promontories, by the various colours by which the damps have stained them.**

Damp would gather fast in these unheated buildings. Often rush matting was placed on the floor to help to soak it up, but in bad weather the congregation would simply have to bear their suffering with good grace. In those churches that offered regular services the clergy would say Morning and Evening Prayer and once a month conduct the Eucharist, offering bread and wine to those who desired it. There was little ceremony or singing. Only in cathedrals were psalms sung; in parish churches they were intoned. What might have been an austere atmosphere in some churches was in others simply dull and soporific. Cowper had more to say:

> The squire of the parish or his ancestors, perhaps to testify their devotion and leave a lasting monument of their magnificence, have adorned the altar-piece with the richest crimson velvet, embroidered with vine leaves and ears of wheat, and have dressed up the pulpit with the same splendour and expense; while the gentleman who fills it is exalted in the midst of all this finery with a surplice as dirty as a farmer's frock.
>
> ... I was more offended with the indecency of worship in others. I could wish that the clergy would inform their congregations that there is no occasion to scream themselves hoarse in making the responses ... The old women too in the aisle might be told that their time would be better employed in attending to the sermon than in fumbling over their tattered testaments till they have found the text; by which time the discourse is near drawing to a conclusion ...
>
> The length of the sermon is also measured by the will of the squire, as formerly by the hour-glass: and I know one parish where the preacher has always the complaisance to conclude his discourse, however abruptly, the minute that the squire gives the signal, by rising up after his nap.

Church was of course the one place where, at least on festive occasions such as Christmas and Easter, everybody who was anybody would be seen, and liked to be seen. Apparel was of the utmost importance in maintaining one's social position in the community. Cowper again cast his mordant eye over the congregation:

> I need not say anything of the behaviour of the congregations in these polite places of religious resort; as the same genteel ceremonies are practiced there as at the most fashionable churches in town. The ladies, immediately on their entrance, breathe a pious ejaculation through their fan-sticks, and the beaux very gravely address themselves to the haberdashers' bills glued upon the linings of their hats. This pious duty is no sooner performed than the exercise of bowing and curtsying succeeds; the locking and unlocking of the pews drowns the reader's voice at the beginning of the service; and the

rustling of silks, added to the whispering and tittering of so much good company, renders him totally unintelligible to the very end of it.

A common custom in towns was for well-to-do families to parade down the streets after church. While living in Bath, Jane Austen might have done the same, as she refers in her letters to members of the congregation at the Octagon church in Milsom Street, where she is likely to have worshipped, strolling along the Royal Crescent after the service. Parson Woodforde once expressed his disapproval of this church which, being a relatively new building, catered for the comfort of its affluent congregation:

It is a handsome building, but not like a place of worship, there being fire-places in it, especially on each side of the Altar, which I cannot think at all decent, it is not liked.

The Octagon, built in 1766–7 and named after the shape of its plan, was a neoclassical building, the fashionable style for 17th- and 18th-century churches popularized by Sir Christopher Wren and Nicholas Hawksmoor. Their interiors tended to be plain. Gone were the soaring arches and gothic tracery of medieval architecture. The new emphasis was on communality of worship and ease, with comfortable boxed pews out of the way of cold draughts. Anglicanism in Georgian England for the most part lacked religious fervour. In this time of national prosperity the majority of churchgoers were happy to be led by clergymen who abided by a creed that espoused heavenly reward for earthly virtue and material success. For their part, parsons paid lip service to their genteel patrons and were recognized as smiling figures of the establishment who rubber-stamped existing power relations. The poet George Crabbe portrayed such a parson in *The Borough*:

But let applause be dealt in all we may,
Our Priest was cheerful, and in season gay;
His frequent visits seldom fail'd to please;
Easy himself, he sought his Neighbour's ease ...
He ever aim'd to please; and to offend
Was ever cautious; for he sought a Friend;
Yet for the Friendship never much would pay,
Content to bow, be silent, and obey,
And by a soothing suff'rance find his way.

Fiddling and Fishing were his arts; at times
He alter'd Sermons, and he aim'd at Rhymes;
And his Fair Friends, not yet intent on Cards,
Oft he amus'd with Riddles and Charades.

With absenteeism among rectors and a law that no longer prosecuted
parishioners for missing church, congregations dwindled as the 18th century
wore on. By 1800 only about one in ten Anglicans took Holy Communion
at Easter. Amid this devotional apathy there emerged various Protestant
minority groups, known as Dissenters (dissenting from the Established
Church of England), who possessed religious zeal and wished to reverse
the trend. Congregationalists, Presbyterians, Unitarians and Baptists all
fell within this group. Added to these were the Quaker and Methodist
movements within the Church of England, though Methodism became a
separate body in 1795. In the last 30 years of the 18th century evangelical
missions everywhere were working to win over disaffected souls. As one
Baptist remarked, 'almost the whole country is open for village preaching'.
John Wesley, who founded the first Methodist chapel in Bristol in 1739, saw
how easily the spiritual life could stagnate, even among his own flock. He
remarked in his *Journal*:

For the Methodists in every place grow diligent and frugal;
consequently they increase in goods. Hence they proportionally
increase in pride, in anger, in the desire of the flesh, the desire of the
eyes, and the pride of life. So, although the form of religion remains,
the spirit is swiftly vanishing away.

The Evangelicals called for a number of changes to religious observance in
daily lives: the saying of grace before meals, higher standards of personal
morality, and regular Sunday worship. One way in which their services
differed significantly from those of the broad church was in hymn-singing.
John and Charles Wesley wrote enough hymns to fill a whole book and
between them contributed to an upturn in church song, as William
Cowper noted:

The good old practice of psalm-singing is, indeed, wonderfully
improved in many country churches. The tunes themselves have been
set to jiggish measures ... and in every county an itinerant band of

> vocal musicians ... make it their business to go round to all
> the churches in their turns, and, after a prelude with the
> pitch-pipe, astonish the audience with hymns set to the new
> Winchester measure.

But growing numbers of converts, in particular to Methodism, produced mixed feelings in society at large. This brand of Christianity was severe. Wesley's sermons from the pulpit became renowned for their uncompromising attitude to moral discipline, for example on the subject of children's obedience to their parents, as this extract from his *Sermon 96* testifies:

> Disobedience is as certain a way to damnation as cursing and swearing.
> Stop him, stop him at first, in the name of God. Do not 'spare the rod,
> and spoil the child.' If you have not the heart of a tiger, do not give up
> your child to his own will, that is, to the devil. Though it be pain to
> yourself, yet pluck your offspring out of the lion's teeth. Make them
> submit, that they may not perish. Break their will, that you may save
> their soul.

Jane Austen herself said in 1809 that she did 'not like the Evangelicals'. Perhaps the following sort of sentiments, from John Wesley's *Sermons on Several Occasions*, might have put her off:

> He who plays when he is a child, will play when he is a man ... avoid
> all lightness as you would avoid hell-fire.

But Wesley also had his moderate side, including, perhaps surprisingly, his attitude to alcohol. Unlike later Methodists, he did not actually disapprove of it. He forbade spirits but happily drank beer and wine, and in fact campaigned for real ale (he objected to the increasing use of hops). He discouraged his followers from drinking tea, thinking that a waste of time and money. Five years later Jane had apparently changed her mind about the Methodists:

> I am by no means convinced that we ought not all to be Evangelicals,
> & am at least persuaded that they who are so from Reason & Feeling,
> must be happiest & safest.

John Wesley's preaching was not always predictable. Perhaps surprisingly he once bemoaned the decline of superstition as a side effect of progressive thinking. In his journal he wrote:

It is true that the English in general, and, indeed, most of the men of learning in Europe, have given up all accounts of witches and apparitions as mere wives' fables. I am sorry for it ... The giving up of witchcraft is in effect giving up the Bible!

Although the witchcraft laws were repealed in 1737, well into Jane Austen's time cases continued to be reported of superstitious villagers adopting their own lynch-law and inflicting severe, sometimes fatal, punishments on suspected witches. As reported in the *Public Advertiser*, one victim in the Wiltshire town of Wilton was lucky to escape in 1761:

One Sarah Jellicoat of this town escaped undergoing the whole discipline [of lynch-law punishment] usually inflicted by the unmerciful & unthinking vulgar on witches, under pretence that she had bewitched a farmer's servant & a tallow chandler's soap, which failed in the operation, only by the interposition of some humane gentlemen & the vigilance of a discreet magistrate, who stopped the proceedings before the violence thereof had gone to a great pitch.

One group that stood out against superstition and all forms of corruption was the Quakers, who were becoming a more prominent force in society than they are today. Poet laureate Robert Southey described their habit and their beliefs:

The most remarkable sect in this land of sectaries is unquestionably that of the Quakers. They wear a peculiar dress, which is in fashion such as grave people wore in the time of their founder [George Fox in the 1650s], and always of sober colour. They never uncover their heads in salutation, nor in their houses of worship; they have no form of worship, no order of priests, and they reject all the Sacraments. In their meeting-houses they assemble and sit in silence, unless any one should be disposed to speak, in which case they suppose him to be immediately moved by the Spirit; and any person is permitted to speak, women as well as men. These, however, are only a few of their peculiarities. They call the days of the week and the months according to their numerical order, saying that their common names are relics of idolatry ... They will not take an oath; and such is the opinion of their moral character, that their affirmation is admitted in courts of justice to have the same force. They will not pay tithes; the priest therefore is obliged to seize their goods for his due. They will not bear arms, neither will they be concerned in any branch of trade or manufactory which is concerned with war ... They prohibit cards and other games, music, dancing, and the theatre. A drunken Quaker is never seen, nor a criminal one ever brought to the bar.

The Georgian Inn

The 18th-century inn was the mainstay of public social life. It served all levels of the community, though less likely the squire with his genteel manners than the 'peasants'. Inns varied in their respectability, just as they might today, from a squalid local boozer to a pristine hotel. As many inns came into existence to serve travellers who needed to rest and replenish during their long journeys, descriptions of these places that many regard as the quintessence of Georgian England came from the pens of visitors from overseas. One such was Washington Irving, from the United States, who poured his impressions into *The Sketch Book of Geoffrey Crayon, Gent*, published in 1820. Here he describes arriving at an inn near Christmas:

In the evening we reached a village where I had determined to pass the night. As we drove into the great gateway of the inn, I saw on one side the light of a rousing kitchen fire beaming through a window. I entered, and admired, for the hundredth time, that picture of convenience, neatness, and broad honest enjoyment, the kitchen of an English inn. It was of spacious dimensions, hung round with copper and tin vessels highly polished, and decorated here and there with a Christmas green. Hams, tongues and flitches of bacon were suspended from the ceiling; a smoke-jack made its ceaseless clanking beside the fireplace, and a clock ticked in one corner.

A well-scoured deal table extended along one side of the kitchen, with a cold round of beef and other hearty viands [food] upon it, over which two foaming tankards of ale seemed mounting guard. Travellers of inferior order were preparing to attack this stout repast, while others sat smoking and gossiping over their ale on two high-backed oaken settles beside the fire. Trim housemaids were hurrying backwards and forwards under the directions of a fresh bustling landlady; but still seizing an occasional moment to exchange a flippant word, and have a rallying laugh with the group round the fire. The scene completely realized Poor Robin's humble idea of the comforts of mid-winter:

> Now trees their leafy hats do bare
> To reverence Winter's silver hair;
> A handsome hostess, merry host,
> A pot of ale now and a toast,
> Tobacco and a good coal fire,
> Are things this season doth require.

A less romantic impression is given by Robert Southey in his *Letters From England* (1807), posing as a Spanish tourist under the pseudonym Don Manuel Alvarez Espriella. Before writing these 'letters' (which Jane Austen read), Southey made several working trips to Spain to help form a foreigner's perspective of English customs and values. He described an inn he entered after landing at Falmouth in Cornwall:

My friend complained that the inn was dirty and uncomfortable. I cannot relish their food: they eat their meat half raw; the vegetables are never boiled enough to be soft; and every thing is insipid except the bread, which is salty, bitter, and disagreeable ... The cheese and butter were more to my taste. Generous wines are inordinately dear, and no others are to be procured; about a dollar a bottle is the price. What you find at the inns is in general miserably bad.

The perpetual stir and bustle in this inn is as surprising as it is wearisome. Doors opening and shutting, bells ringing, voices calling to the waiter from every quarter, while he cries 'Coming,' to one room, and hurries away to another. Everybody is in a hurry here; either they are going off in the packets [steam ferries], and are hastening their preparations to embark; or they have just arrived, and are impatient to be on the road homeward. Every now-and-then a carriage rattles up to the door with a rapidity which makes the very house shake. The man who cleans the boots is running in one direction, the barber with his powder-bag in another; here goes the barber's boy with his hot water and razors; there comes the clean linen from the washerwoman; and the hall is full of porters and sailors bringing in luggage, or bearing it away;—now you hear a horn blow because the post is coming in, and in the middle of the night you are awakened by another because it is going out. Nothing is done in England without a noise, and yet noise is the only thing they forget in the bill!

At other hostelries he was pleasantly surprised by the cordial welcome and received the sort of service expected of a high-class hotel:

Our chaise wheeled under the gateway with a clangor that made the roof ring; the waiter was at the door in an instant; by the time we could let down the glass, he had opened the door and let the steps down. We were shown into a comfortable room; lights were brought, the twilight shut out, the curtains let down, the fire replenished. Instead of oil, they burn candles made of tallow, which in this climate is not offensive; wax is so dear that it is used by only the highest ranks. They burn earth-coal everywhere; which kindles slowly, making much smoke and much ashes; but as all the houses are built with chimneys, it is neither unwholesome nor disagreeable. An Englishman's delight is to stand before the fire; as a means of self-defence against their raw and chilly atmosphere.

Most inns would have a large stable block at the back where spare horses would be managed by an ostler, whose job it was to ensure that enough horses were groomed, fed and watered, ready for ongoing journeys in stagecoaches. Washington Irving described how a bevy of young hands would appear when a stagecoach arrived:

Here he [the coachman] is generally surrounded by an admiring throng of ostlers, stableboys, shoeblacks, and those nameless hangers-on that infest inns and taverns, and run errands, and do all kinds of odd jobs.

Indoors, the taverns would hum with conversation on the subjects of the day: politics, turnips, taxation, footpads (muggers) and highwaymen, and note-swapping on prices of contraband and game. The air would be thick with pipe smoke and wafts of roast meat. Sometimes itinerant musicians would come to scrape their fiddles and if the mood was right some impromptu dancing might start up. And some inns would have indoor games such as skittles; even cockfights were still staged in some places.

On Michaelmas Night (29 September), casual farm labourers would gather at the local inn to be paid and wait in hope to be hired for new work. On these occasions drinking could be heavy and once at Chawton, when the house later occupied by the Austens was still functioning as an inn, a fight broke out resulting in the death of a man.

The village pub or inn could be an unruly place at such times, and the law was toothless to do anything about it in the absence of a regular police force. If the inns were owned by the powers that be, who resided off-premises, there was no restraint on behaviour, as the Somerset rector Revd John Skinner never tired of telling his diary:

> On my way to Wellow to do duty there I spoke to Gay the Landlord of the Red Post Inn, and told him I certainly should represent his house as a disorderly one. He seemed inclined to be impudent, but I did not hear what he said as I rode on directly.
>
> Two or three times previous to this I had represented to Mr. Purnell [the owner and local magistrate] the bad goings on at the Red Post ... but he took no trouble to attend to my representations ... I had also threatened Coombs [the publican at the Camerton Inn] to have his licence taken away, if he permitted such drunkenness and riot. Indeed I consider these two public houses are the principal causes of all the licentiousness and insubordination, poverty and consequent misery of the lower orders; but as there is no Magistrate who is on the spot to restrain them, for Mr. Purnell will do nothing, they go on just as they choose.

Revd Skinner continued to deplore the habitual drunkenness among his parishioners and the harmful effects it had on his community:

> William Britain, of Cridlingcot, died of a consumption, brought on in a great measure by excessive drinking. I attended him several times before his death, and he declared solemnly that the Red Post public house had been his ruin; that frequently on a Sunday he had left his home with the intention of going to Camerton Church, but as he crossed Whitebrooks Lane in his way thither something used to draw

him away as it were, contrary to his better resolutions, and take him up the hill, where there were always a number of people assembled drinking all the Sunday morning: he knew how wrong he had acted ...

The Methodists had been about him, and told him that if he had only a proper faith he should save his soul; but he knew he must repent sincerely, and he only regretted he had not left off his sins before they left him. He seemed to die very penitent.

Drink could be blamed for many an accident, as Skinner recorded frequently in his diary. One incident in 1803 he described as follows:

One pit worker, being much intoxicated on Saturday night was drowned by falling into the Canal ... Aaron Horler, another collier, was killed in a very extraordinary manner. He had been drinking at the public house, whence, after behaving in a violent manner by dancing on the tables and stools, etc., and insulting some of his associates there assembled, he walked to the Lower Pit and, it is supposed, endeavoured to slide down the rope (by which the coal is hauled) to the bottom; but not being able to retain his hold, he fell down many fathoms and was dashed to pieces.

On the Road

The author Thomas de Quincey wrote of coach travel in the late 18th century, when it was normal for the coachman to have to pick his way along a rutty lane:

You stretched a wintry length of lane, with ruts deep enough to fracture the leg of a horse, filled to the brim with standing pools of rain water; and the collateral chambers of these ruts kept from becoming confluent by thin ridges ... the poor off-horse planting his steps with care, and the cautious postillion gently applying his spur, whilst manoeuvring across this system of grooves with some sort of science that looked like a gipsy's palmistry.

The dreadful state of England's roads in the 18th century, caused mostly by the hauling of large loads in huge wagons, restricted most travelling to packhorse. There was no effective highway authority. Absurdly, it was the

PLATE 1. Though this portrait of Jane Austen has not yet been authenticated, some experts believe it was commissioned when she was a young teenager. All the details – style of dress, cropped hair and parasol held in the right hand – are typical of the period. Known as the Rice Portrait, it was inherited by Jane's great nephew, John Morland Rice, who had it reproduced with Lord Brabourne's edition of her letters in 1884.

PLATE 2. This silhouette shows the 16-year-old Edward Austen, Jane's third brother, being presented by his father to Mrs Thomas Knight for adoption. It was not uncommon for a childless titleholder, such as Mr Knight (standing behind his sister), to seek a suitable heir to his estate.

PLATE 3. Godmersham Park in Kent, a grand Palladian estate owned by Thomas Knight, was inherited by Jane's brother Edward. Jane frequently came to stay there after 1798 when he took possession of the property and became a gentleman farmer.

PLATE 4. The Reverend George Austen, Jane's father and rector at Steventon for 44 years, was widely admired for his wisdom and kindliness.

PLATE 5. The Reverend James Austen, pictured c.1790, was Jane's eldest brother, who took over the parsonage at Steventon on his father's retirement.

PLATE 6. The Reverend Henry Austen, c.1820, Jane's fourth brother, became a clergyman after his banking firm collapsed into bankruptcy.

PLATE 7. Captain Francis Austen (known to all as Frank), Jane's fifth brother, is pictured in 1796 during the French Revolutionary Wars.

Plate 8. Eliza de Feuillide was Jane's exuberant cousin. Probably the love child of statesman Warren Hastings, Governor-General of India, her marriage to a French count, later beheaded during the French Revolution, created an exotic if turbulent image in the author's mind. Prone to be coquettish, her outrageous flirting with Jane's brothers at family parties and second marriage to Henry were not greeted with universal approval.

Plate 9. Jane's sister Cassandra's watercolour sketch of Fanny Knight, eldest daughter of Edward, became a family treasure. After the death of her mother when she was a teenager, Fanny grew close to Jane and as a desirable, accomplished young woman, often wrote to her aunt for advice on various suitors. The long and considered replies reveal many of Jane's opinions about love and marriage.

PLATE 10. Steventon Rectory in Hampshire was Jane's home until she was 25, and was where she wrote her first three novels. The house stood in a valley of meadows and winding lanes, with a pretty garden graced by elm trees. Though above average size for a parsonage in those days, the house was later considered insufficient for a rector's family and pulled down.

PLATE 11. Picnics were the new vogue in Georgian society. As this painting of a view to Longleat by the landscape gardener Humphry Repton shows, careful preparation went into such outings which, despite their informal setting, still demanded the observance of polite etiquette. In *Emma*, Jane Austen portrays a similar scene on Box Hill in Surrey; there the heroine becomes exasperated by flattery and fake merriment, and returns home in tears.

PLATE 12. The mornings were spent reading, writing and doing needlework. A mixture of business and pleasure filled the hours of the new middle classes. Letter writing was a major activity. When Jane or Cassandra were away from home, each would write to the other every day with updates on gossip and events.

PLATE 13. Entertainment was made at home. Evenings were often spent round a piano and provided an opportunity for daughters to demonstrate their accomplishments by playing and singing to visitors. The role of men, whom girls tried hard to impress, was to listen and admire.

PLATE 14. By 1810 a well-stocked draper in Pall Mall, London, could display a huge range of fabrics. Dress materials were bought by the yard and handed to a dressmaker who would then discuss styles with her client. No clothes were yet available off the peg, so ladies had to keep abreast of fashions without the aid of window shopping.

PLATE 15. Winchester College, Britain's oldest public school, was attended by several of Jane's relatives. Typical of boarding schools at the time, it supported a Spartan regime of reveille at 5.30am, unremitting study of Greek and Latin, and corporal punishment. An open-plan schoolroom helped masters maintain the strictest discipline.

PLATE 16. A fashion plate of 1794 portrays two young ladies taking an airing in a phaeton. Jane Austen's era was the golden age of horse-drawn carriages. Vehicles reached new heights in elegance and luxury offering the perfect way to be seen in public but not be touched.

PLATE 17. Public transport meant travel by stage coach. Packed to the hilt and uncomfortable, it was rarely occupied by a gentlewoman traveling alone. When visiting relatives, Jane often waited to make such a journey until it was convenient for a brother to escort her.

responsibility of each parish to maintain its roads; but as these were used mostly by travellers from outside the parish, the work was left undone. In recognition of the problem the government licensed the maintenance of stretches of road to private entrepreneurs, known as turnpike companies, whose responsibility it became to keep their road in a good state of repair in return for charging a toll to users. Robert Southey described the system:

> At certain distances gates are erected and toll-houses beside them, where a regular tax is paid for every kind of conveyance in proportion to the number of horses and wheels; horsemen and cattle also are subject to this duty. These gates are rented by auction; they are few or frequent, as the nature of the soil occasions more or less expense in repairs.

By 1750 trunk roads from London to Britain's major cities – Edinburgh, York, Manchester, Bristol, Birmingham – were turnpiked, which, of course, raised the cost of travelling. Typically each passenger was charged two or three pence a mile on a turnpiked road. Over the next 20 years this system of highway maintenance increased fivefold. Although minor roads remained poor by the time Jane Austen was born, major roads had improved so much that public travel had become all the rage among the gentry, who could afford to undertake long journeys for pure pleasure. In *Pride and Prejudice* Elizabeth Bennet, responding to an invitation to visit the picturesque Lake District, is beside herself with joy:

> 'My dear, dear aunt,' she rapturously cried, 'what delight! What felicity! You give me fresh life and vigour. *Adieu* to disappointment and spleen. What are men to rocks and mountains? Oh! What hours of transport shall we spend! And when we *do* return, it shall not be like other travellers, without being able to give one accurate idea of any thing. We *will* know where we have gone—we *will* recollect what we have seen.'

The improvement in travel had a huge impact on society, turning what had been largely agrarian and sedentary into a mobile, opportunistic economy. Trade, both legal and illegal, boomed. Coaching services, inns, horse breeders and a medley of backdoor dealers in game and smuggled goods all benefited. Robert Southey observed in the 1780s:

Poaching is made a trade: the stage coaches carry it from all parts of the kingdom to the metropolis for sale, and the larders of all the great inns are regularly supplied; they who would eagerly punish the poacher, never failing to encourage him by purchasing from his employers.

The net effect of an improved network of transport was a population shift away from the country into the expanding cities. The agricultural writer Arthur Young despaired of the trend as early as 1767 in *The Farmer's Letters to the People of England*:

Giving the power of expeditious travelling depopulates the Kingdom. Young men and women in the country villages enter into service for little else but to raise money enough to go to *London*, which was no such easy matter when a stage-coach was four or five days creeping an hundred miles; the fare and the expenses ran high. *But now!* a country fellow, one hundred miles from *London*, jumps on to a coach-box in the morning, and for eight or ten shillings gets to town by night.

The most common, and affordable, mode of public transport was the stagecoach. This massive contraption of iron, leather and ornamental braiding could fly along improved roads at a fair lick of seven miles an hour. Journeys were broken into 'stages' of about 15 miles, at the end of which an inn was ready to provide refreshments and a change of horses. Tourists at the time were impressed by the efficiency of the system and its peculiarly English charm. Washington Irving described such a journey in his *Sketch Book*:

I rode for a long distance in one of the public coaches, on the day preceding Christmas. The coach was crowded, both inside and out, with passengers. It was loaded also with hampers of game, and baskets and boxes of delicacies; and hares hung dangling their long ears about the coachman's box. I had three fine school-boys for my fellow-passengers inside, returning home for the holidays in high glee.

A stage coach carries animation always with it, and puts the world in motion as it whirls along. The horn, sounded at the entrance of a village, produces a general bustle. Some hasten forth to meet friends, some with bundles and hand-boxes to secure places, and in the hurry of the moment can hardly take leave of the group that accompanies

them. As the coach rattles through the village, every one runs to the window, and you have glances on every side of fresh country faces and blooming giggling girls.

Not all passengers were so enchanted by their experience. Stagecoaches were run by commercial firms eager to squeeze every ounce of profit from each journey. Six passengers went inside, and any number could risk it on the roof or in the luggage basket at the back. Those on top had to make of it the best they could, jolting along with legs dangling over the edge, exposed to all weathers. Top-heavy and subject to unevenness in the road, the overcrowded coaches could easily topple over. The coachman was the key figure in charge of the expedition. He was responsible for the safety of the passengers and delivering them to their destination on time. He tended to be gruff and tough-talking, able to deal with any untoward incidents along the way, and stood for no nonsense from those providing ancillary services. As Irving observed:

I could not but notice the air of bustle and importance of the coachman. He enjoys great consequence and consideration along the road; has frequent conferences with the village housewives, who look upon him as a man of great trust. The moment he arrives where the horses are to be changed, he throws down the reins with something of an air, and abandons the cattle to the care of the ostler; his duty being merely to drive from one stage to another. When off the box, his hands are thrust into the pockets of his great coat, and he rolls about the inn yard with an air of the most absolute lordliness.

Not surprisingly, unaccompanied women tended to avoid travelling by this method unless absolutely necessary. Jane Austen recorded one trip made alone in August, to London, but it was in her local Alton coach and she knew some of the passengers. Still, she was relieved at the end to meet her brother Henry who then escorted her in the 'luxury of a nice large cool Hackney Coach'.

An alternative, better mode of public transport was the post-chaise. Lighter and swifter than stagecoaches, post-chaises were operated by innkeepers who hired them out together with horses and postillions (riders) and were usually keen to stress their superiority. An advertisement placed in a 1791 edition of the *Sussex Advertiser* read:

> There are two modes of conveyance, either by common stages
> or by a post-chaise. By the common stage, you are classed with
> company of every description, and who may very frequently turn
> out disagreeable. You are also paid no attention to at the inns where
> you stop, although you pay exorbitant for refreshment, and are
> frequently insulted by the indecent behaviour of the coachman, and
> besides your fare, you have a considerable sum to pay for luggage.
> On the contrary, if two or three passengers choose to travel together,
> they may, by travelling in a post-chaise, not only avoid all these
> inconveniences – but suit their own convenience in point of time,
> and be at less expence – besides meeting with genteeler treatment
> at the inns on the road.

This age of coach travel proceeded with virtually every year seeing an
advance in speed and efficiency. In the middle years of the 18th century
a good average day's journey was 50 to 60 miles; by the later years of the
century it was twice that mileage. Although carriage design was being refined
all the time, the chief improvement was not in the speed on the road but in
the reduction of stops and in the better service of horses. Cruelty to animals
in service became a political issue of the time. Robert Southey was one of
several critics to bring the public attention to it:

> The life of a post-horse is truly wretched:—there will be cruel
> individuals in all countries, but cruelty here is a matter of
> calculation: the post-masters find it more profitable to overwork
> their beasts and kill them by hard labour in two or three years,
> than to let them do half the work and live out their natural length
> of life. In commerce, even more than in war, both men and beasts
> are considered merely as machines, and sacrificed with even less
> compunction.

One of the most spectacular achievements was John Palmer's mail coaches,
which marked the beginning of a new era in travel as well as postal services.
He discovered that with good horses he could break all existing records
and make the journey between Bath and London inside a day. In 1784 he
challenged existing services by promising a 13-hour service at 28 shillings per
passenger – and at the same time introduced the mail-coach system. Because
a good part of his revenue was generated by conveying mail, he could operate

a lighter coach carrying four passengers, as opposed to six in other vehicles. The advance was reported in the *Bath Chronicle*:

> **The New Mail Coach has travelled with an expedition that has been really astonishing, having seldom exceeded 13 hours in going to or returning from London. It is made very light, carries four passengers, and runs with a pair of horses which are changed every six or eight miles; and as the bags at the different offices on the road are made up against its arrival, there is not the least delay. The Guard rides with the Coachman on the box, and the mail is deposited in the boot. By this means, the inhabitants of this city and Bristol have the London letters a day earlier than usual—a matter of great convenience to all, and of much importance to merchants and traders.**

In 1794 the postal system was reformed and mail coaches ran to a strict schedule. Letters were collected and delivered four to eight times daily for the price of one penny per letter; it was known as the Penny Post. The price doubled in 1805 and by 1812 the cost had risen to four pence per letter for delivery within 15 miles, and up to 17 pence for the northernmost point in Britain – John o' Groats.

Going Private

The gentry and some middle class families would have their own horses and carriage. If not, arrangements would have to be made in advance to have one brought to the house, rather like ordering a taxi. Parson Woodforde regularly journeyed to Norwich about 14 miles away, as he noted in his diary:

> **1789: November 12, Thursday … Sent Ben early this Morning to Norwich to order a Chaise to be sent to my House by 11 o'clock this morning to carry us to Norwich to meet our Somersett Friends there to Morrow. The Chaise came at the time appointed and between one and two this Aft. We went in it to Norwich thank God safe and well by 4. this Afternoon to the Kings Head, and there Nancy and self dined, supped and slept. My Servant Man Briton went with us.**

Two hours, between 11am and one o'clock, would have been enough time to rest the horses and feed them before the return leg. The Austens kept a carriage for various purposes, not least of which was providing transport for family members to attend parties. Jane's nephew wrote:

> A carriage and a pair of horses were kept. The carriage once bought, entailed little further expense; and the horses probably, like Mr Bennet's [in *Pride and Prejudice*], were often employed on farm work. Moreover, it should be remembered that a pair of horses in those days were almost necessary, if ladies were to move about at all; for neither the condition of the roads nor the style of carriage-building admitted of any comfortable vehicle being drawn by a single horse.

Jane Austen refers to various sorts of private carriage in her novels. There were nearly as many different types available as there are cars today, and like cars each model – coach, chaise, gig, landau, landaulette, phaeton, curricle, chariot – represented a different rung on the social ladder. Luxuries were added for longer journeys on cold days, such as hot bricks on the carriage floor, a sheepskin rug over the knees, even a chamber pot. Jane herself enjoyed a ride in a phaeton while staying in London. This was the 'sports car' of the Regency age – an elegant two-seater set high above four wheels, with or without a top, and drawn usually by two horses. In *Northanger Abbey*, Mr Thorpe boasts to Catherine Morland about his gig – a light, two-wheeled open carriage, drawn by one horse, and nothing like as smart as a curricle, which he wishes it were:

> 'What do you think of my gig, Miss Morland? A neat one, is not it? Well hung; town-built; I have not had it a month. It was built for a Christchurch [Oxford college] man, a friend of mine, a very good sort of fellow; he ran it a few weeks, till, I believe, it was convenient to have done with it. I happened just then to be looking out for some light thing of the kind, though I had pretty well determined on a curricle too; but I chanced to meet him on Magdalen Bridge, as he was driving into Oxford, last term: "Ah! Thorpe," said he, "do you happen to want such a little thing as this? It is a capital one of the kind, but I am cursed tired of it."
>
> "Oh! d——," said I, "I am your man; what do you ask?" And how much do you think he did, Miss Morland?'
>
> 'I am sure I cannot guess at all.'

'Curricle-hung, you see; seat, trunk, sword-case, splashing-board, lamps, silver moulding, all you see complete; the iron-work as good as new, or better. He asked fifty guineas; I closed with him directly, threw down the money, and the carriage was mine.'

Needless to say, there was a skill to handling some of the faster, lightweight vehicles, and without sufficient care they could easily overturn when a tight corner was taken at high speed. In *Emma*, Jane Austen describes a scene in Highbury (not, incidentally, the district now in north London) at which an accident has occurred in the past and to which Mr Woodhouse refers as the 'fatal corner'. Highbury is thought to have been modelled on Leatherhead in Surrey and the said corner is identified with one at which a fatal accident actually happened in October 1806 involving the Princess of Wales, Caroline of Brunswick. In both fact and fiction the carriage concerned was a barouche-landau, elegant and swift but notorious for its poor stability. The coroner's inquest was reported in the *Hampshire Chronicle*:

An Inquest was held last Saturday morning, at the Swan Inn, at Leatherhead, on the body of Miss Harriot Mary Cholmondeley, who was killed on Thursday, the 2nd of October instant, about three o'clock in the afternoon, by being thrown out of Her Royal Highness the Princess of Wales's carriage.

The first witness sworn stated that, while standing at his father's door, he heard the noise of a carriage and horses, coming from the Leatherhead Turnpike-gate, towards the spot where he was standing, but was prevented from seeing the carriage by the intervention of the corner of his father's house; he first saw an out-rider or servant, whom he supposed to belong to the persons in the carriage, and perceived the carriage and four turn the corner. The carriage, which was an open barouche-landau, instantly overset, and the top part of it struck against a tree, on the right hand side of the road, exactly opposite the place where he stood. In the carriage were, Her Royal Highness the Princess of Wales, Lady Sheffield, and the deceased Miss Cholmondeley. He instantly crossed over, and found the heads of the ladies lying on the ground, and their bodies in the carriage; he first perceived that Miss Cholmondeley was very much hurt, and that the blood had issued from some part of her head. The Ladies were taken into the Swan Inn, which is about thirty yards from the spot where the carriage was overset. He said that the carriage was coming at a very great rate; and in turning the corner, swang round upon the two off wheels; that the horses broke their traces and ran away, leaving the carriage broken to pieces; that he observed the carriage take a very large sweep against the rising side of the road, which caused it to overturn.

One of the servants at the inn, with assistance from by-standers, took Miss Cholmondeley into the house and laid her on a bed. He thinks she was then alive, but died a few moments afterwards.

Other perils regularly reported in the press included the holding up of coaches by masked robbers. This was the age when the highwayman reached the height of his glory. Every coach carried a guard armed with a blunderbuss (a short musket) to protect passengers in the event of an attack. The Austens were well aware of this danger. For several months in the summer of 1793 a highwayman lurked in the district of Overton just a few miles from Steventon and was never caught. Their friend Wither Bramston was stopped when going home at about ten o'clock one night in June and described the trauma in a letter:

I have been very much frightened lately, by being Stopd returning from drinking tea with Mrs Lefroy, by a footpad, who put his pistol Close to me & said he would blow out my Brains if I did not give him my Money I lost 8 Guineas which I did not like at all, beside its having made my head Ache ever since & I now Start at my own Shadow but am getting better.

In London, highway robbery was so common that members of the public who chose to travel after dark did so prepared for the worst. Lord North, Prime Minister in 1774, recorded:

I was robbed last night as I expected, our loss was not great, but as the postillion did not stop immediately one of the two highwaymen fired at him—It was at the end of Gunnersbury Lane.

Some managed to adopt a more laissez-faire attitude. Horace Walpole, after being shot at in Hyde Park, observed wearily:

One is forced to travel, even at noon, as if one was going to battle.

Crime and Punishment

Outside London there were few professional criminals. Many of the men (rarely women) who committed petty theft were labourers who stole in hard times. The person in charge of dealing with local crime and complaints was the magistrate, or Justice of the Peace (JP). As today, these officials were unpaid. By law, a magistrate had to be a member of the Church of England and the owner of land with an annual income of at least £100. Most were therefore squires, and some were clergymen. The range of judicial and administrative duties they took on varied greatly: from setting the local Poor Rate to issuing warrants for arrest and punishing offenders for all sorts of wrongdoing, such as drunkenness, blasphemy and poaching. As Emma Woodhouse in *Emma* says of Mr Knightley of Donwell Abbey, chief magistrate at Highbury, he had 'all the parish to manage'.

Clergymen worked closely with magistrates on local issues, and between them would arbitrate on disputes in an endeavour to keep the peace. For personalities that thrived on meddling in others' affairs the liaison could create a rich vein of satisfaction, such as that enjoyed by the Revd William Collins and Lady Catherine de Bourgh in *Pride and Prejudice*:

> **Elizabeth [Bennet] soon perceived that, though this great lady was not in the commission of the peace for the county, she was a most active magistrate in her own parish, the minutest concerns of which were carried to her by Mr. Collins; and whenever any of the cottagers were disposed to be quarrelsome, discontented, or too poor, she sallied forth into the village to settle their differences, silence their complaints, and scold them into harmony and plenty.**

Jane's brother Edward Knight became a magistrate and high sheriff in Kent, making frequent visits to the county bench at Canterbury. The sheriff was second to the Lord Lieutenant in the county hierarchy and held considerable political influence on who obtained positions of power. Edward himself was the subject of a long legal battle in 1813 over his inheritance of the Chawton estate, which in the end he managed to hold on to and pass intact to his son.

Serious crimes such as grand larceny and assault were heard by the county magistrates. Punishments for crimes in some places were still brutally medieval. Until 1789 women were occasionally burned alive at the stake for murdering their husbands. Public whipping, pillorying and hanging were all common. In Jane Austen's day every village still had the appropriate equipment, and according to Roberts' *Social History of Southern Counties*:

> **By the side of the duckpond on many village greens stood the stocks, a wooden machine wherein vagrants, strolling players, and those who had imbibed liquor not wisely but too well, were ordinarily secured by the heels until they repented of their former naughtiness.**

On the same spot there might have been the 'ducking' or 'cucking' stool, employed likewise for petty misdemeanours: bakers who served their customers with bread short of the correct weight, old crones suspected of witchcraft, or scolding wives could all be administered this corrective treatment (sometimes preliminary to imprisonment) by which the culprit was strapped to a seat and lowered 'over some deep water into which they were thrice let down to cool their choler and heat'. A man from Northamptonshire published a poem in 1780 about the ducking stool as a remedy for irate harridans:

> **Down in the deep the stool descends,**
> **But here at first we miss our ends;**
> **She mounts again and rages more**
> **Than ever vixen did before.**
> **So throwing water on the fire,**
> **Will make it burn up but the higher.**
> **If so, my friends, pray let her take**
> **A second turn into the lake,**
> **And rather than your patient lose,**
> **Thrice and again repeat the dose;**
> **No brawling wives, no furious wenches,**
> **No fire so hot, but water quenches.**

The whipping-post, set up next to the stocks, had offenders chained to it for public display. Alternatively, men and women were whipped at the 'cart's tail', that is, they were tied to the back of a cart and whipped as it was driven slowly through the streets followed by a noisy crowd. The parish register of Barnstaple in Devon gives these details of punishments dealt to women when Jane Austen was alive:

1776. Mary Jones for larceny—'being very ill'—sentenced to be sent
to the workhouse till she recovered, and then to be whipped.
1778. Elizabeth Thorne, to be severely whipped the two next market
days until bloody.
1787. Elizabeth Vaughan, to be whipped at the cart's tail on Friday,
from prison to Northgate and back, on her naked back, until her body
is bloody.

These barbaric sentences were not outlawed until 1820. Public humiliation
was considered an effective measure in keeping down crime and bad
behaviour. Notices in advance of due punishments were carried in the press,
and the *Bath Herald* ran these two pieces in 1792:

[7 April:] Barnet the Baker will be made a public example tomorrow,
by being whipped through the streets of the city, agreeably to a part
of his sentence.
[14 April:] The immense croud that attended the flagellation of
Barnett, last Saturday, made a new method of punishment necessary,
which undoubtedly ought to be ranked with our modern improvements.
The criminal was placed in the cart, which not only gave the Beadle
[parish official] an opportunity of bestowing the lashings unchecked by
the pressure of the croud, but at the same time made the punishment
more public, as everybody had a view of the offence.

Reformers lobbied Parliament to modernize punitive measures but these
attempts were often met with resistance from the establishment, as Dr
Johnson's biographer James Boswell described when one evening in 1783
someone ventured to argue with Johnson that executions should not be
public spectacles. The old sage of Fleet Street replied in fury:

They object that the old method drew together a number of spectators.
Sir, executions are intended to draw spectators. If they do not draw
spectators, they don't answer their purpose. The old method was most
satisfactory to all parties: *the public was gratified by a procession; the
criminal was supported by it.* Why is all this to be swept away?

The problem was that crime was on the increase and something had to
be done to keep it in check. As an irate Arthur Young remarked (in *The*

Farmer's Letters to the People of England) when observing the goings-on in a locality of Oxfordshire:

> The vicinity is filled with poachers, deer-stealers, thieves, and pilferers of every kind: offences of almost every description abound so much that the offenders are a terror to all quiet and well-disposed persons.

There were two reasons for meting out punishment: one was to protect the community and grant it satisfaction; the second was to safeguard landowners' capital. Of the two, the second carried more weight. As the playwright Oliver Goldsmith once declared, 'Laws grind the poor, and rich men rule the law.' The number of crimes upgraded to the status of capital offences increased massively in the second half of the 18th century. The Austens' local newspaper, the *Hampshire Chronicle*, carried this notice in July 1776:

> Oxford—William and Thomas Smith, two brothers, were capitally convicted and received sentence of death, for robbing H Harrison, Esq; Gentleman-Commoner of Trinity College, on the highway, near Witney in this county, of about nine guineas and a metal watch.

Even petty theft, such as shop-lifting or pick-pocketing, now carried the death sentence. Destruction of property, likewise, met with exemplary severity. An Act of Parliament in 1803 prescribed death for poachers who resisted arrest with firearms.

A novel punishment of the Georgian era was to transport nuisance criminals to a distant land. At the time when the British crown was losing its sovereign grip of America, a new dumping ground for convicted criminals was needed. The timely discovery of Australia by Captain Cook a few years before Jane Austen's birth meant that this vast continent could instead be adopted for the purpose. The first dispatch of more than 700 convicts was made in 1788 and hundreds of thousands more followed over the next 80 years, usually in appalling conditions.

Transportation was a prospect facing Jane Austen's aunt Mrs Leigh-Perrot in 1800 when she was tried for shop-lifting in Bath. She was accused of stealing some white lace, which had become wrapped in a parcel of purchases she had made while shopping with her husband. It seems that some time after the couple had left the premises, the shop assistant, on seeing them pass, crossed the street and accosted Mrs Leigh-Perrot, who recalled the incident thus:

'I beg pardon, Madam, [said the shop assistant] but was there by mistake a card of white lace put up with the black you bought?' I answered I could not tell as I had not been home but she might satisfy herself as the parcel had never been out of my hand—on saying which I gave it to her, She open'd it, and there was a Card of White Edging which She took out saying 'Oh here it is' and returned to the Shop. This did not surprise me as I thought it might have proceeded from Shop hurry or Negligence, but before we had got to the Abbey Church Yard the Man who had taken my [black] Lace away to fold up, came after us to desire to know my Name and place of Abode as he never had put up that card of White Edging. This alarmed me a good deal because I had neither asked for White Lace nor had I seen any such thing in the Shop.

A charge was laid to the Bath magistrates, much to their embarrassment as they knew Mrs Leigh-Perrot personally. It turned out that the original shop owner had gone bankrupt and the business was now being run by a couple who were trying to make extra cash by illicit means and had attempted to blackmail this wealthy lady. Being a woman of principle she determined to stand trial and proclaim her innocence, and risk the penalty, rather than submit to this dastardly deed.

In the meantime the magistrates had no alternative but to remand her in custody at Ilchester jail in Somerset until the trial seven months later, though the jailor allowed her to stay in his house, with her husband, rather than suffer the degradation of prison life. How much this gesture was motivated by pure kindness and deference to the higher classes is doubtful; he certainly received money from her cousins. The squalid conditions of the stay were hard enough for poor Mrs Leigh-Perrot. She described their plight after the visit of a friend:

It is not in the power of anyone to lessen *materially* the many Evils we must unavoidably endure in this House of Misery ... he [the jailor] told me that the Dining Room I was to consider as my own whenever I chose to be alone—and so it was till Fires began; but this Room joins to a Room where the Children all lie, and not Bedlam itself can be half so noisy, beside which as not one particle of Smoke goes up the Chimney, I leave you to judge of the Comfort I can enjoy in such a Room ... My dearest Perrot with his sweet composure adds to my Philosophy ... Cleanliness has ever been his greatest delight and yet he sees the greasy toast laid by the dirty Children on his Knees, and feels the small Beer trickle down his sleeves on its way across the table unmoved. Mrs Scadding's [the jailor's wife's] Knife well licked to clean it from fried onions helps me now and then—you may believe how the Mess I am helped to is disposed of—here are *two dogs and three cats* always as hungry as myself.

As the value of the lace in question was more than one shilling, the crime Mrs Leigh-Perrot was accused of amounted to grand larceny and was therefore, in theory, punishable by death. In practice the worst she could probably have expected was transportation to Botany Bay for 14 years, a grim enough prospect admittedly. As can be imagined, the scandal surrounding the case kept tongues wagging for the whole duration of the defendant's incarceration. When the trial was finally heard at Taunton Assizes in March 1800, the Great Hall of the castle was packed as it had never been since the infamous Judge Jeffreys held his Bloody Assize after the Monmouth Rebellion in 1685. The *Bath Chronicle* reported the scene:

No fewer than 2000 persons could be present; the throng, tumult and confusion of this vast, promiscuous multitude was so great that at least half an hour elapsed before any proceedings could be heard.

The trial lasted seven hours and the jury took ten minutes to return a verdict of not guilty, at which announcement the court burst into spontaneous applause. The couple were free to go but despite winning their case they still had to pay hefty costs, as Mrs Leigh-Perrot declared:

The frightful expense I cannot Estimate. I am told it will be nearer *two* than one thousand pounds and from the large demands already made only for conveying the Witnesses (and the two days' Expenses for the House and Eating at Taunton which alone amounted to £93 odd money), I can easily suppose it will be full that sum.

Crime at the upper end of the social scale was not uncommon, especially in places of entertainment where one might temporarily let down one's guard. In the 1790s Bath was rife with gentlemen thieves, as the writer Edward Clarke observed in dismay:

> **There is perhaps no part of the world, setting aside the infernal purlieus of St James's [of London], where gaming is carried to so high a pitch as at Bath. This is owing, in great measure, to that swarm of daemons, who under the general name of *blacklegs*, or *sharpers*, infest all places of public amusement. In Bath one is never secure from the insidious designs of these indefatigable harpies. They infest the rooms, the promenades, nay, inconsistent as it may seem, the very churches are not free from the profanation of these vermin ... What is our Police? Where are our magistrates? ... why sleeps the rod of justice? When scoundrels with white hairs are suffered to patrole our streets, arm in arm with the flower of our nobility, whom they pillage at their leisure, under the assumed and specious mask of gentlemen.**

Even some members of the gentry might find themselves sentenced to imprisonment for their crimes. One notable example was the newspaper editor and publisher Leigh Hunt, who was jailed for three years for libelling the Prince Regent. But in general, prisons of the time were almost entirely used to hold the accused awaiting trial. In the 1770s only about one sentence in 50 went to internment.

Jails were generally very unpleasant places; some of the newer ones had cells and a degree of humanity but traditional ones were open-plan dens of drunken disorder and disease, with no segregation of the sexes. One description of inmates in Middlesex prisons in 1776 reads like a caricature of a medieval dungeon:

> **Vagrants and disorderly women of the very lowest and most wretched class of human beings, almost naked, with only a few filthy rags almost alive with vermin, their bodies rotting with distemper, and covered with itch, scorbutic and venereal ulcers.**

By the turn of the 19th century philanthropists were arguing for urgent prison reform. Elizabeth Fry, a Quaker preacher, became famous in this respect. Her visit to Newgate prison in 1813 was a key moment as she witnessed the horrific conditions under which women, sometimes accompanied by their children, were detained. In her *Memoir*, she described the following experience:

> **I have just returned from a most melancholy visit to Newgate, where I have been at the request of Elizabeth Fricker [condemned for robbery], previous to her execution tomorrow morning, at eight o'clock. I found her much hurried, distressed and tormented in mind. Her hands cold and covered with something like the perspiration preceding death and in a universal tremor. The women with her said she had been so outrageous before our going that they thought a man must be sent for to manage her. However, after a serious time with her, her troubled soul became calmed ... Besides this poor woman there are also six men to be hanged, one of whom has a wife near her confinement, also condemned and six young children. Since the awful report came down he has become quite mad, from horror of mind. A strait waistcoat could not keep him within bounds: he had just bitten the turnkey [prison warder].**

Women and children were crammed like sardines in a tin, many sleeping naked on the floor without bedding. Some, driven mad by deprivation, had become wild and dangerous. Despite the risks, Fry and the helpers that she enlisted spent several days making clothes and bedding for the inmates and went inside the prison to offer solace and their prayers. The experience was so shocking that Fry determined to do all she could to bring about reform – and indeed she succeeded. She helped to establish individual prison cells, segregation of the sexes and female supervision for women. More generally, a new attitude turned minds away from vengeance to thinking of prisons as places of correction, following her guiding principle that 'punishment is not for revenge, but to lessen crime and reform the criminal'. Evangelical reformers and secular Unitarians started to see it as their social duty to visit prisoners in an effort to turn them into good citizens.

Unfair Play and Vice Squads

Cruelty to animals in service has been mentioned earlier. Equally inhumane were the animal shows and blood sports of the Georgian era put on to amuse country folk. A survey by the antiquary and engraver Joseph Strutt, *Sports*

and Pastimes of the People of England, published in 1801, described
the following:

> One great part of the joculator's profession was the teaching of bears,
> apes, horses, dogs, and other animals, to imitate the actions of men,
> to tumble, to dance, and to perform a variety of tricks contrary to
> their nature ... The dancing bears have retained their place to the
> present time, and they frequently perform in the public streets for
> the amusement of the multitude.

Tricks included training a bear to stand on its head and to dance with a
monkey on its back; usually bears were muzzled to prevent them biting.
Robert Southey was one among several detractors who publicly protested
against blood sports, as late as 1801:

> The practice of bull-baiting is not merely permitted, it is even enjoined
> by the municipal law in some places. Attempts have twice been
> made in the legislature to suppress this barbarous custom: they were
> baffled and ridiculed, and some of the most distinguished members
> were absurd enough to assert that if such sports were abolished there
> would be an end of the national courage ... This English sport is
> even more cowardly than the bull-fights of the Portugueze. The men
> are exposed to no danger whatever; they fasten the animal to a ring,
> and the amusement is to see him toss the dogs, and the dogs lacerate
> his nostrils, till they are weary of torturing him, and then he is led
> to the slaughter-house. The bear and the badger are baited with the
> same barbarity; and if the rabble can get nothing else, they will divert
> themselves by worrying cats to death.

Another public entertainment popular in Jane Austen's day, though officially
outlawed, was boxing. Magistrates were often loath to interfere with a
fight that had been publicized in advance in the press, with a good turnout
expected. Prize-fighters would do the round of country fairs challenging any
local talent who might like to put up his fists. Gamblers and pundits would
place their bets on which of the two fighters would prevail. A referee was
appointed to ensure fair play and also to keep the crowd from interfering.
If their man was losing, backers would sometimes come into the ring and
deliver a few softening-up blows to the opponent. In time a small stage

was erected and roped off to prevent this sort of thing happening. Of equal brutality, another sport sometimes staged at fairs was cudgelling. Two participants would each brandish a club with a basket-handguard. The first to draw blood from his opponent's head was the winner.

There were forces working against the perpetuation of these old traditional customs and also of seasonal fairs and feasts. Many of the activities took place on village commons and were jovial occasions involving a fair bit of drinking and carousing, which tended to sport an unruly element. The agricultural enclosure movement took away much of this public land literally from under their feet.

Another key factor was the emergence late in the 18th century of what became known as Vice Societies. Two institutions in particular, patronized by wealthy businessmen and peers, aimed to combat what they regarded as a proliferation of vice. The Proclamation Society, founded in 1787, and the Society for the Suppressing of Vice, founded in 1802, brought thousands of prosecutions for various moral and religious offences, including gaming, drunkenness, blasphemy, pornography, prostitution, swearing and profanation of the Sabbath. The Revd Sydney Smith had this to say about the Vice Society (usually referring to the latter of the two):

> **It is a corporation of informers supported by large contributions bent on suppressing not the vices of the rich but the pleasures of the poor. A man of £10,000 a year may worry a fox for as much as he pleases, encourage the breed of a mischievous animal on purpose to worry it: & a poor labourer is carried before a magistrate for paying a sixpence to see an exhibition of courage between a dog and a bear.**

As more and more prosecutions were made and public recreations were suppressed, so these societies, who were really the successors to earlier Puritans in their intolerance, brought hatred and ridicule upon themselves. In time they recommended that all fairs whatsoever should be outlawed. At the start of the new century one clergyman, Revd Richard Warner, was glad things were changing, to his mind for the better, as a whole medley of indecent pastimes were suppressed:

> **The pranks, the feats of jugglers, tumblers and dancers, the jests of itinerant *mimes* or mummers, and the dangerous amusement of the quintane [joust], diversified occasionally by the pageant and the**

masque, or the *elegant* pastimes of bullbaiting, cock-fighting, cock-scaling, pig-racing, bowling, football, grinning through a horse-collar, and swallowing scalding hot frumenty, these rude athletick [*sic*] sports or gross sensual amusements, satisfied our ancestors.

Now public amusements were becoming more refined: cards, balls and plays replaced the rude sports and sensual amusements more typical of the early Georgian period.

In a similar vein of intolerance of public nuisance, magistrates in built-up areas cracked down on gin shops selling the spirit by the glass to members of the public. Gin-swilling had reached epidemic proportions in the 18th century, especially in cities, where low excise tariffs made it cheaper than beer, turning it into the poor man's curse. The following notice in the *Bath Chronicle* in 1788 highlighted the problem:

The Magistrates of this city, at the last licensing day, signified their determination to the retailers of spirits, that after the present year no licence would be granted, allowing the retail of spirits in SMALL quantities;—so that the worst of all nuisances (the petty gin-shops) will, by this resolution, be abolished.

The Rhythm
of the Year

The Austens, like other rural families, moved to the rhythm of the farming year. By 1800 only one-fifth of England's population of nine million lived in towns, so the vast majority depended on the rural economy. Though transport was improving, food and manufactured goods were still produced for local consumption. The seasons and weather conditions were everybody's concern, whether landlord or peasant, and the whole community would be involved in the most important seasonal tasks, such as hay-making and harvesting. The men took care of the primary stages of agriculture, producing wheat, corn and meat for food, straw thatch and bedding for animals, and wool and hides for clothing. Women tended the domestic animals and performed as many seasonal tasks as possible out of doors to make use of daylight hours. All this outside activity made the landscape and villages much more peopled than generally is the case today.

Parties would celebrate the completion of key seasonal activities such as sheep-shearing in the spring, hay-making in the summer, and of course the harvest festivals of early autumn. One commentator of the time was Joseph Strutt, the author of *Sports and Pastimes of the People of England* (first published in 1801), who wrote:

There are two feasts annually held among the farmers of this country, which are regularly made in the spring, and at the end of the summer, or the beginning of autumn, but not confined to any particular day. The first is the sheep-shearing, and the second the harvest-home; both of them were celebrated in ancient times with feasting and variety of rustic pastimes; at present, excepting a dinner, or more frequently a supper, at the conclusion of the sheep-shearing and the harvest, we have little remains of the former customs.

Some old customs had died out, or were now prohibited, like the May Fair of London which gave way to the wishes of its affluent residents. But many in the country were still actively celebrated by folk never slow to take the opportunity to indulge in some country revels. At Whitsuntide, merrymaking fairs called the Whitsun Ales were occasions for sports, plays and competitions. A popular custom in Oxfordshire, described by Strutt, celebrated the spring season of lambs, at which a 'lady's feast' of roasted lamb was enjoyed by everyone:

> A fat lamb was provided, and the maidens of the town, having their thumbs tied behind them, were permitted to run after it, and she who with her mouth took hold of the lamb was declared the Lady of the Lamb, which, being killed and cleaned, but with the skin hanging upon it, was carried on a long pole before the lady and her companions to the [village] green, attended with music, and a morisco [morris] dance of men, and another of women. The rest of the day was spent in mirth and merry glee.

Some of the customs Strutt described are still familiar today:

> The morris-dance was sometimes performed by itself, but was much more frequently joined to processions and pageants, and especially to those appropriated for the celebration of the May-games. On these occasions, the hobby-horse, or a dragon, with Robin Hood, the maid Marian, and other characters, supposed to have been the companions of that famous outlaw, made a part of the dance ... The garments of the morris-dancers were adorned with bells ... A set of morris-dancers went about the country, consisting of ten men who danced, besides the maid Marian, and one who played upon the pipe and tabor.

Another custom observed at this time of year was described in *The Spectator*:

> It is at this time, in May, that we see the brisk young wenches, in the country parishes, dancing round the maypole. It is likewise on the first day of this month that we see the ruddy milkmaid exerting herself in a most sprightly manner under a pyramid of silver tankards, and, like the virgin Tarpeia, oppressed by the costly ornaments which her benefactors lay upon her.

Bat, Ball and Turf

Formerly the province of peasants, many sports were adopted by their squires and glamorized in the latter part of the 18th century. Peers sponsored events for the benefit of lords and commoners alike, and outdoor sports became big attractions, with gambling often the key feature. Even a gentle sport like cricket became a betting game as county teams competed for high stakes before huge crowds. If tradition is correct, the first cricket club was founded at Hambledon in Hampshire; disbanded in the 1790s, its members dispersed to other counties and helped to spread organized cricket. The Marylebone Cricket Club (MCC) was founded in 1787 at Thomas Lord's ground in Marylebone, now the headquarters of English cricket, and by the end of the century cricket had become so popular that it was hailed as the national sport. The *Gentleman's Magazine* in 1833 gave this summary:

> **Cricket is the pride and the privilege of the Englishman alone. Into this, his noble and favourite amusement, no other people ever pretended to penetrate: a Frenchman or a German would not know which end of a bat they were to hold; and so fine, so scientific, and so elaborate is the skill regarding it, that only a small part of England have as yet acquired a knowledge of it. In this, Kent has always stood proudly pre-eminent; Kent is emphatically the field of the cricketer's glory. Sussex, Hampshire, and Surrey, next follow in the list; and Middlesex owes its present fame to the establishment of the Marylebone Club within its boundaries.**

Unlike some other sports, cricket was not confined to the genteel in society. The gentry and nobles regarded a cricket match as an opportunity to fraternize with the lower classes in a way that did not happen in other countries of Europe. The historian George Trevelyan once said, 'If only the French noblesse had been capable of playing cricket with their peasants their chateaux would never have been burnt.' On the field of play codes of dress distinguished amateurs (the gentlemen) from professional players, as the *Gentleman's Magazine* continued:

> **The *gentlemen* always played in breeches and silk stockings; the *players*, as Lord Winchelsea's, wore hats with gold binding, and ribbons of particular colour.**

According to Jane Austen's niece Fanny Knight, her brothers were 'mad about cricket', and Jane herself preferred it to many of the traditional female pastimes, a liking she echoes in the character of the teenaged Catherine Morland in *Northanger Abbey*:

> **She was fond of all boys' plays, and greatly preferred cricket not merely to dolls, but to the more heroic enjoyments of infancy, nursing a dormouse, feeding a canary-bird, or watering a rose-bush ...**
> **[Mrs Morland's] elder daughters were left to shift for themselves; and it was not very wonderful that Catherine who had by nature nothing heroic about her, should prefer cricket, base ball, riding on horseback, and running about the country at the age of fourteen, to books ...**

Horse racing on the flat developed apace in Jane Austen's day, becoming a highly popular recreation for the public in late summer. The Prince of Wales was a big fan, a fact that in turn attracted more nobles and gentry to race meetings. The first Thoroughbred racehorses were bred by crossing imported Arab stallions and English mares, and before long the sport turned professional. With its fast and furious competition, horse racing proved ideal for gamblers and a commercial goldmine for the organizers. The Classic races, so popular today, were founded in this period. Following the first major 'flat' race held at Doncaster in 1776 came the Oaks at Epsom and the Epsom Derby by 1800. Soon afterwards the Newmarket 2000 Guineas and 1000 Guineas were inaugurated. The *Bath Chronicle* reported tremendous enthusiasm for this novel sport as race-goers flocked to Claverton Down in the 1770s:

> **We have the pleasure to assure our polite readers and the Lovers of the Turf, that our Races have not been honoured (since their first institution) with such a numerous and brilliant appearance of Company as at this time.—It is computed that about 800 carriages, and not less than 20,000 persons on horseback and a-foot, were on the Down yesterday, when, it was generally allowed, the sport was equal to any ever seen on a race-course in one day.**

The Austens were also caught up in this new fad, which was as much a social occasion as a spectator sport. Fanny Knight reported of a good day at the races in 1806 from her home at Godmersham Park in Kent:

Were you at any part of the Races? I shall be vexed to death if you were at the course, any day, particularly Wednesday, which day we were there, that is to say Capt[n] and Mrs H[y] Austen, the three boys, & I to meet the Goodnestone Party, which was very pleasant. Have you heard who were the Belles of the Races?

Other sports of the time included archery, real tennis (a game confined to the aristocracy and played in a specially designed indoor court), rackets, fives (Parson Woodforde played this with colleagues against the rectory wall), bowls on village greens, pall-mall (a game similar to today's croquet) and football to some extent, though it generally suffered from a ruffianly image – so no change there!

At the Seaside

Excursions to the sea for a holiday of two or three weeks were a novelty in Jane Austen's time. The idea developed in the mid-18th century when Londoners took advantage of improved transport to visit the south coast, the nearest beach being at Brighton, then only a small fishing village called Brighthelmstone. When the Prince of Wales popularized the idea, Brighton became the most fashionable of the few seaside resorts, especially among the upper classes. In a rash of exuberance the whimsical prince commissioned the exotic Regency Pavilion overlooking the sea, and one of his favourite pastimes while on holiday was challenging his friends to race chariots along the pebbly shore.

Not to be outdone by his son, King George III decided to go sea-bathing as well, partly on the advice of his doctor that taking sea air and salt water would be good for his health. The king chose to explore further afield and discovered what he was sure was a superior location to Brighton. Thus was born the seaside resort of Weymouth. So excited were the traders and residents of this humble village that everyone everywhere seemed to have turned into an ardent royalist. The novelist Fanny Burney, who was staying there as a member of Queen Charlotte's entourage, described the scene in her diary in 1789:

The loyalty of this place is excessive; they have dressed out every street with labels of 'God save the King'; all the shops have it over the doors; all the children wear it in their caps—all the labourers in

their hats, and all the sailors *in their voices*; for they never approach the house without shouting it aloud—nor see the King, or his shadow, without beginning to huzza, and going on to three cheers. The bathing-machines made it their motto over all the windows; and those bathers that belong to the royal dippers wear it in bandeaux on their bonnets, to go into the sea; and have it again, in large letters, round their waists, to encounter the waves ... Nor is this all. Think but of the surprise of His Majesty when, the first time of his bathing, he had no sooner popped his royal head under water than a band of music, concealed in a neighbouring machine, struck up 'God save great George our King'.

Needless to say, the king's course of action, expedited as it was on medical grounds, gave the royal seal of approval to the idea of seaside recuperation, and doctors everywhere began prescribing such stints to cure all sorts of ailments, just as the inland spa town, notably Bath, had earlier in the century been asserted to be the panacea for all ills. Suddenly, all the world was taking to the sea. William Cowper put the craze to verse in his poem 'Retirement' in 1782:

But now alike, gay widow, virgin, wife,
Ingenious to diversify dull life,
In coaches, chaises, caravans, and hoys,
Fly to the coast for daily, nightly joys,
And all, impatient of dry land, agree
With one consent to rush into the sea.

The result of this new mass tourism was a ribbon development of resorts all the way along the south coast from Margate in the east to Teignmouth in the west. Jane Austen even based *Sanditon* on such a place. One Dr Augustus Granville, who wrote a guide to English spas, remarked:

Since George III introduced the fashion of regularly going to the southern coast for health, doctors have been advising it in all consumptive cases. The particular spot designated for this purpose has extended west and south, farther and farther every eight or ten years; from Weymouth to Sidmouth, from Sidmouth to Exmouth, and so on to Dawlish and Teignmouth.

By the 19th century, Weymouth had already fallen out of favour. One notoriously crusty landowner, the Hon. John Byng, detested the affected vulgarity of the place and wrote in his *Torrington Diaries*:

A sandy shore, being excellent for bathing, has first induced the neighbours to come; and since, by fashion, and by the Duke of Gloucester's having built a house [where George III stayed], is become the resort of the giddy and the gay: where the Irish beau, the gouty peer, and the genteel shopkeeper blend in folly and fine breeding.

When she had read her sister Cassandra's report of it, Jane Austen was equally dismissive:

Weymouth is altogether a shocking place I perceive, without recommendation of any kind, & worthy only of being frequented by the inhabitants of Gloucester.—I am really very glad that we did not go there.

Instead Jane and her parents went to Lyme for a few weeks in September, which they enjoyed so much that they returned for a second holiday. Jane was clearly impressed by the scenery around Lyme and the nearby villages of Charmouth and Colyton. She chose to set *Persuasion* in the resort and describes its environs with greater relish than she does the settings of her other novels:

... as there is nothing to admire in the buildings themselves, the remarkable situation of the town, the principal street almost hurrying into the water, the walk to the Cobb, skirting round the pleasant little bay, which in the season is animated with bathing machines and company, the Cobb itself, its old wonders and new improvements, with the very beautiful line of cliffs stretching out to the east of the town, are what the stranger's eye will seek; and a very strange stranger it must be, who does not see charms in the immediate environs of Lyme, to make him wish to know it better. The scenes in its neighbourhood, Charmouth, with its high grounds and extensive sweeps of country, and still more its sweet retired bay, backed by dark cliffs, where fragments of low rock among the sands make it the happiest spot for watching the flow of the tide, for sitting in unwearied contemplation; the woody varieties of the cheerful village of Up Lyme, and above all, Pinny,

with its green chasms between romantic rocks, where the scattered
forest trees and orchards of luxuriant growth declare that many
a generation must have passed away since the first partial falling
of the cliff prepared the ground for such a state, where a scene so
wonderful and so lovely is exhibited, as may more than equal any
of the resembling scenes of the far-famed Isle of Wight: these
places must be visited, and visited again, to make the worth of
Lyme understood.

Because Jane Austen's period predates the time of mass tourism, for which
hotels were built to cater in the Victorian period, holiday-makers would
rent lodgings for their stay. These would probably be situated by the sea with
easy access to the beach for bathing. Genteel families would wish to hire a
Georgian invention known as the bathing machine, in which to change in
private. Servants would push this contraption, a portable vestibule, down
the sandy beach and into a sufficient depth of water. A cord would then be
pulled to release the rear flap allowing the bather to step out into the sea.
The Austens probably hired such a device, as Jane liked to bathe when she
could. In a letter to Cassandra she describes the family holiday taken in mid-
September 1804:

We are quite settled in our Lodgings by this time, as you may suppose,
& everything goes on in the usual order. The servants behave very
well & make no difficulties, tho' nothing certainly can exceed the
inconvenience of the Offices, except the general Dirtiness of the
House & furniture, & all its Inhabitants.—Hitherto the weather has
been just what we could wish;—the continuance of the dry Season is
very necessary to our comfort.—I endeavour as far as I can to supply
your place, & be useful & keep things in order ... The Bathing was so
delightful this morning & Molly so pressing with me to enjoy myself
that I believe I staid in rather too long, as since the middle of the day
I have felt unreasonably tired. I shall be more careful another time, &
shall not bathe tomorrow.

Holidays were sociable times when families introduced themselves to each
other and might dance together at local balls held in the town assembly
rooms. On this occasion the Austen family went frequently to the dances
held every night at Lyme:

We all of us attended [the balls], both on Wednesday Evening, & last Evening—My Mother had her pool of Commerce [card game] each night. … My Mother & I staid about an hour later [than Mr Austen]. Nobody asked me the first two dances—the next two I danced with Mr Granville, Mrs Granville's son—whom my dear friend Miss Armstrong offered to introduce to me—or with a new, odd looking Man who had been eyeing me for some time, & at last without any introduction asked me if I meant to dance again.—I think he must be Irish by his ease …

Before swimming became a pleasure activity there was a school of thought that said bathing in cold sea water was particularly good for the health, especially early in the morning. For this reason holidays were formerly taken in the autumn. Fanny Burney's diary entry for 20 November 1782 described such an expedition with Dr Johnson's friend Mrs Thrale and her daughters:

Mrs. Thrale and the three Miss Thrales and myself all arose at six o'clock in the morning, and 'by the pale blink of the moon' we went to the seaside, where we had bespoke the bathing-women to be ready for us, and into the ocean we plunged. It was cold, but pleasant. I have bathed so often as to lose my dread of the operation, which now gives me nothing but animation and vigour. We then returned home, and dressed by candle-light, and, as soon as we could get Dr. Johnson ready, we set out upon our journey, in a coach and a chaise, and arrived in Argyll Street at dinner time. Mrs. Thrale has there fixed her tent for this short winter, which will end with the beginning of April, when her foreign journey takes place.

Gathering in the Harvest

Autumn was a busy time for farmers as they gathered the harvest and prepared for the cold months ahead. A burst of activity in late September ensured that hops were picked and put into baskets for drying, and fruits harvested and stored. Wheat would already have been reaped with scythes and threshed with flails, and children would have gathered up the chaff for animal bedding. Fattened geese and turkeys were walked in droves to the market.

Traditionally autumn was the time for a wholesale slaughtering of livestock for the winter meat supply. Carcasses of cattle, sheep and pigs were salted for preservation and stored in huge brick-lined pits. The only animals to survive the winter were breeding stock. But through the 18th century, new winter feeds for animals were making their way into farming practice, as Dr Samuel Johnson observed in A *Journey to the Western Isles of Scotland* in 1775:

> **Young *Col* ... has introduced the culture of turnips, of which he has a field ... His intention is to provide food for his cattle in the winter. This innovation was considered by Mr. *Macsweyn* as the idle project of a young head, heated by English fancies; but he has now found that turnips will really grow, and that hungry sheep and cows will really eat them.**

Since the mass cultivation of new green crops, originated by the wealthy Norfolk farmer Charles 'Turnip' Townshend, animal stock could now be kept through the winter and slaughtered as required. An additional benefit was the increased amount of manure that fertilized the soil and so increased yields. Together with more sophisticated methods, agriculture became a lot more intensive during Jane Austen's lifetime (for the most significant advance, the enclosures, see page 234).

Everyone in the community had their particular seasonal task to perform, with a name to indicate it: the messer oversaw the corn harvest; the hayward removed fences from the fields after harvest to allow cattle and sheep to graze; livestock managers included the coward and calvert, who looked after cows and calves; the shepherd, ewart and tupper tended the sheep, and a poynder impounded any stray sheep.

Hunting and Shooting

The country squire's traditional attachment to his land naturally led to the development of hunting and shooting as country sports. Hunting was mainly of fox, deer and hare and was so popular that the season extended from September right round to April. Fox hunting – the preserve of the landowning gentry – was largely a Georgian invention, with the fox being added to the deer as a suitable quarry from the middle of the 18th century. Just as horse breeding and training improved performances on the race course, so horses were bred for the chase, for which stamina and the ability to jump hedges were vital attributes. Hounds also were reared to follow scent, and landowners would keep permanent packs for regular hunts, some acquiring nationwide reputations by the 1770s. There was no doubting the enthusiasm for blood sports, as Robert Southey described:

> There is certainly no race of people, not even the hunting tribes of savages, who delight so passionately as the English in fox-hunting. The fox-hunter is a character as utterly unlike any other in society, and as totally absorbed in his own pursuits as the alchemist. His whole thoughts were respecting his hounds and horses; his whole anxiety, that the weather might be favourable for the sport; his whole conversation was of the kennel and stable, and of the history of his chases ... here the pleasure is in the pursuit. It is no uncommon thing to read in the newspapers of a chase of ten or twelve leagues [30 or 35 miles] – remember, all this at full speed, and without intermission – dogs, men, women and horses equally eager and equally delighted, though not equally fatigued.

James Austen was keen on hunting and kept a pack of hounds during his early days as a curate. One of his regular hunting partners was the Prince of Wales who, until 1795, held hunting parties at Kempshott Park, near Basingstoke in Hampshire. At the time of the French Revolution (1789–99), a large party of aristrocratic *émigrés* was entertained at Kempshott. On one occasion a great stag-hunt was arranged for their amusement, involving some 500 horsemen. The guests were equipped in the familiar French style with long twisted horns over their shoulders; their bizarre appearance is said to have caused some hearty laughter among the Hampshire farmers. Any gentleman who could keep up with the chase was invited to join a hunt, though mere farmers would probably be excluded on social grounds. James's son, James Edward Austen-Leigh, became a keen hunter like his father and joined the famous Vine Hunt, which rode locally on a grand Tudor estate.

Jane Austen deplored excessive indulgence in blood sports, and preferred her nephews to get it out of their systems at Godmersham Park rather than anywhere local to her. Fanny Knight wrote in her diary about her eldest brothers shooting partridge there in 1809 when no more than 15 years old:

> The two eldest boys went out shooting this September for the first time & had pretty good success for young beginners. Edward killed in all 3 brace & George 1 brace besides Hares, Rabbits etc. They had only 5 days partridge shooting.

While Jane understood the need to keep down vermin and to kill game for food, far more birds were shot for sport than consumption. In *Mansfield Park*, Tom, son of Sir Thomas Bertram, has a good time shooting pheasants in his father's wood:

'The first day I went over Mansfield Wood, and Edmund took the copses beyond Easton, and we brought home six brace between us, and might each have killed six times as many, but we respect your pheasants, sir, I assure you, as much as you could desire. I do not think you will find your woods by any means worse stocked than they were. I never saw Mansfield Wood so full of pheasants in my life as this year. I hope you will take a day's sport there yourself, sir, soon.

Just as they are today, hunts and shoots were social occasions, with parties held afterwards to celebrate the day's kill. During the summer recess of Parliament, which extended into October, Horace Walpole would invite his friends up to his lodge in Norfolk, according to Lord Hervey:

To hunt, be noisy, jolly, drunk, comical and pure merry ... We used to sit down to dinner a little snug party of about thirty odd, up to the chin in beef, venison, geese, turkeys, etc; and generally over the chin in claret, strong beer, and punch. We have Lords Spiritual and Temporal, besides commoners, parsons, and freeholders innumerable.

Some adventuresome ladies might take part in the chase but on the whole it was not thought to be suitable for women. Furthermore, they frequently had to put up with their men going on and on about their conquests in the field or some other incident, conversations that Jane Austen herself probably found tiresome at times. In *Mansfield Park* she describes Maria Bertram's plight as the incorrigible Mr Rushworth beleaguers her with endless tales of his sporting exploits:

Maria, with only Mr. Rushworth to attend to her, and doomed to the repeated details of his day's sport, good or bad, his boast of his dogs, his jealousy of his neighbours, his doubts of their [hunting] qualifications, and his zeal after poachers—subjects which will not find their way to female feelings without some talent on one side, or some attachment on the other, had missed Mr. Crawford grievously.

Plate 18. King George III set a trend in sea-bathing when he took to the waters off the coast of Weymouth in 1789. His doctor had advised the health benefits of immersion in salt water and so a craze for the seaside began. It soon became a pleasure activity, with many fishing villages being turned into resorts.

Plate 19. Lyme Regis became a popular resort in the late Georgian period. Jane Austen spent two happy holidays here with her family, in 1803 and 1804, and used the seaside town as the setting for her novel *Persuasion*.

PLATE 20. From September to April most landowners engaged in field sports, especially hunting and shooting. This 1789 etching of a squire and his fellows shooting ducks, by artist George Morland, celebrates one of the all-male pastimes. Jane herself found men's boasting of the morning quarry most tiresome when repeated ad nauseam.

PLATE 21. Cross country horse races, with hedges as jumps, were held in late summer when the ground was hard. Most provincial towns had a racecourse where the local gentry organized a festive race week rounded off by a ball.

PLATE 22. Thomas Rowlandson's 1800 series of paintings, *The Comforts of Bath* included this one depicting the latter day squalor of the baths. What was once a health resort for members of high society wishing to 'take the cure' offered by natural spring water degenerated into an everyday pool for the hoi polloi.

PLATE 23. Many historic landmarks in Bath known to us today were built in the Georgian era. Robert Adam's Pulteney Bridge, styled on the Ponte Vecchio in Florence was, when the Austens lived in Bath, one of the latest architectural treasures of the period.

PLATE 24. The dandy was a curious phenomenon of the Regency period. Gentlemen affecting extreme elegance in their clothes and manners promenaded the fashionable streets of London.

PLATE 25. Evening dress in the Regency style was classically elegant. High-waisted gowns, combined with hair pinned up and fine accessories, created an air of demure sophistication.

PLATE 26. Dancing classes were popular among the young wishing to impress their partners at balls. The waltz in particular, with its entwining arm movements, was an exciting new development at the turn of the 19th century.

PLATE 27. Most provincial towns had Assembly Rooms where society met for the season. Balls provided the main opportunities for young ladies and gentlemen to be introduced to each other. In her novels Jane Austen described in detail the thrills and disappointments inherent in such occasions.

PLATE 28. In her 30s Jane Austen lived at Chawton Cottage in Hampshire with her widowed mother, her sister Cassandra and their friend Martha Lloyd. With virtually no income following George Austen's death, they relied on family for support. Fortunately Jane's brother Edward Knight had inherited the Chawton estate and could let them live there in modest comfort.

PLATE 29. The threat of invasion from Revolutionary France meant pressing paupers into military service by offering the king's shilling in return for their enlistment. This practice earned ordinary soldiers the Duke of Wellington's famous epithet of 'the scum of the earth'.

PLATE 30. Jane Austen's brothers, Francis and Charles, both took part in naval campaigns against the French. For most of Jane's life England was at war with its neighbour and the welfare of her male relatives was for her, as for many women, a frequent preoccupation.

PLATE 31. The former House of Commons (burned down in 1834) had much to debate in a period of great social injustice. Parliamentary protection of the gentry's privileges held fast at a time when the vote was still restricted to male landowners.

PLATE 32. Despite Parliament's abolition of the slave trade in 1807, the British colonies continued to use slave labour. This scene of felling sugar cane in Antigua might well have formed the background to Jane Austen's novel *Mansfield Park* in which Sir Thomas Bertram owns such a plantation on this Caribbean island.

PLATE 33. Standing over the speaker's chair in the House of Commons is Pitt the Younger, British prime minister for much of Jane Austen's lifetime. In James Gillray's cartoon of 1797 his pockets bulge with taxes and war bills while he tramples the opposition.

PLATE 34. Late Georgian society saw a new genre of illustration: the political cartoon. No subject pleased James Gillray more than the future George IV, or 'the Prince of Whales', as he was mocked for his overindulgent lifestyle and ever-expanding waistline.

PLATE 35. 'I have a secret art to cure, each malady which me endure.' Apothecaries everywhere professed a remedy for every ailment. As the general practitioners of their day, and cheaper than calling in a physician, these spurious chemists were apt to thrive on their trade.

In November, celebrations of Guy Fawkes Night took place. The Gunpowder Plot had been commemorated ever since the failed attempt to blow up the Houses of Parliament in 1605, during the reign of James II. Such a festive occasion would deserve some appropriate toasts, for which typically a strong brandy punch was brewed, garnished usually with bread and nutmeg.

Bath in Winter

The Georgians had a great capacity for enjoying themselves. The winter 'season' of their year involved a good deal of socializing: entertaining and being entertained at private houses and resorts. The main season in Bath lasted from September to December, with a second, lesser one in the spring, from April to June. These were times when the gentry could cement their position in society by renewing relations with other families within the same class. A few weeks or even months might be spent in Bath, or some other fashionable spa such as Cheltenham or Tunbridge Wells, and later in London. In *Persuasion*, Lady Russell relishes the busy atmosphere of Bath after a prolonged period in the country:

> ... and driving through the long concourse of streets from the Old Bridge to Camden Place, amidst the dash of other carriages, the heavy rumble of carts and drays, the bawling of news-men, muffin-men and milkmen, and the ceaseless clink of pattens [wooden overshoes], she made no complaint. No, these were noises which belonged to the winter pleasures; her spirits rose under their influence; and like Mrs Musgrove she was feeling, though not saying, that after being long in the country, nothing could be so good for her as a little quiet cheerfulness.

Bath was second only to London as a Mecca for wealthy hedonists. Ever since the gambling entrepreneur Richard 'Beau' Nash had established Bath, with its therapeutic spring water, as a fashionable health resort early in the 18th century, the city had bloomed in Georgian splendour. Many of the buildings for which Bath became famous went up in Jane Austen's day: the Royal Crescent, the Assembly Rooms and Robert Adam's Pulteney Bridge were all built in the 1770s. One impressed visitor was the French traveller and American immigrant Louis Simond, who wrote this description in 1810, a short while after Jane Austen had lived there:

Bath is certainly very beautiful. It is built of freestone, of a fine cream-colour, and contains several public edifices, in a good taste. We remarked a circular place called the Crescent, another called the Circus ... This town looks as if it had been cast in a mould all at once; so new, so fresh, so regular. The building where the medical water is drank, and where the baths are, exhibits very different objects; human nature, old, infirm or in ruins, or weary and ennuyé. [The Roman baths, though discovered by this time, were not excavated until the 1880s.] Bath is a sort of monastery, inhabited by single people, particularly superannuated females. No trade, no manufactures, no occupations of any sort, except that of killing time, the most laborious of all. Half of the inhabitants do nothing, the other half supply them with nothings: multitude of splendid shops, full of all that wealth and luxury can desire, arranged with all the arts of seduction.

Visiting families must have revelled in the atmosphere of high style and affluence, of casual window-shopping on firm pavements and sauntering through the public parks, such as Sydney Gardens where an orchestra might be playing and fireworks be set off after dark. Delightful scenes no doubt, but the city had a reputation for becoming dreadfully hot in summer. As a result the residents tended to take their holidays then, and the shopkeepers did their stock-taking. The Scottish poet and essayist James Beattie described the conditions:

Bath is situated in the bottom of a deep and narrow valley; so that there is hardly such a thing to be felt there as a fresh breeze. The soil is white chalk, which on the surface of the ground is pounded, by the feet of animals, and the wheels of carriages, into a fine powder, which, in dry weather, is continually flying about; and, drawn in the breath, proved most offensive to my lungs; in wet weather, it covers all the level and narrow streets with a deep mire. The heat of the place is very great; and the air much more close and stifling than that of London.

Expansion was exponential in the 1790s, when more than a thousand townhouses went up to provide accommodation for the ever-increasing tourists. Crescent upon crescent stepped up the north side of the city, each one commanding a grander view and a higher price, such that Sir Walter Elliot in *Persuasion* could boast of his 'lofty, dignified situation' in Camden

Place. The city's amenities had to keep up too. In the same novel, Lady Dalrymple is portrayed as a typical gentlewoman of the time, who takes a house for three months knowing that the Assembly Rooms would offer the entertainments described in the *Bath Guide of 1802*:

> **There are two dress balls every week, viz. on Monday at the New Rooms [Upper Rooms], and Friday at the Lower Rooms ... There are also two Fancy Balls every week, viz. at the Lower Rooms on Tuesday and at the New Rooms on Thursday, nine subscription concerts, and three choral nights, in the winter at the New Rooms, on Wednesday.**

Jane Austen made her first visit to Bath in 1797 as a guest of her aunt and uncle, the Leigh-Perrots (a couple of years before their unfortunate court case). Two years later Jane and her mother accompanied her brother Edward there in May; he was a sufficiently important personage (being heir to a large estate) to be detailed in the *Bath Chronicle*'s list of visitors. Such worthy persons were invited to sign their name and address of lodging in the visitors' book in the Pump Room, so that the Master of Ceremonies might find an opportunity to meet them. One group of visitors, described by the Scottish novelist Tobias Smollett in *The Expedition of Humphrey Clinker* and including the fictitious Matthew Bramble, were enchanted by the charm and courtesy they encountered during their stay in April:

> **Bath is to me a new world—All is gaiety, good-humour, and diversion. The eye is continually entertained with splendour of dress and equipage; and the ear with the sound of coaches, chaises, chairs, and other carriages.** *The merry bells ring round,* **from morn till night. Then we are welcomed by the city-waits in our own lodgings ... As soon as we were settled in, we were visited by the Master of the Ceremonies; a pretty little gentleman, so fine, so civil, so polite, that in our country he would pass for the prince of Wales; then he talks so charmingly, both in verse and prose ... He did us the favour to dine with us, by my uncle's invitation; and the next day 'squired my aunt and me to every part of Bath ...**

Those who could afford sedan chairs were ferried all over the city, up and down its many steep hills, by strong Irish bearers. The compactness and manoeuvrability of the chairs made them a convenient method of getting around a crowded city, and enabled the bearers to deliver their client to virtually any destination required. This was an account of them from a German tourist, Count Friedrich Kielmansegge, visiting Bath in the 1760s:

> A large number of sedan-chair men—at present over a hundred—find sufficient subsistence, and charge a moderate fare; for a distance of 500 yards, sixpence; for an English mile, one shilling ... Few people, or scarcely any, use carriages in the town, except to take a drive; many who do not live far off, or do not use the waters, go on foot in fine weather. For going to the waters there are specially made sedan chairs, which are quite small and low, bowed at below so as to give room, and with very short poles, for the purpose of carrying the people straight out of their beds, in their bathing costume, right into their baths.

According to Smollett's Matthew Bramble, the day began early for the chattering classes:

> At eight in the morning, we go in dishabille to the Pump-room; which is crowded like a Welsh fair; and there you see the highest quality and the lowest trades folks, jostling each other, without ceremony. The noise of the musick playing in the gallery, the heat and flavour of such a crowd, and the hum and buz of their conversation, gave me the head-ach, but afterwards all these things became familiar, and even agreeable.

The Pump Room windows looked out over the King's Bath, a huge cistern with 'patients' up to their necks in hot spring water. Another visitor, the Englishman Samuel Gale, gave an account of the correct form for bathers in his *Tour Through Several Parts of England*:

> The manner of going in is for the gentlemen and ladies to dress themselves in their proper habits in their own apartments; the first in fine canvas waistcoats of a sandy colour, edged and trimmed with black ribbands or ferreting, and tied down before with strings of the same colour, having on canvas drawers and slippers, and a lawn linen cap; the latter in canvas gowns and petticoats, with pieces of lead affixed at the bottom, to keep them down under the water.
> Being thus dressed they are brought in chairs, sometimes close covered up in their morning gowns, and are set down in the passages

which lead into the bath, shut at each end by a door for more privacy. The descent from the passage or entrance is by stone steps, at which one of the guides attending the bath meets you to conduct you in. The first we visited was the Cross-bath ... Two sides of the bath have galleries, one for the spectators, one for the music. This bath is the most frequented by the quality of both sexes, where, with the greatest order and decency, the gentlemen keep to one side of the bath, and the ladies to the other. No gentleman whatever must presume to bathe in the ladies' district; the ladies are supposed to be so modest as not to come near the gentlemen ...

The ladies bring with them japanned bowls or basons, tied to their arms with ribbands, which swim upon the surface of the water, and are to keep their handkerchiefs, nosegays, perfumes, and spirits, in case the exhalations of the water should be too prevalent. The usual compliment, when any one goes into the bath, is to wish them a good bath; and the company, while bathing, generally regale themselves with chocolate.

'Taking the waters' at Bath involved imbibing as well as bathing. On arrival at the Pump Room visitors would drink a few glasses of the mineral water and perhaps eat a Bath Oliver biscuit to remove the slightly bitter taste. These biscuits, stamped with the inventor's portrait, had first been made by Dr William Oliver earlier in the 18th century but became very popular in Jane Austen's time when his assistant set up a shop in the city to compete with Sally Lunn's famous bakery. Shopping was an important activity during a stay in Bath. Ladies would tend to wait until they arrived before deciding what to wear. Just as today we browse boutiques to see the latest fashions, so Georgian ladies would do the same to avoid being caught out of date with their styles (see page 179).

Of all the diversions and entertainments available in Bath – concerts, plays, gaming, shopping, eating cake, or just gossiping – the most exhilarating was dancing. Jane Austen declares in *Emma* that it is as addictive as a drug:

It may be possible to do without dancing entirely. Instances have been known of young people passing many, many months successively, without being at any ball of any description, and no material injury accrue either to body or mind;—but when a beginning is made—when the felicities of rapid motion have once been, though slightly, felt—it must be a very heavy set that does not ask for more.

Dances were as subject to fashion as modes of dress. So important was it to be accomplished on the ballroom floor that all the latest moves could be learned at dance classes if you lived near a city. This advertisement appeared in a London newspaper, *The Morning Herald and Daily Advertiser*, in January 1784:

DANCING, FENCING, AND MUSIC
Taught on the most reasonable Terms, at Hatton House ...
where Ladies and Gentlemen, every day, and at any hour they chuse to appoint, will be punctually attended, and privately instructed, in the Minuet, Minuet de la Cour, Cotillons, &c.
A School, for Ladies only, open at Hatton House, every Wednesday and Saturday afternoon, from four till eight.
English Country Dances perfected in three evenings, with Liberty of practising twice a week during three months, for only 2l. 2s. at Hatton House. A Public Assembly will likewise be opened every Monday, Wednesday and Friday. Subscription for four tickets, each admitting a Lady and Gentleman, 10s. 6d.—Ticket only 3s.—Ladies and Gentlemen attended at their own apartments, by
J. WALL Du VAL and Co.

The name 'country dance' did not signify something practised in the country as opposed to town; it was derived from the French *contre-danse*, which describes the formation of dancers in two lines standing opposite each other, the men on one side, the women on the other. The leading couple would then move down the central aisle created by the two lines, followed by successive couples, and move off to weave patterns across the floor. Jane Austen was familiar with various dance movements, including reels, the stately minuet and the hornpipe (a popular dance in the war years, accompanied by horn blowing). Her favourite was the cotillion, which she thought a superior dance to the new Parisian quadrille, designed to be danced by a quartet of couples. The new sensation in the 1790s was the German waltz, a favourite topic in newspapers of the time:

The Balls at Southampton are exceedingly lively and well-attended. The young Ladies are particularly favourable to a German Dance, called the *Volse*; for squeezing, hugging, &c, it is excellent in its kind, and more than one Lady has actually fainted in the middle of it.

It was at the fashionable Upper Assembly Rooms that Jane danced beneath crystal chandeliers in the magnificent green and gold ballroom. The ballroom provided a respectable environment in which carefully chaperoned girls and unmarried men could meet; the dance floor was virtually the only place where potential marriage partners could be identified and courted – it was the marriage market of Georgian society and as such was the most thrilling stage in the world. Well-bred young ladies might wait for such occasions to 'come out': to make their first formal appearance in public on reaching womanhood. Jane captures the sense of anticipation in this scene from *Northanger Abbey* with Catherine Morland and Isabella Thorpe:

The party from Pulteney-street reached the Upper-rooms in very good time … Isabella having gone through the usual ceremonial of meeting her friend with the most smiling and affectionate haste, of admiring the set of her gown, and envying the curl of her hair, they followed their chaperons, arm in arm, into the ballroom, whispering to each other whenever a thought occurred, and supplying the place of many ideas by a squeeze of the hand or a smile of affection.

Elizabeth Canning, a real-life debutante more confident than Catherine Morland, wrote the following in a letter to her mother in December 1792. Any first-night nerves were assuaged by a sense of wonder at the occasion, despite, unusually, not having a partner for the evening:

I was dressed the same as for the Concert, except that I wore the Lawn, which was much admired, instead of my Muslin Jacket, & petticoat. At length a little past Seven arrived, we *set Sail*, were soon safe landed, at the upper Rooms, by that time I felt all impatience to be in the Ball Room, & was picturing to myself all the charms I could conceive such a Place to have; when we entered it, I was fully gratified, for to be sure I never [saw] so brilliant an assembly. It was amazingly crouded although the minuets had not begun; so much so, that we found some difficulty to get seats—I was very much

entertained with the bad minuet-dancers, especially with a
Mr Badcock who was obliged to stand up with seven, or eight
Ladies successively, to the great diversion of the Spectators.

Tea might sometimes be taken for refreshment at the Assembly Rooms just
as it would be drunk at home in the evening. No alcohol would have been
consumed. The debutante continued her first night account:

I believe there were twenty minuets which was rather tiresome, but
at last the Country dances began, there was great humming, & hawing
whether or no I should dance ... & I declared ... that I should like
to wait till after Tea; when we went into the Tea room, we could
not get a Table, so they agreed to go to cards, till some of the people
returned into the Ball Room ... while at Cards Mrs Leigh sent some
good Man to look for some dapper little personage for me, & indeed
he succeeded very well, for he soon brought us a Young *Gem'mon* of
about *fifteen* ... [However] the pride of the Old Aunts was up at the
Idea of my making my first Essay with a Boy ... Your poor little picksy
was obliged to content herself without cutting capers ... but the next
time I go to a Ball now that I know the Manoeuvres of it, I shall get
them to look out for a partner earlier in the Evening, & then I shall
have a better chance.

At least if one ball went badly an aspiring belle could try another in a few
days' time, and make sure she 'manoeuvred' effectively, either before the ball
or during it, to secure a suitable partner for the evening. But come the spring,
time would be running out. When Jane danced at the Upper Rooms in May
there was more than a whiff of low-season in the air, as she reported to her
sister Cassandra:

I dressed as well as I could, & had all my finery much admired at
home. By nine o'clock my Uncle, Aunt & I entered the rooms &
linked Miss Winstone on to us.—Before tea, it was rather a dull affair;
but then the beforetea did not last long, for there was only one dance,
danced by four couple.—Think of four couple, surrounded by about
an hundred people, dancing in the upper rooms at Bath!—After tea we
cheered up; the breaking up of private parties sent scores more to the
Ball, & tho' it was shockingly & inhumanly thin for this place, there

were people enough I suppose to have made five or six very pretty
Basingstoke assemblies.

At the height of the season in excess of a thousand might attend a ball,
which was open to all who could afford it. When Jane Austen moved to Bath
in 1801, by which time the city had swelled to 30,000 inhabitants, becoming
the ninth largest in England, much of the upper gentry stayed away on
account of the numerous *hoi polloi*. Even 30 years earlier, Tobias Smollett
complained in *The Expedition of Humphry Clinker* about the type of person
now frequenting the city:

> Every upstart of fortune presents himself at Bath ... planters, negro-
> drivers, hucksters from our American plantations; usurers, brokers,
> and jobbers of every kind; men of low birth and no breeding, have
> found themselves suddenly translated into a state of affluence,
> unknown to former ages; and no wonder that their brains should be
> intoxicated with pride, vanity and presumption ... And all of them
> hurry to Bath, because here, without any further qualification, they
> can mingle with the princes and nobles of the land. Even the wives
> and daughters of low tradesmen ... are infected with the same rage
> of displaying their importance; and insist upon being conveyed to
> Bath where they may hobble country dances and cotillons among
> lordlings, squires, counsellors and clergy.

Between Jane Austen's writing of *Northanger Abbey* in 1798 and *Persuasion*
in 1815, Bath had seriously gone out of fashion with the well bred. No longer
might you see the likes of a Thomas Gainsborough or Horace Walpole or
Admiral Horatio Nelson sauntering down the main shopping thoroughfare
of Milsom Street. Jane Austen depicts Sir Walter Elliot in *Persuasion* as
typical of those who, having known Bath in its heyday, were disenchanted
by what they now saw around them:

> The worst of Bath was the number of its plain women. He did not
> mean to say that there were no pretty women, but the number of
> the plain was out of all proportion. He had frequently observed,
> as he walked, that one handsome face would be followed by thirty,
> or five-and-thirty, frights; and once, as he had stood in the shop in
> Bond Street, he had counted eighty-seven women go by, one after

another, without there being a tolerable face among them. It had been a frosty morning, to be sure, a sharp frost, which hardly one woman in a thousand could stand the test of. But still, there certainly were a dreadful multitude of ugly women in Bath; and as for the men! they were infinitely worse. Such scarecrows as the streets were full of!

By the Regency period, if the elite of society visited at all it would be for health reasons, to 'take the cure' – the drinking of natural mineral water that maintained its reputation for healing all manner of illnesses and conditions. One somewhat reluctant patient was the Prince of Wales, who suffered from, among other things, royal ennui. In a letter to the Queen he lamented:

... of all the dull séjours I have experience'd, this certainly at the present moment is the dullest. Perhaps my having been a good deal indispos'd since I have been here makes me consider this place as stupider than it really is. However, I understand that in the opinions of most people it really *is* so, & perhaps the more so, from the comparative very gay & crowded winter which has fallen to the lot of this water-drinking place during the last three or four months ... I go as little out as I possibly can; one must occasionally go to the Rooms, or, properly speaking, to the Balls, for half an hour, which is the utmost time I have staid, as there is hardly a creature I ever saw before in my life that go there, & the two Balls that I have hitherto been at so crowded, so hot, & so stinking, that I was absolutely gasping for fresh air, & dying to get away from the moment I came into the Rooms.

A Georgian Christmas

Christmas was the highlight of the year for the gentry. It was the one time when their houses were sure to be filled with relatives, who stayed for weeks being amused by entertainments every evening. On Christmas Eve holly would be laid out on window ledges, and the preparation of festive dishes and turkey would be in hand, with some delicacies bought in, as Robert Southey noted in his *Letters from England*:

Just at this time shops are filled with large plum-cakes, which are crusted over with sugar, and ornamented in every possible way. These

are for the festival of the kings, it being part of an Englishman's religion to eat plum-cake on this day, and to have pies at Christmas made of meat [mincemeat] and plums.

Carols would be sung, and Christmas morning in Steventon saw George Austen setting off up the hill to his tiny unheated church of St Nicholas to deliver the lesson and serve the bread and wine to those parishioners who might turn up. Afterwards the gentlemen might enjoy a spot of rabbit and snipe shooting across the morning frost. Jane records in a letter that the only thing better than eating turkey was giving parcels of food and clothing to the poor in the community, a customary practice of the time. The tradition was followed in England, as it was throughout Europe, of exchanging presents on St Nicholas' Day, 6 December. Gifts were also exchanged in the New Year (the two were later condensed to form a single custom of gifting on Christmas Day). Jane once made a little needle bag for a friend who had stayed for Christmas and accompanied it with a short verse:

**This little bag, I hope, will prove
To be not vainly made;
For should you thread and needles want,
It will afford you aid.**

**And, as we are about to part,
'Twill serve another end:
For, when you look upon this bag,
You'll recollect your friend.**

A good deal of entertainment would be had from simple fireside gossip among all the relatives gathered at Christmas. In 1786 there was an especially lively Christmas at Steventon Rectory. The newly wed Eliza, now Comtesse de Feuillide, made her much-awaited entrance together with her noisy baby, Hastings (named after his godfather Warren), and her mother Philadelphia. A pianoforte was borrowed for the occasion, as Eliza was accomplished in that department and gave daily recitals. Other cousins, the Coopers, who lived nearby, came over too, and impromptu dances in the parlour added to the family fun.

What would have interested Jane probably more than anything would have been the accounts of foreign travel. Eliza would not have been short of tales about the court of Versailles and Marie Antoinette's exquisite costumes, while her mother would no doubt have made the most of exotic Calcutta where her poor husband languished in the East India Company. Soon there would be reports of naval expeditions from Jane's two brothers, Frank and Charles, back from buccaneering adventures on the high seas. And any number of other relations and friends might carry stories from the British dominions.

It need hardly be said that the main order of the day of a Georgian Christmas was not religious observance but playing games. Card games were very popular, but so were many other kinds, which made the atmosphere resemble a children's party. Fanny Knight described the festive season in 1812:

> **We have in general had cards, snapdragons, Bullet pudding, etc. on any particular evening, and Whist, Commerce and others and Tickets were the favourite games. I think when cards failed, the boys played every evening at Drafts, Chess and Backgammon. On Twelfth night we had a delightful evening …**

Bullet Pudding deserves a special mention. It was a typically lively game, loved particularly for the indignity it inflicted on the loser. Fanny described it:

> **You must have a large pewter dish filled with flour which you must pile up into a sort of pudding with a peak at top; you must then lay a Bullet at top & everybody cuts a slice of it & the person that is cutting it when the Bullet falls must poke about with their noses & chins till they find it & then take it out with their mouths which makes them strange figures all covered with flour but the worst is that you must not laugh for fear of the flour getting up your nose & mouth & choking you …**

When James Austen returned from Oxford for Christmas in 1782 at the age of 17, he insisted on following the fashion of the time by staging an amateur theatrical. This would become a regular feature of their Christmases at Steventon rectory for the rest of the decade. At first plays were presented in the dining room; later, as their efforts became more ambitious, the rectory barn was converted to provide a makeshift stage. The first play was a dark tragedy, *Matilda*, set in the time of the Norman Conquest with passion, intrigue and murder; and James wrote a prologue and epilogue to accompany it. As the years went by, their choices lightened up somewhat. One farce, *High Life Below Stairs*, was a pastiche on etiquette and told the story of a household of idle servants who mimic their absent masters by drinking, flirting and arguing. The play inspired Jane, at the age of 14, to compose a short vignette herself, entitled *The Visit*, which she dedicated to her brother James in honour of his seasonal extravaganzas. These acquired a reputation among their relations. Eliza tried to persuade her cousin Phylly to come to Steventon one Christmas, but being too nervous of what would be expected of her she couldn't face it. As she wrote in a letter to her brother James in 1787:

> They go at Xmas to Steventon and mean to act a play 'Which is the Man' and 'Bon Ton' [by Garrick]. My uncle's barn is fitting up quite like a theatre and all the young folks are to take their part ... They wish me much of the party and offer to carry me, but I do not think of it. I should like to be a spectator, but am sure I should not have the courage to act a part.

In Georgian times the climax to all the fun was Twelfth Night. The spirit of this final evening of Christmas, the Feast of the Epiphany, took its cue from the visit of the Three Wise Kings, with everyone wearing fancy dress and mask. This was the masque ball of the winter season, also called the Children's Ball because it was usual to 'draw' two children to be king and queen for the evening (an ancient notion dating back to Roman times when master changed places with slave). It was their task to preside over a masquerade in which everybody had to dress as a character from a myth or fairy-tale. It was a popular idea to dress as members of the opposite sex, as in a pantomime; at Godmersham some members of the family would ride into Canterbury to buy suitable masks for the occasion. Fanny Knight described one such event in a letter to her ex-governess, Dorothy Chapman:

> Godmersham Park, 12 January 1806
> My dear Miss Chapman ... On Twelfth day we were all agreeably surprised with a sort of masquerade, all being dressed in character, and then we were conducted into the library, which was all lighted up and at one end a throne, surrounded with a grove of Orange Trees, and other shrubs, and all this was totally unknown to us all! Was it not delightful? I should have liked you very much to have been of the

party. Now I will tell you our different characters. Edward and I were a Shepherd King and Queen; Mama a Savoyarde with a Hurdy-Gurdy; Marianne and William her children with a Tambourine and Triangle; Papa and Aunt Louisa—Sir Bertram and Lady Beadmasc one hundred years old—Uncle H. Austen—a Jew; Uncle E—a Jewess; Miss Sharpe—a Witch; Elizabeth—a flowergirl; Sophia—a fruitgirl; Fanny Cage—a Haymaker; George—Harlequin; Henry—clown; and Charley a Cupid! Was it not a good one for him, sweet fellow! He had a little pair of wings and a bow and arrow! and looked charming.

And Up to London

The London season began for country squires in the New Year and went on for up to four months. Nobles and the gentry would keep a house solely for their entertainment during this time of high life in the bustling capital. By the Regency period travel up to the capital was no longer the once-in-a-lifetime wonder of the early Georgians. The Frenchman Louis Simond was amazed at the mobility of the English:

> Nobody is provincial in this country ... Nobody above poverty has not visited London once in his life; and most of those who can, visit it once a year. To go up to town from 100 or 200 miles distance, is a thing done on a sudden, and without any previous deliberation. In France the people of the provinces used to make their will before they undertook such an expedition.

Sophisticated soirées in Georgian townhouses now replaced the rustic repasts of country squiredom. Plays, concerts, exhibitions, smart shops, elegant carriages and fashionable promenading through John Nash's Regency developments in Piccadilly, St James's and Regents Park were the stuff of life while sojourning in London.

And so it was for Jane. At the end of March in 1811, she went to stay with her brother Henry and cousin Eliza (now his wife) at their new home in Sloane Street. She was there until May correcting proofs of her first novel to be published, *Sense and Sensibility*, and during this time met many of Henry's friends at tea and dinner parties, which she said she found very pleasant. In April Eliza gave a large party, engaging professional musicians for their entertainment, and inviting old friends and family connections to meet Jane.

In a letter to Cassandra, Jane described the event, which was of sufficient social importance to be reported in the press the next day:

> Our party went extremely well ... The rooms were dressed up with flowers &c, & looked very pretty.—A glass for the Mantlepiece was lent, by the Man who is making their own. Mr Egerton & Mr Walter came at ½ past 5, & the festivities began with a p^r of very fine Soals ... At ½ past 7 arrived the Musicians in two Hackney coaches, & by 8 the lordly Company began to appear ... The Draw^g room being soon hotter than we liked, we placed ourselves in the connecting Passage, which was comparatively cool, & gave us all the advantage of the Music at a pleasant distance, as well as that of the first view of every new comer.—I was quite surrounded by acquaintance, especially Gentlemen ... I had as much upon my hands as I could do ... We were all delight & cordiality of course. Miss M. seems very happy, but has not beauty enough to figure in London.—Including everybody we were 66—which was considerably more than Eliza was expecting ... The Music was extremely good ... It opened with (tell Fanny) 'Prike pe Parp pin Praise pof Prapella' [Jane and her niece Fanny created a nonsense language in which they would put 'p' in front of every word]—... Between the Songs were Lessons on the Harp, or Harp & Piano Forte together ... There was one female singer, a short Miss Davis all in blue, whose voice was said to be very fine indeed; & all the Performers gave great satisfaction by doing what they were paid for, & giving themselves no airs.—No amateur could be persuaded to do anything.—The House was not clear till after 12 ...

Jane spent her time visiting the sights of London and walking in parks, which she noted were in bloom earlier than they were in Kent, where Cassandra was staying:

> Your Lilacs are in leaf, *ours* are in bloom.—The Horse chestnuts are quite out, & the Elms almost.—I had a pleasant walk in Kensington G^s on Sunday with Henry, Mr Smith and Mr Tilson—everything was fresh and beautiful.

She particularly enjoyed the theatre, which was experiencing something of a golden age of stage comedy in the West End, with great shows performed at the Theatre Royal in Drury Lane and the King's Theatre in the Haymarket. Actors and actresses were the celebrities of the period and included such big names as David Garrick (after whom the club in Covent Garden was named) and Sarah Siddons, who was immortalized as *The Tragic Muse* in a portrait by Sir Joshua Reynolds after her impassioned performances in *Macbeth*. Jane had her own favourites whom she made every effort to see. Her letter to Cassandra continued:

> We *did* go to the play after all on Saturday, we went to the Lyceum, & saw the Hypocrite, an old play taken from Moliere's *Tartuffe*, & were well entertained ... I have no chance of seeing Mrs Siddons.—She *did* act on Monday, but as Henry was told by the Boxkeeper that he did not think she would, the places were given up ... I should particularly have liked to see her in Constance, & could swear at her with little effort for disappointing me.—Henry has been to the Watercolour Exhibition, which open'd on Monday, & is to meet us there again some morn^g—If Eliza cannot go—(& she has a cold at the moment) Miss Beaty will be invited to be my companion.

However, some poor souls from the country could not keep up with the pace of life in the capital. After one trip Mrs Austen complained there was no time to do things, that everything was done in such a hurry:

> Here I am once more in this scene of dissipation and vice, and I begin already to find my morals corrupted.

Even the great social animal Eliza de Feuillide had to put the brakes on sometimes in her younger days. She had rented a smart house in the West End for the season and invited Jane's 16-year-old brother Henry to stay at her house. Perhaps the seeds of their love were sown at this early stage, albeit ten years before they would eventually marry. At any rate, her status as a French countess eased her entry into all sorts of places in high society, as she declared in an excited but exhausted state to her Kentish cousin Phylly Walter one morning in April 1787:

> As to me I have been for some time past the greatest rake imaginable & really wonder how such a meagre creature as I am can support so much fatigue, for I only stood from two to four in the Drawing Room

& ... went to the Dutchess of Cumberland's in the evening, & from thence to Almack's where I staid till five in the morning; all this I did not many days ago, & am yet alive to tell you of it. I believe tho' I should not be able to support London hours, & all the racketing of a London life for a year together.

Almack's was one of London's most exclusive clubs – even the Duke of Wellington was once turned away. Founded in 1764, it became a social centre for elite gatherings for gambling, dancing and gossip. This was the era of gentlemen's clubs where little nocturnal assemblies would litter the capital till all hours. Other notable venues were the Whigs' Kit-Kat club, White's (which Henry Austen once attended with royalty), Boodle's and the greatest of all gambling dens, Waiter's, opened in 1805. The story has it that the Prince of Wales, being dissatisfied with the quality of food at existing clubs, called for a waiter and instructed him to take a house and turn it into a club, which he did, and so was founded Waiter's. One famous member was Lord Byron, and he recalled the days when he rubbed along with the fops of the Regency period:

I had gamed and drunk, and taken my degrees in most dissipations, and having no pedantry, and not being overbearing, we ran on quietly together. I knew them all, more or less, and they made me a member of Waiter's (a superb club at that time), being, as I take it, the only literary man ... Our masquerade was a grand one, so was the Dandy ball too.

Fashion and Etiquette

It was not until the 18th century that such a concept as fashion existed in the sense we know it today. But in the consumerist society of late Georgian England the way you dressed and behaved were strong indicators of your fortune and status. Jane Austen was a keen follower of fashion – as revealed in her letters to Cassandra, which are peppered with details of dressmaking and alterations and purchases made to keep abreast with fast-changing modes. Despite high inflation caused by the Napoleonic Wars, there had never been so much money sloshing around the fashionable arcades. In one letter she tells of her expedition in London to a popular draper's shop, Grafton House:

> We set off immediately after breakfast & must have reached Grafton House by ½ past 11—, but when we entered the Shop, the whole Counter was thronged, & we waited *full* half an hour before we c^d be attended to. When we were served however, I was very well satisfied with my purchases.

Once the Prince of Wales was made Regent in 1811 and became the leader of fashion, styles altered even more quickly. Whether in art, architecture, poetry or costume, they became exuberant and daring. Low necklines, French cosmetics and German waltzes were all the rage and the upper classes disported with an air of licentiousness unknown in living memory. The social reformer William Cobbett saw nothing good in the current frippery:

> It was, for hundreds of years, amongst the characteristics of the English people, that their taste was, in all matters, for things solid, and good; for the *useful*, the *decent*, the *cleanly* in dress, and not for the *showy*. Let us hope, that this may be the taste again.

But Cobbett was destined to be disappointed, for fashion was here to stay; and not only for the benefit of affluent city dwellers. Its tendrils would reach the furthest recesses of village England, as William Cowper observed:

> **In a village church, the squire's lady or the vicar's wife are perhaps the only females that are stared at for their finery … In towns where the newest fashions are brought down weekly by the stage-coach or wagon, all the wives and daughters of the most topping tradesmen vie with each other every Sunday in the elegance of their apparel.**

The Belle's Assemblage

For decades Georgian attire had been stiff and formal. When Jane Austen was a little girl, ladies went to parties wearing heavy silk dresses with garish brocades and ruffles. Wide hoop-petticoats and a bustle would make these dresses balloon out like parachutes and cause considerable inconvenience at every turn – eating, for example, would be done sitting sideways to the table. The crowning glory was the hair set, a towering showpiece of amazing complexity. It was all a great source of amusement to Robert Southey, among others:

> **The smaller the waist the more beautiful it was esteemed. To be shaped like a wasp was therefore the object of the female ambition; and so tight did they lace themselves, or rather so tightly were they laced, for it required assistant strength to fasten their girths, that women have frequently fainted from the pressure, and some actually perished by this monstrous kind of suicide …**
>
> **They all wore powder; the hair at the sides was stuck out in stiff curls, or rolls, tier above tier, fastened with long double black pins; behind it was matted with pomatum [perfumed ointment] into one broad flat mass, which was doubled back and pinned upon a cushion, against which the toupee was frizzed up, and the whole frosted over with powder white, brown, pink, or yellow.**

Cartoonists caricatured court ladies by drawing pictures of them wearing ships in full sail and windmills on their heads. In her novel *Evelina*, published in 1778, Fanny Burney expressed the despair some women felt at the vogue for this bizarre flourish, which could take hours to prepare:

I have just had my hair dressed. You can't think how oddly my head feels, full of powder and black pins, and a great cushion on the top of it. I believe you would hardly know me, for my face looks quite different to what it did before my hair was dressed. When I shall be able to make use of a comb for myself I cannot tell, for my hair is so much entangled, frizzled they call it, that I fear it will be very difficult.

This peculiar idea had originated in France, as did many styles of clothing. Until the French Revolution it was the height of English fashion to be 'Frenchified', as Jane's cousin Eliza, Comtesse de Feuillide never tired of reminding everyone:

There is perhaps no place in the world where dress is so well understood & carried to so great a perfection as in Paris, & no wonder it should be so since people make it the chief business & study of their lives. Powder is universally worn, & in very large quantities, no one would dare to appear in public without it.

News of the latest look spread chiefly by word of mouth and letters. Sophisticated young gentlewomen might browse pocket books such as *La Belle Assemblée* and some of the earliest fashion magazines to find out what was being worn in Paris. But these modes cut no ice with the British authorities at public assembly rooms, where strict observance of their dress code was expected of all guests when attending balls, especially for the most formal of dances, the minuet, which required the wearing of clean white gloves and decorative flaps (lappets) on the headdress. At Bath the Master of Ceremonies made it clear in the *Bath Chronicle* in 1776 that he was not standing for any French nonsense:

The Master of the Ceremonies begs leave to remind the Ladies who chuse to dance Minuets at the Dress-Balls, that a suit of cloaths, or a full-trimmed negligé with lappets and hoops, are the only dresses proper for the occasion; that all other fancy dresses, such as polonèse [a type of French gown], French night-gown, &c. however elegant, are not sufficient dresses, and are highly improper to be worn with lappets. He likewise begs leave to request the parents of young ladies, who are in robe coats, that their cloaths be full trimmed, and to be

worn with a hoop; all other fancy dresses are not proper for a minuet at the dress balls at Bath.

During the last quarter of the 18th century styles became simpler and more refined, moving towards the Regency's columnar style that took as its model the classical dress of ancient Greece. Waistlines went up, hair came down, and textiles became lighter and thinner, sometimes almost see-through, much to the delight of the gentlemen. One Colonel George Hanger remarked in his memoirs:

I must confess, I am a great admirer of short waists and thin clothing; formerly, when the women wore strong stiff stays [corsets stiffened with whalebone] and cork rumps, you might as well sit with your arm round an oaken tree with the bark on, as around a lady's waist; but now, as you have seldom any more covering but your shift and gown of a cold day, your waist is extremely comfortable to the feel.

Cotton and calico were imported from India and eclipsed wool as the primary material for garments (except in the case of fine cashmere shawls, also from India). A pamphlet of 1782 reads:

As for the ladies, they wear scarcely anything now but cotton, calicoes, muslin, or silks, and think no more of woolen stuffs than we think of an old almanac. We have scarcely any woolens now about our beds but blankets, and they would most likely be thrown aside, could we keep our bodies warm without them.

When Jane was a young lady and ready to wear her first ball gown, she would have worn a 'round gown', a loose-fitting dress with a high waistline to conceal the figure, and short sleeves. Although plain colours might be worn, white was considered most proper for the evening. In May of 1801 Jane had a new white gown made up in anticipation of going to the Assembly Rooms. She certainly knew her own mind when it came to fashion, what she liked and disliked. Once while attending a ball she deplored seeing so many young women not only standing around without dancing partners but 'each of them with two ugly naked shoulders'. Some 13 years later, in a letter to Cassandra, she said more on the subject:

> I learnt from Mrs Tickar's young Lady, to my amusement, that the
> stays now are not made to force the Bosom up at all;—*that* was a very
> unbecoming, unnatural fashion. I was really glad to hear that they are
> not to be so much off the shoulders as they were.

Come the Regency period, fashion was moving on so fast that Jane became
anxious one evening in the following spring about what clothes might be
suitable for London society:

> I wear my gauze [diaphanous fabric with twisted weave] gown today,
> long sleeves & all; I shall see how they succeed, but as yet I have no
> reason to suppose long sleeves are allowable.—I have lowered the
> bosom especially at the corners, & plaited black satin ribbon round
> the top … Mrs Tilson had long sleeves too, & she assured me that they
> are worn in the evening by many. I was glad to hear this.

Ensuring that ladies up from the country got the style right and did not
appear parochial on such occasions required the dedicated eye of a spy. Six
months later Jane reported again, this time to her friend Martha Lloyd:

> I was at a little party last night at Mrs Latouche's, where dress is a good
> deal attended to, & these are my observations from it.—Petticoats
> short, & generally, tho' not always, flounced … the coloured
> petticoats with braces over the white Spencers [short jackets cut like
> the bodice] & enormous Bonnets upon the full stretch, are quite
> entertaining. It seems to me a more marked change than one has lately
> seen.—Long sleeves appear universal, even as Dress, the Waists short,
> and as far as I have been able to judge, the Bosom covered.

Intelligence once gathered, ladies could make their forays to the shops. In
Northanger Abbey Catherine Morland and Mrs Allen typically did not go
to the Assembly Rooms until they had found out what was 'in' that season.
Even possession of this knowledge might not prevent a good deal more
anxiety when trying to hone down the precise ensemble for an occasion
– something that Jane, though herself unworried by such concerns, saw only
too often upset ladies around her. She voices a typical dilemma plaguing the
mind of Catherine Morland, arguably the heroine most afflicted by matters
of appearance, as she contemplates a forthcoming ball:

What gown and what head-dress she should wear on the occasion became her chief concern. She cannot be justified in it. Dress is at all times a frivolous distinction, and excessive solicitude about it often destroys its own aim. Catherine knew all this very well; her great aunt had read her a lecture on the subject only the Christmas before; and yet she lay awake ten minutes on Wednesday night debating between her spotted and her tamboured [embroidered] muslin, and nothing but the shortness of the time prevented her buying a new one for the evening.

Yet, as the author warns, men are too often blind to such subtleties of distinction in the opposite sex and all the effort might hardly be worth the candle:

This would have been an error in judgment ... from which one of the other sex rather than her own, a brother rather than a great aunt, might have warned her, for man only can be aware of the insensibility of man towards a new gown. It would be mortifying to the feelings of many ladies, could they be made to understand how little the heart of man is affected by what is costly or new in their attire; how little it is biased by the texture of their muslin, and how unsusceptible of peculiar tenderness towards the spotted, the sprigged, the mull [sheer cotton fabric], or the jackonet [thin glazed cotton fabric]. Woman is fine for her own satisfaction alone. No man will admire her the more, no woman will like her the better for it. Neatness and fashion are enough for the former, and a something of shabbiness or impropriety will be most endearing to the latter.

Envy was always a trait to beware, and guests had to mind they did not upstage their hosts or even senior sisters. Choosing the right fabrics for turning into dresses was all important and required great care, as they were costly and their quality varied, especially muslins, which were prone to falling out of shape – a hazard Jane often refers to through her characters. Questions of texture, weight, colour and pattern all had to be considered before deciding which fabric was the most suitable for the time of the year. Commissioning a dressmaker might also have its difficulties, as Jane implied in a letter to Cassandra in 1801:

I will engage Mrs Mussell as you desire. She made my dark gown very well & may therefore be trusted I hope with Yours—but she does not always succeed with lighter Colours.—My white one I was obliged to alter a good deal.

Choosing hats was an altogether simpler task. Many women made their own, and there were other advantages in covering the head, as Jane told Cassandra in 1798:

I have made myself two or three caps to wear of evenings since I came home, and they save me a world of torment as to hair-dressing, which at present gives me no trouble beyond washing and brushing, for my long hair is always plaited up out of sight, and my short hair curls well enough to want no papering [curlers]. I have had it cut lately by Mr Butler [her hairdresser from Basingstoke].

It was fashionable by the 19th century to wear the hair short at the front and to curl it using papers. Ladies had their hair styled either by a maid or, for special occasions, by a professional hairdresser, who was of course the more expensive option. If he had to travel some distance to tend to his clients he might have to be offered board and lodging before making the return journey. The sums were sometimes cause for concern for the poor Austen ladies, as Jane admitted:

Mr Hall walked off this morng. to Ospringe, with no inconsiderable Booty. He charged Eliz:th 5s for every time of dressing her hair, & 5s for every lesson to Sace [lady's maid], allowing nothing for the pleasures of his visit here, for meat drink & Lodging, the benefit of Country air ... Towards me he was as considerate, as I had hoped for, from my relationship to you, charging me only 2s.6d for cutting my hair, tho' it was as thoroughly dress'd after being cut for Eastwell [neighbouring house], as it had been for the Ashford Assembly.—He certainly respects either our Youth or our poverty.

Some time later Jane had her hair curled but thought it looked 'hideous and longed for a snug cap' to hide it.

Like the hairdos of the previous generation, hats could be extravagant affairs. Eliza's rather plain cousin Phylly Walter told her brother James how she was given one while on a shopping spree with Eliza and her mother in Tunbridge Wells in 1787:

> On Friday morning the Comtesse [Eliza] and I hunted all the Milliner's shops for hats: she presented me with a very pretty fancy hat to wear behind the hair, on one side, and as a mixture of colors is quite the thing, I chose green and pink with a wreath of pink roses and feathers; but the taste is for all the most frightful colors.

Headwear was a fashion that courted excess, as hats were adorned with all manner of artificial flowers and fruits – much to Jane's amusement, which she shared with Cassandra in 1799:

> Flowers are very much worn, & Fruit is still more the thing. Eliz. has a bunch of Strawberries, & I have seen Grapes, Cherries, Plumbs & Apricots—There are likewise Almonds & raisins, French plumbs & Tamarinds at the Grocers, but I have never seen any of them in hats.—A plumb or greengage would cost three shillings;—Cherries & grapes about 5 I believe—but this is at some of the dearest shops; —My aunt has told me of a very cheap one near Walcot Church, to which I shall go in quest of something for you.

The Georgian era was big on cosmetics too. Radical changes were made during Jane's lifetime, just as they were in other departments of fashion. In the earlier part of her life it was usual for women to wear a white 'mask' of paste made from kaolin clay or talc; cheeks were rouged and lips red; eyebrows were trimmed and blackened for dramatic effect, and a regular ingredient used in cosmetics was white lead – it was not unknown for ladies who had habitually whitened their faces with this substance to die of lead poisoning. Powder and paint were liberally applied to render a variety of effects; sometimes black patches were affixed to the face as 'beauty spots', often to hide unwelcome blemishes. Fashionable ladies and gentlemen could be very particular about what was welcome and what was not. In *Persuasion*, Sir Walter Elliot's daughter Elizabeth talks to her sister Anne about facial features:

> 'Freckles do not disgust me so very much as they do him [her father]: I have known a face not materially disfigured by a few, but

he abominates them. You must have heard him notice Mrs. Clay's freckles.'

'There is hardly any personal defect,' replied Anne, 'which an agreeable manner might not gradually reconcile one to.'

'I think very differently,' answered Elizabeth, shortly; 'an agreeable manner may set off handsome features, but can never alter plain ones …'

On Sir Walter's recommendation, Mrs Clay has used a skin cream, Gowland's Lotion, much used at the time for treating skin complaints; and his daughter Anne's looks have so improved of late that he cannot believe this is not also due to the dependable Gowland. The narrative continues:

In the course of the same morning, Anne and her father chancing to be alone together, he began to compliment her on her improved looks; he thought her 'less thin in her person, in her cheeks; her skin, her complexion, greatly improved—clearer, fresher. Had she been using any thing in particular?' 'No, nothing.' 'Merely Gowland,' he supposed. 'No, nothing at all.' 'Ha! he was surprised at that;' and added, 'Certainly you cannot do better than to continue as you are; you cannot be better than well; or I should recommend Gowland, the constant use of Gowland, during the spring months. Mrs. Clay has been using it at my recommendation, and you see what it has done for her. You see how it has carried away her freckles.'

Sir Walter reckoned the application simply removed superficial scurf, enabling the skin underneath to breathe again. In fact the recipe for this famous concoction, conceived by apothecary John Gowland, would have had today's health watchdogs howling in protest: the most active ingredient was mercuric chloride, which stripped off the top layer of skin. A gentler application was lavender water, used for scent and to soothe aches and pains; jasmine was also used regularly as scent.

A range of jewellery and trinkets could be purchased by ladies of means to complement their appearance at parties. One indispensable accessory was the fan, but wielded in the wrong hands it might be more of a burden than an ornament. The art of 'fluttering' could take several months to learn and, once mastered, would serve almost as a second language, capable of expressing all sorts of emotions. Needless to say, fans came in various styles and were often beautifully decorated with nature scenes, flowers, cherubs or illuminated poetry; some were even studded with diamonds and other jewels. One fashionable shop in Bath advertised its wares in the press, including several recognized brands of fan for the period:

MOORE'S UNIVERSAL TOY-SHOP

Among the new Articles are the Cestuses, Mulbrowk, Balloon, Gibraltar, and other Fans, pocket-books, boxes, gold-pins, lockets, bracelets, trinkets, ear-rings, tooth-pick cases, purses, Paris irons, combs that will not split ... a valuable assortment of penknives and scissars.

Dressing the Beau

The male's counterpart to the fan was his sword, an accoutrement worthy of only the best-bred gentlemen, and a common element of formal attire until the 1780s. The composer Haydn played at a concert with a sword buckled at his side; and when Warren Hastings began his trial at Westminster Hall in 1791 (see page 225) he wore a puce silk coat, a bag wig and a diamond-hilted sword. Edward Austen-Leigh recalled the fashion:

> **The graceful carriage of each weapon [sword and fan] was considered a test of high breeding. The clownish man was in danger of being tripped up by his sword getting between his legs ...**
>
> **Old gentlemen who had survived the fashion of wearing swords were known to regret the disuse of that custom, because it put an end to one way of distinguishing those who had, from those who had not, been used to good society. To wear the sword easily was an art which, like swimming and skating, required to be learned in youth. Children could practise it early with their toy swords adapted to their size.**

The appearance most characteristic of the upper class male of the Regency period was that of the fop, or dandy. While Napoleon rampaged over Europe, the English gentleman reached his apogee in this rarefied creature who made a profession out of idleness. Jane Austen's novels are littered with them: Sir Walter Elliott in *Persuasion*, Frank Churchill in *Emma*, and in *Mansfield Park* the characters of Henry Crawford and Mr Yates. In real life, no one exemplified the form better than 'Beau' Brummell (1778–1840), the celebrated master of taste whose immortal motto ran:

To be truly elegant one should not be noticed.

The hallmark of elegance for George Brummell was sober perfection, not the showy display so popular among his predecessors. The following description, in William Gardiner's *Music and Friends*, of a 'gay Lionel' of the 1780s was typical of a flashy gentleman of the time:

His coat was a bright grey mixture, approaching to white, with a black silk collar and silver cord buttons, black satin small-clothes, with sky-blue ribbed silk stockings. At the knee-band was a small diamond buckle, and a larger and costly one ornamented the toe of the shoe. Rich lace ruffles set off the hand, and a cocked hat surmounted a head of hair dressed in the height of French fashion [powdered, with curls around the face].

One of the most flamboyant of men was the Prince of Wales who, according to Gardiner, dressed for the opening of Parliament in November 1783 in:

Black velvet, most richly embroidered with gold, and pink spangles, and lined with pink satin. His shoes had pink heels; his hair was pressed much at the sides, and very full frizzed, with two very small curls at the bottom.

In the 1790s all this fancy ornamentation was abolished, largely as a result of Brummell's example, which first Londoners and then country squires took as their lead. An immaculate, well-tailored appearance came to distinguish the cultured gentleman from his shabbier contemporaries. The coat was cut away to form a swallowtail at the back, allowing it to be worn easily on horseback. This morning dress, so called because it was worn in the morning when gentlemen went out riding, remained the standard style well into the Regency period. Knee breeches were replaced by pantaloons tucked into hussar or 'Wellington' boots; the cut of the trouser and shape of the man's leg became all important – so much so that some gentlemen wore artificial calves to improve their curvature. Particularly fastidious men tended to remain standing at parties, to avoid any creasing.

Having a 'fine leg' was one of Brummell's chief concerns. According to the writer William Hazlitt, the essence of dandyism is contained in the story that Brummell passed his morning hours trying to decide which was his favourite leg. Punctiliousness in dress and manners was the by-word for the dandy. Brummell's biographer and personal assistant Captain Jesse gave this account of the man whom he had observed at close quarters for many years:

> **His chief aim was to avoid anything marked; one of his aphorisms being that the severest mortification a gentleman could incur was to attract observation in the street by his outward appearance. He exercised the most correct taste in the selection of each article of apparel … The collar was so large that, before being folded down, it completely hid his head and face … Brummell was one of the first who revived and improved the taste for dress, and his great innovation was effected upon neckcloths … if the cravat was not properly tied at the first effort, or inspired impulse, it was always rejected. His valet was coming downstairs one day with a quantity of tumbled neckcloths under his arm, and being interrogated on the subject, solemnly replied: 'Oh, they are our failures.' Practice like this, of course, made him perfect, and his tie soon became a model that was imitated.**

The trick was to dress down at the same time as dressing up. By presenting himself so uniformly, and with such military precision, any deviation from the norm was calculated for effect. In a playful way Brummell would allow the understatement in his attire to flirt dangerously with overstatement. Jesse explains that his costume went as follows:

> **In the morning his outward man was quiet, and never varied; it consisted of a snuff-coloured surtout [frock coat], with a velvet collar a shade darker, and a real cashmere waistcoat … Dark blue trousers, very pointed boots, the unrivalled white neckcloth, a black hat a little larger at the crown than at the circumference of his head, and primrose kid gloves, completed his attire. In summer the cashmere waistcoat was exchanged for a light Valentia one.**

Though an admirer of the Beau, Jesse had many a chuckle about his eccentricity and could easily spend a couple of hours secretly watching his master perform the morning ritual:

The door of his bedroom being always left a little open to carry
on the conversation, the secrets of his dressing-table were, much
to my entertainment, revealed in the glass upon the mantelpiece
of his salon. I think I see him now, standing without his wig, in
his dressing-trousers, before the glass, going through the manual
exercise of the flesh-brush ... when the strigil of pig's bristles was
laid aside, he looked very much like a man in the scarlet-fever, and
a flannel was accordingly put on ... Before 'robing', the Beau took
a dentist's mirror in one hand, and a pair of tweezers in the other,
and thus nobly armed, closely scanned his forehead and well-shaved
chin, and did not lay them down till he had drawn, with a resolution
and perseverance truly extraordinary, and totally regardless of the
exquisite pain the removal of each elegant extract must have caused
him—every stray hair that could be detected on the surface of his
venerable mug!
... Every hair being at last in its right place, and his hat a little on
one side, with an umbrella under his arm, his body slightly bent, and
his tie reflected in his lucent boots, he proceeded, creeping, snail-like
down the street.
... In the street, Brummell never took off his hat to any one, not
even to a lady; it would have been difficult to replace it in the same
position, for it was invariably put on with care, and at a prescribed
angle; added to which his wig might have been disturbed—a
catastrophe too dreadful to be wantonly encountered.

Manners Makyth Man

Once abroad in the clubs, balls, coffee-houses and private houses of society,
Brummell was equally influential on matters of etiquette. He rarely made
any pronouncements on fashion, preferring instead to give an enigmatic
shrug or a wince or utter a rhetorical remark. Sometimes he might let an
aspiring dandy know that his trousers had 'bad knees', without ever letting
it be known what good knees were. He disliked rural life and thought eating
vegetables was quite vulgar, once declaring that he had had to reject an
aristocratic candidate for marriage when he discovered she ate cabbage. A
similar cause for outrage was the pea, which it was customary to eat off the
back of one's knife. A famous anecdote about Brummell was recalled by
Edward Austen-Leigh:

When he was questioned about his parents, he replied that it was long since he had heard of them, but that he imagined the worthy couple must have cut their own throats by that time, because when he last saw them they were eating peas with their knives. Yet Brummell's father had probably lived in good society; and was certainly able to put his son into a fashionable regiment, and to leave him £30,000.

On manners in general the Whig statesman Edmund Burke spoke for conventional wisdom, which considered them to be essential to society's well-being; they represented nothing less than the accumulated wisdom of civilization. If morals were the principles by which right should be distinguished from wrong, manners were the outward expression of these principles in relationships. Not surprisingly, therefore, people were expected to pay heed to this code of behaviour in whatever situation they found themselves, public or private. Manners were even more important than the law, as Burke expressed in 1795 in one of his *Letters on a Regicide Peace*:

The law touches us but here and there, and now and then. Manners are what vex and soothe us, corrupt or purify, exalt or debase, barbarize or refine us, by a constant, steady, uniform, insensible operation, like that of the air we breathe in. They give their whole form and colour to our lives.

Contemporary thinking ran along the lines that virtues were more likely to gain affection if they were presented in well-mannered behaviour. Jane Austen advised her niece Fanny Knight not to marry John Plumptre; even though his undoubted virtues made him a good prospect in theory, Fanny could not forget his awkwardness. Lord Chesterfield expanded on the issue in one of his many letters of advice to his son in 1774:

An awkward address [social manner], ungraceful attitudes and actions, and a certain left-handiness (if I may use that word) loudly proclaim low education and low company; for it is impossible to suppose that a man can have frequented good company, without having catched something, at least, of their air and motions ... The very accoutrements of a man of fashion are grievous incumbrances to a vulgar man. He is at a loss what to do with his hat, when it is not upon his head; his cane (if unfortunately he wears one) is at perpetual war with every cup of tea or coffee he drinks; destroys them first, and then accompanies them in their fall … His clothes fit him so ill, and constrain him so much, that he seems rather their prisoner than their proprietor. He presents himself in company, like a criminal in a court of justice; his very air condemns him.

In *Emma*, Emma Woodhouse and Harriet Smith discuss the relative merits, in terms of gentlemanly assets, of the near-perfect Mr Knightley and the tenant farmer and aspiring gentleman Mr Martin. Harriet speaks first, attempting to defend Mr Martin, to whom she is attracted (and will eventually marry):

'Certainly, he is not like Mr. Knightley. He has not such a fine air and way of walking as Mr. Knightley. I see the difference plain enough. But Mr. Knightley is so very fine a man!'

'Mr. Knightley's air is so remarkably good that it is not fair to compare Mr. Martin with him. You might not see one in a hundred with gentleman so plainly written as in Mr. Knightley. But he is not the only gentleman you have been lately used to. What say you to Mr. Weston and Mr. Elton? Compare Mr. Martin with either of them. Compare their manner of carrying themselves; of walking; of speaking; of being silent. You must see the difference.'

'Oh yes!—there is a great difference. But Mr. Weston is almost an old man. Mr. Weston must be between forty and fifty.'

'Which makes his good manners the more valuable. The older a person grows, Harriet, the more important it is that their manners should not be bad; the more glaring and disgusting any loudness, or coarseness, or awkwardness becomes. What is passable in youth is detestable in later age. Mr. Martin is now [aged 24] awkward and abrupt; what will he be at Mr. Weston's time of life?'

In and Out for Dinner

Restricted means of travel in Jane Austen's day and the relatively few members of the gentry living within easy reach made hosting a dinner party a somewhat repetitive affair. As the author declares in *Persuasion* through the character of Mary Musgrove, 'One knows beforehand what the dinner will be like, and who will be there.' Mrs Leigh-Perrot boasted of having 30 families to dine with in her affluent area near Bath; but in most neighbourhoods there would have been far fewer and the same families tended to be invited again and again.

However well known the guests, conventions had to be observed throughout the duration of a dinner party. Once all the guests had arrived and were ready to eat, they would proceed to the dining room in a set order, though the form for this was changing during Jane Austen's lifetime. Traditionally all the ladies entered first, followed by the men. In *Pride and Prejudice*, written in 1796, the ladies at Mrs Bennet's dinner party are already seated when the men come into the dining room and Mr Bingley therefore has the opportunity to choose who to sit next to, and naturally it is Jane Bennet. Later etiquette dictated that each gentleman should offer an arm to his chosen or allotted lady and they would enter the room together. The host always escorted the female guest of the highest social position, a custom the appalling Mrs Elton in *Emma* cannot wait to take advantage of to show off her newly elevated status:

> **Dinner was on table. Mrs. Elton, before she could be spoken to, was ready; and before Mr. Woodhouse had reached her with his request to be allowed to hand her into the dinner-parlour, was saying— 'Must I go first? I really am ashamed of always leading the way.'**

The principal male and female guests were seated next to their respective hostess and host, while the rest of the company sat with whom they liked in alternating genders. At large houses two full courses might be offered, of which each consisted of a huge range of dishes, as described earlier. Between courses private conversation paused while servants with sharp hearing cleared away the dishes, empty or otherwise. At the outset of this *service à la Française*, guests would be told whether or not to expect a second course so they could pace themselves. At the end of the second course the entire table was cleared, including the tablecloth, and the dessert brought. (The word 'dessert' is derived from the French *desservir*, meaning 'to clear the table'.)

Dessert usually consisted of sweet finger-food. By the 19th century cheese had made its appearance on the dining table. Wine did not usually appear until this stage. A gentleman would pour a glass for the lady next to him and himself and drink a toast of his choice. After one or, at most, two glasses of wine, the ladies would withdraw. The appropriate time for this was judged by the hostess, who would rise to her feet and be followed out of the dining room by her female guests. Again, the order for departure followed a strict order of precedence, by rank and age. It did sometimes happen that seniority in one category might clash with that in the other. In *Mansfield Park*, Mrs Norris spitefully advises her niece Fanny on what she must and must not do when invited out to dine:

> The nonsense and folly of people's stepping out of their rank and trying to appear above themselves, makes me think it right to give *you* a hint, Fanny, now that you are going into company without any of us; and I do beseech and entreat you not to be putting yourself forward, and talking and giving your opinion as if you were one of your cousins— ... *That* will never do, believe me. Remember, wherever you are, you must be the lowest and last; and though Miss Crawford is in a manner at home at the Parsonage, you are not to be taking place of her. And as to coming away at night, you are to stay just as long as Edmund chuses. Leave him to settle that.

Married women took precedence over the unmarried. This could cause a good deal of resentment in an elder sister if the younger one should marry before her and take her place in the family hierarchy.

After the women had withdrawn, the men could spend an hour or so drinking and talking without inhibition. The women meanwhile were pitched together in the drawing room with no alcohol or male company. In *Sense and Sensibility*, the author describes the scene at the Dashwoods' dinner party where there was an unfortunate 'poverty of conversation':

> When the ladies withdrew to the drawing-room after dinner, this poverty was particularly evident, for the gentlemen had supplied the discourse with some variety—the variety of politics, inclosing land, and breaking horses—but then it was all over, and one subject only engaged the ladies till coffee came in, which was the comparative heights of Harry Dashwood, and Lady Middleton's second son William, who were nearly of the same age.
>
> Had both the children been there, the affair might have been determined too easily by measuring them at once; but as Harry only was present, it was all conjectural assertion on both sides, and everybody had a right to be equally positive in their opinion, and to repeat it over and over again as often as they liked.

Conversation was the all-important ingredient of dinner parties for Jane Austen and there are many references in her novels to the stultifying boredom they commonly induced. Her own experiences must have provided plenty of material, the details of which she would often pass on to Cassandra in her letters. One dinner party held locally in the nearby village of Ashe in November 1800 is an example:

> **We sat down 14 to dinner in the study, the dining room being not habitable from the Storm's having blown down its chimney.—Mrs Bramston talked a good deal of nonsense, which Mr Bramston & Mr Clerk seemed almost equally to enjoy. There was a whist & a casino table, & six outsiders.—Rice & Lucy made love, Mat Robinson fell asleep, James & Mrs Augusta alternately read Dr Jenner's pamphlet on the cow pox, & I bestowed my company by turns on all.**

The expression 'made love' in Jane's letter does not mean what it does today. Courting couples would make love by kissing and touching affectionately, and would not have sexual intercourse until the wedding night. The interest in Dr Jenner here refers to his recent discovery of a vaccine against smallpox using a serum from the corresponding disease suffered by cows (the word 'vaccine' comes from the Latin for cow, *vaccus* – more on this and other diseases in the last chapter).

The final part of a dinner party would see the gentlemen rejoining the ladies in the drawing room. Formerly they would have gone through as a group, but by the end of the century the normal habit was for individuals to drift in when they wished. In summer the period known as the afternoon, between dinner and tea, might be spent out of doors, perhaps going for a walk in the early evening. 'Tea' was the name of the ceremony but coffee might be drunk instead. Dinner parties that went off particularly well might conclude with some impromptu dancing to the scraping of a fiddle or the tinkling of a harpsichord or piano.

Although there were many rules of etiquette to be followed, polite society in earlier generations had dictated a much stiffer, more formal regime than Jane Austen's contemporaries had to tolerate. Compared with other European nations, the English were perceived to have an easygoing air with regard to their manners and conversation. In the 1780s a French visitor to England, François de la Rochefoucauld, observed the general lack of strict protocol:

Formality counts for nothing and for the greater part of the time one pays no attention to it. Thus, judged by French standards, the English, and especially the women, seem lacking in polite behaviour. All the young people whom I have met in society in Bury [Bury St Edmunds, Suffolk] give the impression of being what we should call badly brought up: they hum under their breath, they whistle, they sit down in a large armchair and put their feet on another, they sit on any table in the room and do a thousand other things which would be ridiculous in France, but are done quite naturally in England.

Private Balls

Private balls were held at various times for local friends to attend. Wherever possible they would be scheduled to coincide with the appearance of the full moon, which, in the absence of street lighting, provided sufficient illumination for coachmen to see their way. If it was too dark or too muddy, some coachmen would refuse to travel.

Considering the amount of time spent by the average rural Georgian in routine living, an invitation to a local ball must have been a welcome diversion. The chief dances on these occasions were the hornpipe, cotillion, reels, country dance and, most majestic of all, the minuet, a difficult dance that often drew an admiring audience, as Jane Austen's nephew Edward Austen-Leigh recalled:

The stately minuet reigned supreme; and every regular ball commenced with it. It was a slow and solemn movement, expressive of grace and dignity, rather than of merriment. It abounded in formal bows and courtesies, with measured paces, forwards, backwards and sideways, and many complicated gyrations. It was executed by one lady and gentleman, amidst the admiration, or the criticism, of surrounding spectators ... Those ladies who intended to dance minuets, used to distinguish themselves from the others by wearing a particular kind of lappet on their head-dress ... Gloves immaculately clean were considered requisite for its due performance, while gloves a little soiled were thought good enough for a country dance; and accordingly some prudent ladies provided themselves with two pairs for their several purposes.

In Fanny Burney's novel *Camilla*, the vulgar Mr Dubster is not allowed to dance with Camilla, to her relief, because he has mislaid one of his gloves:

> **The chief occupation of the evening was the interminable country dance, in which all could join in. This dance presented a great show of enjoyment, but it was not without its peculiar troubles. The ladies and gentlemen were ranged apart from each other in opposite rows, so that the facilities for flirtation, or interesting intercourse, were not so great as might have been desired by both parties. Much heart-burning and discontent sometimes arose as to who should stand above whom, and especially as to who was entitled to the high privilege of calling and leading off the first dance: and no little indignation was felt at the lower end of the room when any of the leading couples retired prematurely from their duties, and did not condescend to dance up and down the whole set.**

Traditionally ladies were condemned to dance for the whole evening with the same partner, an aspect of ballroom etiquette that persisted in some circles, though less so by the time Jane Austen was dancing. Eliza Hancock, that happy-go-lucky Francophile, expressed her dismay at the staid custom in a letter to her cousin Phylly in 1780:

> **Upon the whole your ball must have been a very agreeable one. The circumstance however of not being able to dance with the person you wished must have lessened your amusement. It is a vexation you would not have had in this country [France] as it is the custom to change your partner every dance ... I should think it must be the most tiresome thing in the whole world to have the same partner (& maybe a bad one) the whole evening, while perhaps there are twenty others in the room whom you would have preferred.**

The rebellious streak that lurked within Jane's nature caused her to flout these rules when she apparently became obsessed about dancing with the Irishman Tom Lefroy at a local ball. Her sister had warned Jane by letter not to be 'too particular' in her attention to him, thereby risking 'exposing' her feelings to him.

At the end of a ball when dancers were flagging, it was usual for hosts to provide supper before guests embarked on perhaps a long and cold journey home. Everyone would sit down to a reasonably hearty hot snack. Anything lighter might be thought skimping on one's hosting duties – Mrs Weston's proposal in *Emma* to serve merely sandwiches at the end of a private ball is pronounced 'an infamous fraud upon the rights of men and women'.

Courting Rules and Transgressions

In general Jane supported the conventions of her time that dictated the conduct of relationships between the sexes and was critical of those who did not obey them, because of the possible stress and humiliation that might be caused. It was certainly not normal to pay so much attention to a man as Jane did to Mr Lefroy without his first having proposed to her. Her experience may have inspired something in the scene in *Sense and Sensibility* when Marianne, the character representing the romantic and wild 'sensibility' in woman, throws caution to the wind and lets her emotions fly to the wonderful Mr Willoughby:

> **She had no eyes for anyone else. Everything he did was right, everything he said was clever. If dancing formed the amusement of the night, they were partners for half the time; and when obliged to separate for a couple of dances, were careful to stand together and scarcely spoke a word to anybody else. Such conduct made them of course most exceedingly laughed at; but ridicule could not shame, and seemed hardly to provoke them.**

Conventions in courtship were established to protect a female, in particular, and to some extent a male, from falling foul of improper conduct on the part of the other sex. A man who paid too much attention to women without being serious about his intentions could make a fool of a young lady who was taken in by his advances. In *Persuasion* the honourable Captain Wentworth makes the mistake of paying too much attention to Louisa Musgrove and all her friends expect him to propose. Various complications prevent him from openly asking his real love Anne Elliot for her hand and in his desperation to declare himself to her before he has to leave on naval duty he breaks another code of etiquette by hastily conveying his message in writing. Men and women who were not engaged were forbidden by custom to send letters to each other. Jane Austen went so far as to say that those people who conducted relationships without due regard to courting etiquette, such as those with 'lively' manners, were likely also to be immoral, or at least lack discretion.

All this made conversation more difficult than it might have been without any social restraints. Couples had to be extremely careful about what they said to each other and people could not express any personal interest in members of the opposite sex, which might be construed as indicating some intent to marry. Certainly young men and women who were not related could not be left alone to talk in private, or share a carriage together.

Body language and gestures, such as nods, frowns, smiles, bows and curtsies, were all useful ways of conveying one's feelings discreetly. A handshake was not a mode of greeting but an expression of some intimacy which would only be made in a situation of confidence. In *Pride and Prejudice* Elizabeth Bennet tries talking to the taciturn Darcy at a private ball:

> They stood for some time without speaking a word; and she began to imagine that their silence was to last through the two dances, and at first was resolved not to break it; till suddenly fancying that it would be the greater punishment to her partner to oblige him to talk, she made some slight observation on the dance. He replied, and was again silent. After a pause of some minutes, she addressed him a second time with:
>
> 'It is *your* turn to say something now, Mr. Darcy—I talked about the dance, and *you* ought to make some kind of remark on the size of the room, or the number of couples.'
>
> He smiled, and assured her that whatever she wished him to say should be said. 'Very well.—That reply will do for the present.— Perhaps by and by I may observe that private balls are much pleasanter than public ones.—But *now* we may be silent.'
>
> 'Do you talk by rule then, while you are dancing?'

A rather more flirtatious conversation is related in *Northanger Abbey* between Catherine Morland and Henry Tilney, her partner at a ball in Bath:

> I have hitherto been very remiss, madam, in the proper attentions of a partner here; I have not yet asked you how long you have been in Bath; whether you were ever here before; whether you have been at the Upper Rooms, the theatre, and the concert; and how you like the

place altogether. I have been very negligent—but are you now at leisure to satisfy me in these particulars? If you are I will begin directly.

After a series of questions and answers about these matters, Mr Tilney continues in mock humility:

'I see what you think of me,' said he gravely—'I shall make but a poor figure in your journal tomorrow.'

'My journal!'

'Yes, I know exactly what you will say: Friday, went to the Lower Rooms; wore my sprigged muslin robe with blue trimmings—plain black shoes—appeared to much advantage; but was strangely harassed by a queer, half-witted man, who would make me dance with him, and distressed me by his nonsense.'

'Indeed I shall say no such thing.'

'Shall I tell you what you ought to say?'

'If you please.'

'I danced with a very agreeable young man, introduced by Mr. King; had a great deal of conversation with him—seems a most extraordinary genius—hope I may know more of him. *That*, madam, is what I *wish* you to say.'

'But, perhaps, I keep no journal.'

'Perhaps you are not sitting in this room, and I am not sitting by you. These are points in which a doubt is equally possible.

Catherine at this point is making her formal debut in society as a young woman, whereupon all the qualities of her breeding and upbringing will be scrutinized by every interested party. By being admitted to the grown-up social events for the first time she is effectively entering the 'marriage market'. The time chosen to 'come out' varied depending on the status of other siblings. If an elder sister remained unmarried, a younger one might be held back a year or so until her sister was established in a relationship. It did sometimes happen that guests at private parties were unsure whether a young lady was formally 'out' or not, as in the case of Fanny Price in *Mansfield Park*. Mary Crawford asks the question:

'I begin now to understand you all, except Miss Price,' said Miss Crawford, as she was walking with the Mr. Bertrams [Tom and

Edmund]. 'Pray, is she out, or is she not?—I am puzzled.—She dined at the Parsonage, with the rest of you, which seemed like being *out*; and yet she says so little, that I can hardly suppose she *is*.'

Edmund, to whom this was chiefly addressed, replied, 'I believe I know what you mean—but I will not undertake to answer the question. My cousin is grown up. She has the age and sense of a woman, but the outs and not outs are beyond me.'

When it came to the crunch time of proposing marriage, a man had two options: the verbal 'sudden-death' approach, or the more formal method of writing it in a letter. To propose verbally, the man would have to do some manoeuvring to be alone with the woman of his choice, something which in itself would betray his intentions. The proposal would need to establish the suitor's credentials, including whatever means he could offer to support her, but financial negotiations, including the size of her marriage portion, would be conducted later with her father if the outcome was positive. Should the man be rejected, the woman was bound to keep the matter under wraps. Such secrecy did allow a gentleman to try his luck again were circumstances to change for the better. In *Pride and Prejudice* Jane Austen portrays the pig-headed arrogance of some gentlemen who, like her character the Revd Mr Collins in his pursuit of Elizabeth Bennet, would not take 'No' for an answer:

'You must give me leave to flatter myself that your refusal of my addresses is merely words of course. My reasons for believing it are briefly these:—It does not appear to me that the establishment I can offer would be any other than highly desirable; and you should take it into farther consideration that in spite of your manifold attractions, it is by no means certain that another offer of marriage may ever be made you. Your portion is unhappily so small that it will in all likelihood undo the effects of your loveliness and amiable qualifications. As I must therefore conclude that you are not serious in your rejection of me, I shall chuse to attribute it to your wish of increasing my love by suspense, according to the usual practice of elegant females.'

A proposal by letter could be addressed directly to the lady in question or to her father. Jane's niece Fanny Knight (daughter of her brother Edward) received such a letter from Sir Edward Knatchbull:

Dear Miss Knight
Much as I flatter myself that a favourable reception will be given
to this communication; it is quite impossible for me to conceal the
anxiety with which I shall await your reply ... It is not from any
professions which I can make that I shall venture to found any claim
to your esteem. Allow me to say that you are the only person in whose
Society I can find Happiness and to whose example and care I could
entrust the welfare of my children.

Once engaged, the couple might still find it difficult to be alone. One means
of escape was a country walk; another, strangely, was the dance floor. With
the help of accompanying music and with their friends and relations seated
out of earshot, the couple could talk and hold hands more freely than in any
other social context.

Breaking off an engagement constituted a serious breach of etiquette and
was inadmissible for a gentleman, and only just allowable for a lady if she had
a good reason.

The Plain Wedding

There was no pomp and pageantry attached to weddings in Jane Austen's
day, all that being thought old-fashioned and vulgar. As the author said
of Emma Woodhouse's wedding, 'the parties have no taste for finery or
parade'. They were simple affairs, perfunctorily performed with due respect
to etiquette. Jane's niece Caroline recalled her half-sister Anna's wedding in
November 1814 to Ben Lefroy at Steventon (of which their father, James,
was still rector) as being typical of the time for genteel families. The occasion
began with the family setting off from the rectory for the church half a mile
down the road, with the women riding in the carriage and the men on foot.
Apart from the immediate family there seemed to be no other guests in the
church, which looked hardly different from normal:

[There was] no stove to give warmth, no flowers to give colour or
brightness, no friends, high or low, to offer their good wishes and
so to claim some interest in the great events of the day—all these
circumstances and deficiencies must, I think, have given a gloomy
air to our wedding. Mr Lefroy read the service, my father gave
his daughter away. The Clerk of course was there altho' I do not

> particularly remember him; but I am quite sure there was no one else
> in the church, nor was anyone else asked to the [wedding] breakfast,
> to which we sat down as soon as we got back [from the church] …
> The breakfast was such as best breakfasts then were: some variety of
> bread, hot rolls, buttered toast, tongue or ham and eggs. The addition
> of chocolate at one end of the table, and the wedding cake in the
> middle, marked the speciality of the day … Soon after breakfast, the
> bride and groom departed. They had a long day's journey before them,
> to Hendon [north of London]; the other Lefroys went home; and in
> the afternoon my mother and I went to Chawton … The servants had
> cake and punch in the evening … Such were the wedding festivities of
> Steventon in 1814.

It seems that not until after the couple had departed was their happiness
toasted. Some weddings did not even put on a special reception and the
newly-weds drove directly from the church to their new home. The wedding
dress would have been elegant but nothing spectacular, and could well have
been 'Sunday best'. A description of Anna's bridal gown on this occasion at
Steventon was given later by one of her own daughters. The dress was of:

> Fine white muslin, and over it a soft silk shawl, white, shot with
> primrose, with embossed white satin flowers.

What was of most importance to the bride, and for that matter the mother
too, was the trousseau. The bride's clothes might well have required a special
trip to London to find suitable outfits for early married life, and perhaps a
honeymoon, though the latter was not yet customary outside the aristocracy
and even then would not necessarily be undertaken in private. Early married
life, likewise, might include a sister of the bride sharing the couple's home.

Calling Cards

On moving into a new area, people of the genteel classes would make
their arrival known to other members of their class in the neighbourhood
by calling on them and leaving their calling, or visiting, card. By this
means they could introduce themselves and perhaps leave an invitation.
In *Persuasion* the Elliots, upon moving into their new home in Bath, are
inundated with callers:

Bath more than answered their expectations in every respect. Their house was undoubtedly the best in Camden Place, their drawing-rooms had many decided advantages over all the others which they had either seen or heard of, and the superiority was not less in the style of the fitting-up, or the taste of the furniture. Their acquaintance was exceedingly sought after. Every body was wanting to visit them. They had drawn back from many introductions, and still were perpetually having cards left by people of whom they knew nothing.

Similar to a business card today, a calling card bore the visitor's name, title and residence, and would have been conveyed by the maid to the mistress of the house, who then decided whether or not to receive the caller. The card system operated effectively as a method of social screening, to admit the acceptable and reject the undesirable. If the reply was 'not at home', this was code for not wishing to make the acquaintance. If a reciprocal card was formally presented to the visitor, this indicated there was a chance for the relationship to develop. The safest course for a visitor was to leave his or her card, usually placed on a silver tray in the hall, without asking if the mistress was at home. This would then oblige the mistress to reciprocate the call if she wished to pursue relations.

The Picturesque and the Gothic

If a 'bridal tour' was taken for a few weeks after a couple were married, it was fashionable at the end of the 18th century to view what was termed 'picturesque landscapes', most notably those of the Lake District. Now that roads and carriages had improved, it was easier to go on sight-seeing jaunts to different regions and to see at first hand the scenery recreated in paintings on exhibition in art galleries.

These were the years of the great Romantic painters: Turner, Constable, Reynolds, Gainsborough – all shared the view, through landscapes and portraits, that nature was something sublime. Love of the countryside and its representation in idyllic pastoral scenes moved young men and women everywhere to try their own hands at the new style, and 'package' the product into something picturesque. The poet William Combe set the task to verse in *The Tour of Dr Syntax in Search of the Picturesque*, published in 1809:

> What man of taste my right will doubt,
> To put things in, or leave things out?
> 'Tis more than right, it is a duty,
> If we consider landscape beauty:
> He ne'er will as an artist shine
> Who copies nature line by line;
> Whoe'er from nature takes a view
> Must copy and improve it too:
> To heighten ev'ry work of art,
> Fancy should take an active part.

Much depended on how one beheld the view before one's eyes. Jane Austen must have heard her contemporaries earnestly discussing the issues in arty language – mere dabblers risked finding themselves out of their depth, as she describes in *Northanger Abbey*:

> They were viewing the country with the eyes of persons accustomed to drawing, and decided on its capability of being formed into pictures, with all the eagerness of real taste. Here Catherine was quite lost. She knew nothing of drawing—nothing of taste: and she listened to them with an attention which brought her little profit, for they talked in phrases which conveyed scarcely any idea to her. The little which she could understand, however, appeared to contradict the very few notions she had entertained on the matter before. It seemed as if a good view were no longer to be taken from the top of an high hill, and that a clear blue sky was no longer a proof of a fine day. She was heartily ashamed of her ignorance.

As for Jane, her enjoyment at exhibitions was not restricted to viewing the paintings themselves. In 1811 she mentioned in a letter to Cassandra that she visited the gallery of the British Institution in Pall Mall, where her 'preference for Men & Women always inclines me to attend more to the company than the sight [of the paintings]'. At an exhibition of portraits two years later she played another game, this time identifying characters in her novels:

> Henry & I went to the [Society of Painters] Exhibition in Spring Gardens. It is not thought a good collection, but I was very well

pleased—particularly (pray tell Fanny) with a small portrait of Mrs. Bingley, excessively like her. I went in hopes of seeing one of her sister, but there was no Mrs. Darcy;—perhaps however, I may find her in the Great Exhibition [at the British Academy in Somerset Place] which we shall go to, if we have time;—I have no chance of her in the collection of Sir Joshua Reynolds's Paintings which is now shewing in Pall Mall, & which we are also to visit. Mrs. Bingley's is exactly herself, size, shaped face, features & sweetness; there never was a greater likeness. She is dressed in a white gown, with green ornaments, which convinces me of what I had always supposed, that green was a favourite colour with her. I daresay Mrs D. will be in Yellow.

By the turn of the 19th century the Romantic spirit, which had started out producing soft tranquil landscapes, had evolved into a more radical movement in which the avant-garde rejected the establishment and its authority and instead the imagination of the individual triumphed. The beauty and power of nature, as represented in paintings such as Turner's *Snowstorm: Hannibal and His Army Crossing the Alps*, was being corrupted by the new money-making ethics of urban life. Poets such as William Blake, William Wordsworth and Samuel Taylor Coleridge saw in such upheavals as the French Revolution an attempt to liberate humanity from the curse of rational order and industrial 'progress', which they believed disturbed the wonderful harmony of nature, as William Wordsworth wrote in 1805 in his lines on the French Revolution:

Bliss was it in that dawn to be alive,
But to be young was very heaven!—Oh! times,
In which the meagre, stale, forbidding ways
Of custom, law, and statute, took at once
The attraction of a country in romance!
When Reason seemed the most to assert her rights,
When most intent on making of herself
A prime Enchantress—to assist the work,
Which then was going forward in her name!
Not favoured spots alone, but the whole earth,
The beauty wore of promise, that which sets
(As at some moment might not be unfelt

Among the bowers of paradise itself)
The budding rose above the rose full blown.
What temper at the prospect did not wake
To happiness unthought of? The inert
Were roused, and lively natures rapt away!
... Not in Utopia, subterranean fields,
Or some secreted island, Heaven knows where!
But in the very world, which is the world
Of all of us,—the place where in the end
We find our happiness, or not at all!

The next generation of Romantic poets – Shelley, Byron, Keats – developed the theme and helped to make the poetry of Chaucer and Milton fashionable again. From the preface to Blake's long poem *Milton* came the words of the famous anthem *Jerusalem*, contrasting his beatific vision of ancient Albion with the present land of 'dark satanic mills' created by the Industrial Revolution.

An offshoot of this radical mood was the proliferation of Gothic novels – romantic mysteries set in remote ghostly places. One of the first of the type, and a harbinger of the Romantic movement, was Horace Walpole's nightmare-inspired novel *The Castle of Otranto*, published in 1764. Similar melodramatic tales, which flooded the market in the next few decades, caused a certain amount of alarm among parents and teachers about the influence this popular fiction was having on young adults, principally young women. An article that appeared in 1799 in *The Lady's Monthly Museum* from a fictitious mother about her teenage daughter expressed this concern. Her daughter ...

... has acquired a most unfortunate propensity to reading;– not that I disapprove of reading, Madam; but she subscribes to a circulating library, and reads nothing in the world but novels – nothing but novels, Madam, from morning to night. – She is about eighteen; has been a year and a half from school ... I am afraid she will read herself into a consumption for she already looks so pale ... The maid is generally dispatched to the library two or three times in the day, to change books. One week she will read in the following order: *Excessive Sensibility, Refined Delicacy, Disinterested Love, Sentimental Beauty,* etc. In the next come *Horrid Mysteries, Haunted*

Caverns, Black Towers, Direful Incantations, and an endless list
of similar titles.

Her father finds fault; I scold; but all in vain.

One very popular Gothic writer of the time was Ann Radcliffe, whose *The Mysteries of Udolpho* (1794) Jane Austen satirized in *Northanger Abbey*. The following extract from Radcliffe's novel reads like countless horror stories written since, but at the time it was a new style of writing:

A return of the noise again disturbed her; it seemed to come from that part of the room which communicated with the private staircase, and she instantly remembered the odd circumstance of the door having been fastened, during the preceding night, by some unknown hand. Her late alarming suspicion concerning its communication also occurred to her. Her heart became faint with terror. Half raising herself from the bed, and gently drawing aside the curtain, she looked towards the door of the staircase, but the lamp that burned on the hearth spread so feeble a light through the apartment, that the remote parts of it were lost in shadow. The noise, however, which she was convinced came from the door, continued. It seemed like that made by the undrawing of rusty bolts, and often ceased, and was then renewed more gently, as if the hand that occasioned it was restrained by a fear of discovery. While Emily kept her eyes fixed on that spot, she saw the door move, and then slowly open, and perceived something enter the room, but the extreme duskiness prevented her distinguishing what it was. Almost fainting with terror, she had yet sufficient command over herself to check the shriek that was escaping from her lips, and letting the curtain drop from her hand, continued to observe in silence the motions of the mysterious form she saw. It seemed to glide along the remote obscurity of the apartment, then paused, and, as it approached the hearth, she perceived, in the stronger light, what appeared to be a human figure.

More serious fiction took the form of social realism, which had only begun in novel form earlier in the century through such writers as Daniel Defoe (*Robinson Crusoe*), Samuel Richardson (*Sir Charles Grandison*), Henry Fielding (*Tom Jones*) and Oliver Goldsmith (*The Vicar of Wakefield*). Their female counterparts were now developing the genre. Fanny Burney and

Maria Edgeworth, like Jane Austen after them, wrote about contemporary morals and manners and especially how they affected the lives of women. Of Burney's novels, *Evelina* was an instant hit with the public and remained the best loved of that genre until Jane Austen took up the mantle. In France, Laclos' scandalous novel, *Les Liaisons Dangereuses*, was published in 1782 and quite possibly influenced Jane Austen in her drafting of the unpublished *Lady Susan*, about a woman who is a bad mother and a dazzling temptress.

The Romantic and Gothic styles, which began in literature and spread to art, naturally extended their influence into architecture and landscape gardening. While classical symmetry remained the predominant theme in Georgian England, a growing interest in irregular picturesque forms took hold of people's imaginations. Horace Walpole himself designed his rococo villa at Strawberry Hill, Twickenham, by combining the classical with Gothic fantasy:

One must have taste to be sensible of the beauties of Grecian architecture; one only wants passions to feel Gothic ... It is difficult for the noblest Grecian temple to convey half so many impressions to the mind as a cathedral does of the best Gothic taste ... The priests exhausted their knowledge of the passions in composing edifices whose pomp, mechanism, vaults, tombs, painted windows, gloom and perspective infused such sensations of romantic devotion.

Elements of this Gothic style spread out across English gardens in the form of temples, bridges, follies and fake ruins set amid undulating lawns, streams and cascades. This was the age of the great Lancelot 'Capability' Brown (1715–83), whose nickname derived from his assessments of his clients' land as having 'great capability of improvement'. Brown endeavoured to capture the rambling spirit of nature in a picturesque setting that could be appreciated in the view from the house. The park at Chatsworth in Derbyshire is probably the most famous example of his work and in *Pride and Prejudice* Elizabeth Bennet visits the gardens while on her northern tour. The fictional estate of Pemberley, belonging to Mr Darcy, is also described as having the sort of features typical of Brown's designs. There was a general open-door policy among the owners of grand houses that allowed strangers to be shown round their estates at any reasonable hour without appointment.

Brown's talented successor, Humphry Repton, developed his work by introducing a transitional stage between house and garden in the form of ornamented terraces, covered walkways and conservatories. One notable example was Adlestrop Park, set in the lovely Gloucestershire Cotswolds and similar in spirit to Walpole's Strawberry Hill. This had been the ancestral home of the Leigh family since the Reformation; Jane Austen's maternal grandfather was born there and her cousin James-Henry Leigh owned it while she was alive. Jane mentions Repton in *Mansfield Park* when urgent improvements to Sotherton Court are discussed. Mr Rushworth says of his fictional Elizabethan pile in Northamptonshire:

I declare, when I got back to Sotherton yesterday, it looked like a prison—quite a dismal old prison.'

'Oh! for shame!' cried Mrs. Norris. 'A prison, indeed! Sotherton Court is the noblest old place in the world.'

'It wants improvement, ma'am, beyond any thing. I never saw a place that wanted so much improvement in my life; and it is so forlorn that I do not know what can be done with it ... I hope I shall have some good friend to help me.'

'Your best friend upon such an occasion,' said Miss Bertram calmly, 'would be Mr. Repton, I imagine.'

'That is what I was thinking of. As he has done so well by Smith, I think I had better have him at once. His terms are five guineas a day.'

When the Napoleonic Wars resumed in 1803 with a renewed threat of invasion, many businesses, including landscape design, went into decline until a degree of economic stability returned.

Politics, War and Industry

The House of Commons, filled as it was with landowning aristocrats, behaved more like an exclusive club than a body representing the people. As the division between rich and poor became ever wider, so the cries for reform grew louder, while new industrial entrepreneurs wanted a slice of power – and respect – for themselves. Despite being ensconced in a rural backwater for much of her life, Jane Austen was an acute observer of how the old order was changing.

The aristocratic Whig party was splintering, a new Conservative party was gaining ground, and alert political consciences spawned various radical groups. The Austen family and their friends were among those who owned colonial plantations in the West Indies, which, on the back of slave labour, produced 80 per cent of England's imports. Britain was at war for much of Jane's lifetime. America won its independence the year after she was born. The Napoleonic Wars boosted national pride but peace came at a price, with a spiralling National Debt and attendant consequences for the labouring classes. When writing to his son, Lord Chesterfield advised him to avoid certain subjects in conversation: one was religion, the other politics. It was a view shared by many in Jane's circle, as she indicates in this passage from *Northanger Abbey*. Henry Tilney is talking to Catherine Morland and finds that his original topic of conversation about painting landscapes runs into a cul-de-sac:

> ... fearful of wearying her with too much wisdom at once, Henry suffered the subject to decline, and by an easy transition from a piece of rocky fragment and the withered oak which he had placed near its summit, to oaks in general, to forests, the enclosure of them, waste lands, crown lands and government, he shortly found himself arrived at politics; and from politics, it was an easy step to silence.

At War With France

Silence was the privilege of those not involved in running the country.
When Jane was an adolescent, the political barometer rose steadily with the
unfolding of events across the Channel that were to have a profound effect
on Britain for the rest of her life. The beginning of the French Revolution is
taken as 14 July1789, when the royal fortress prison of the Bastille, a hated
symbol of oppression, was stormed by the Parisian mob. Initial sympathy
went with the revolutionaries, whose valiant slogan 'Liberté, Egalité,
Fraternité' appealed to English idealists. William Blake championed their
cause and Charles James Fox, leader of the Whig party, called it 'the greatest
event that ever happened in the world'. But support ebbed away as reports
from refugees arriving at English ports hidden in fishing boats revealed
the true horror of the bloody massacre. The guillotining of the French
king produced shock and outrage in English statesmen, many of whom
determined to oppose this Reign of Terror. Whig politician Edmund Burke
stormed into the House of Commons and threw down a dagger on to the
floor, exclaiming:

> There's French fraternity for you! Such is the weapon which French
> Jacobins [hard-core Revolutionaries] would plunge into the heart of
> our beloved king.

But even in times of national alarm, Georgian politicians retained their
sense of humour. The playwright and politician Richard Sheridan spoiled
Burke's dramatic effect and set the House in uproar when he retorted:

> The gentleman, I see, has brought his knife with him, but where is
> his fork?

Parson Woodforde was in sombre mood when news of the French king's
execution reached him in his Norfolk rectory five days after the event,
as he recorded in his diary on 26 January 1793:

> I breakfasted, dined, &c. again at home. Nancy breakfasted, dined, &c.
> again at home. Dinner today Souse, Veal Pye and Calfs Heart rosted.
> Billy Bidewells People brought our Newspapers from Norwich. The
> King of France Louis 16 inhumanly and unjustly beheaded on Monday

last by his cruel, blood-thirsty Subjects. Dreadful times I am afraid are approaching to all Europe. France the foundation of all of it.

English Roman Catholics mourned the king's death in their churches up and down the country. The *Bath Chronicle* reported on 31 January:

> Sunday in several of our churches and other places of religious worship, funeral sermons were preached on the death of the unfortunate Louis; and on Monday the Catholic Chapel was hung with black, and solemn mass was said; at which all the French refugee Clergy now in Bath assisted; all the people of that nation, who have here found a shelter from the distractions in their own unhappy country, were also there. The scene was distressing – not a dry eye was within the walls of the Chapel.

Days after the death of Louis XVI a French Republic was formed and war was declared against Britain. For most of the next 20 years Britain, and other nations of Europe, would be at war with France, fighting battles halfway round the world, from India to the Caribbean. Curiously, nothing of this conflict is mentioned by Jane Austen in her letters and little in her novels. Yet it certainly impacted on her family.

Cassandra was engaged to be married to Tom Fowle, a former pupil of her father's, who was sent as chaplain with the British Expeditionary Force to the West Indies. He died there of yellow fever, and she remained unmarried for the rest of her life. Henry gave up studying to be a clergyman and signed up with the homebound Oxford Militia as a 'Gentleman to be Lieutenant'. For the next seven years he moved from base to base with his regiment, ready to defend the coast in the event of invasion. Francis and Charles were on naval duty in both the Revolutionary Wars (1793–1801) and the Napoleonic Wars fought at sea, from 1803 until the enemy fleets were destroyed at Trafalgar two years later. In February 1794 Eliza's husband, Jean Capot de Feuillide, was arrested in Paris and within hours of his trial was guillotined.

Having only recently spent eight years fighting the American War of Independence at great expense to the exchequer, one might ask why England should wish to go to war again, as indeed the radical William Cobbett argued:

> The obstacles to war were very great. There was the DEBT, which, by the unsuccessful American war, had been made to amount to *six*

times the amount of taxes in the reign of James II [1685–8]. There were, besides, heavy burdens entailed upon the country by that war on account of half-pay and of other things. The interests of the *people* of England manifestly pointed to peace: their wishes too were in favour of peace.

So what was the case for war? Cobbett described the predicament that Parliament was facing:

At the time when this war began, 1793, William Pitt, a son of the late Earl of Chatham, was Prime Minister. He had established what he called a SINKING FUND, and had adopted other measures for reducing the amount of the DEBT, which had now reached the fearful amount of *two hundred millions* and upwards. A new war was wholly incompatible with Pitt's schemes of reduction; and he, of course, would be, and he *really was, opposed to the war of* 1793, though he carried it on ... until the day of his death, which took place in 1806. And here we behold the all-ruling power of the aristocracy!

This body had, for many years, been divided into two 'parties', as they called them, bearing the two nick-names of Tories and Whigs. The Tories affected very great attachment to the *throne and the church*; the Whigs affected perfect *loyalty*, indeed, but surprising devotion to the *rights of the people*, though it was they who ... had made the Riot Act [a law of 1715 saying that if 12 or more disturb the peace they must disperse or be charged with felony]; so that, if they were the friends of the people, what must their enemies have been! The truth is, there was no difference, as far as regarded the people, between these two factions; their real quarrels were solely about *the division of the spoil*; for, whenever any contest arose between the *aristocracy* and the *people*, the two factions had always united in favour of the former; and thus it was in regard to that all-important question, the war against Republican France.

A revolution happening so near to their own shores scared the living daylights out of English politicians, not to mention King George III, who feared that insurrection fever might spread to England. Furthermore, there were enough propagandists working to this end. The most famous was the fearless journalist Thomas Paine, who had helped America to win its fight for independence from British sovereignty. Now back in England, Paine issued a robust defence of the ideals of the French Revolution in a book entitled *The Rights of Man* (1791), which was so incendiary that his printer refused to publish it for fear of prosecution. His treatise took the form of a reply to Burke's attack on the Revolution and he addressed it to George Washington, first president of the United States, as a model democratic republican. It is a very long tract and only the briefest extracts can be reproduced here:

> Mr. Burke with his usual outrage, abused the Declaration of the Rights of Man, published by the National Assembly of France, as the basis on which the constitution of France is built. This he calls 'paltry and blurred sheets of paper about the rights of man.' Does Mr. Burke mean to deny that man has any rights? If he does, then he must mean that there are no such things as rights anywhere, and that he has none himself; for who is there in the world but man? But if Mr. Burke means to admit that man has rights, the question then will be: What are those rights, and how man came by them originally?
>
> Though I mean not to touch upon any sectarian principle of religion, yet it may be worth observing, that the genealogy of Christ is traced to Adam. Why then not trace the rights of man to the creation of man? I will answer the question. Because there have been upstart governments, thrusting themselves between, and presumptuously working to un-make man ... Every history of the creation, and every traditionary account, whether from the lettered or unlettered world, however they may vary in their opinion or belief of certain particulars, agree in establishing one point: all men are born equal, and with equal natural right.

Paine went on to talk about man's rights as a member of society. Logically these natural rights extended to civil ones and together the members of a society should have the collective power to enforce their will. The obstacle to this usually lay in government:

> In casting our eyes over the world, it is extremely easy to distinguish the governments which have arisen out of society, or out of the social compact, from those which have not ... They may be all comprehended under three heads. First, Superstition. Secondly,

Power. Thirdly, the common interest of society and the common rights of man. The first was a government of priestcraft, the second of conquerors, and the third of reason.

He then came to the focus of his argument – the legitimacy of the English constitution:

A constitution is not a thing in name only, but in fact. It has not an ideal, but a real existence; and wherever it cannot be produced in a visible form, there is none. A constitution is a thing antecedent to a government, and a government is only the creature of a constitution. The constitution of a country is not the act of its government, but of the people constituting its government. It is the body of elements, to which you can refer, and quote article by article; and which contains the principles on which the government shall be established ... Can, then, Mr. Burke produce the English Constitution? If he cannot, we may fairly conclude that though it has been so much talked about, no such thing as a constitution exists, or ever did exist, and consequently that the people have yet a constitution to form.

... Mr. Burke will not, I presume, deny the position I have already advanced – namely, that governments arise either out of the people or over the people. The English Government is one of those which arose out of a conquest [the Norman Conquest of 1066], and not out of society, and consequently it arose over the people; and though it has been much modified from the opportunity of circumstances since the time of William the Conqueror, the country has never yet regenerated itself, and is therefore without a constitution.

... Much is to be learned from the French Constitution. Conquest and tyranny transplanted themselves with William the Conqueror from Normandy into England, and the country is yet disfigured with the marks. May, then, the example of all France contribute to regenerate the freedom which a province of it destroyed!

In the second part of his treatise Paine demanded a programme of social reforms to address the shocking condition of the poor, and on its eventual publication the provocateur became an instant celebrity, a champion of the ordinary man's right to a better life. The following year the French issued their Edict of Fraternity inviting the working classes of all nations to rise up and join the Revolution, and Paine was forced to flee. In his absence he was charged with treason and never returned to England.

There were good reasons why politicians should have feared an uprising in England. The vast majority of the population had no say in choosing their representatives in Parliament. Unless a man owned land – and seven out of eight did not – he could not vote. And no women, of course, had the vote. The ratio of Members of Parliament to the electorate was grossly disproportionate. Some boroughs with a small population returned several MPs, whereas new cities, such as Birmingham and Manchester, still had no constituency and therefore no representation in Westminster. With no system in place to regulate electoral boundaries, the situation became a scandal. One notorious example of these so-called 'rotten boroughs' was the old port of Dunwich in Suffolk, which, even after most of it had fallen into the sea and it was left with just 32 inhabitants, nevertheless kept its two MPs. Protesters cried out for reform, which did not come until 1832. As Cobbett said of this nationwide problem:

> The [English] people had begun, even during the American war [1775–83], to demand a REFORM IN THE COMMONS HOUSE OF PARLIAMENT as the only cure for existing evils. When the standard of the right of representation had been raised by thirty millions of people only twenty miles from them [i.e. in France], those of England could not be expected to be dead to the call. They were not; and it took no long time to convince our aristocracy that one of two things must take place; namely, that the French people must be compelled to return under their ancient yoke; or, that a change must take place in England, restoring to the people *the right of freely choosing their representatives.*
>
> ... The alternative was: *Parliamentary Reform,* or *put down the Republic of France.* The former ought to have been chosen; but the latter was resolved on, in spite of the acknowledged risk of failure; for, so much did the aristocracy dread the other alternative, that failure, compared with that, lost all its terrors. To war then they went; in war they continued for twenty-two years.

This attitude translated at a local level into pockets of absolute rule at the hands of the squire of the manor who behaved like a little king in his village. Jane Austen depicted a squire who was also an MP in Sir Thomas Bertram

(*Mansfield Park*). Like him, MPs would hope to count on the political support of their tenants and neighbouring landowners, who in return for their favour could rely on the MP's promotion in Parliament of their rights as landowners, which in turn gave them more power – effectively they ran the country.

When it came to war, all the machinery of recruitment was set in motion. Generals were responsible for manning their own regiments. Their recruiting officers, who would be local businessmen, went round persuading all and sundry to accept the king's shilling (the money paid to volunteers for joining up); while the Royal Navy press-ganged men in the ports. The attitudes of English folk to war were ambivalent at the time, as Robert Southey wrote early in the 19th century in one of his letters:

> They [the English] are ready and almost eager for the commencement of hostilities, because they are persuaded that war is unavoidable. The tremendous power of France seems rather to provoke than alarm them: volunteers are arming every where; and though every man shakes his head when he hears the taxes talked of, it is evident that they are ready to part with half they have, if the national exigencies call for it. A grievous evil in their military system is that there is so limited time of service. Hence arises the difficulty which the English find in recruiting their armies. The bounty money offered for a recruit during the war amounted sometimes to as much as twenty pieces of eight, a sum, burthensome indeed to the nation when paid to whole regiments, but little enough if it be considered as the price for which a man sells his liberty, for life. There would be no lack of soldiers were they enlisted for seven years. Half the peasantry in the country would like to wear a fine coat from the age of eighteen till five-and-twenty, and to see the world at the king's expense.

It was well known that the regular army in Britain was tiny compared with that of other European states. A year after the beginning of hostilities with France it stood at 45,000, compared with Prussia's 190,000. Not surprisingly, when at last it came to the final showdown with Napoleon at the Battle of Waterloo in 1815, the allied Anglo-Dutch force would have succumbed to the superior might of France had it not been for the intervention of Blücher's Prussian army at the eleventh hour.

Whereas regular soldiers enlisted indefinitely, those in the militias, such as Jane Austen's brother Henry, would have committed for seven years only and were restricted to home service. Every district in the country also had its association of volunteers, who were obliged by government to make contingency plans in case of invasion. The *Hampshire Chronicle* carried the following notice in 1798 detailing the minutes of the North Hampshire committee meeting, at which Jane's eldest brother James Austen was present:

At a MEETING of the COMMITTEE of the NORTH HANTS ASSOCIATION, held at the Town Hall, in Basingstoke, on Wednesday, the 23rd of May 1798.

Present,

THOMAS HALL, Esq. Chairman.

[Incls:] John Harwood, Esq., John Lovett, Esq., Rev. Mr Lefroy, Rev. Mr Powlett jun., Rev. John Harwood, Rev. James Austin [*sic*], Rev. Mr Dyson.

Resolved that under the existing circumstances, the underwritten Engagements shall be properly printed on separate sheets and a sufficient number be distributed to every Parish in this Northern District.

We, the undersigned, do engage, for the protection of our lives and properties, to supply Government with Waggons, Carts, and Horses, whensoever we are called upon by proper authority.

We do engage to form ourselves into Voluntary Association of Pioneers, under the Command of such Leaders, chosen from ourselves for every twenty-five men, as may be appointed by the Civil Authority of the County, and upon such Allowances as shall be generally arranged throughout the County.

We do engage to drive and take care of such Live Stock to such places of safety as may be directed.

We do engage, in case Government should find it necessary, to suffer ourselves to be trained to the Use of Arms in our Neighbourhood, once in every week, and that in case of an actual-Invasion, or Appearance of the Enemy, we will perform such Military Duties as shall be required within this Military District, which extends to no other Coast than those of Hants and Dorset, and to no inland County except Wilts.

After ten years of war with France, which never actually resulted in invasion of Britain, the Peace of Amiens was signed in 1802. Napoleon seemed to have established a stable government but 14 months later he declared himself Emperor of France and was really only drawing breath before waging the next onslaught, known as the Napoleonic Wars (which would last another 12 years, to 1815). In 1804 he assembled a large fleet ready to invade Britain. Fortunately the Royal Navy was equal to the task and chased the French ships from the Mediterranean to the Caribbean and back again, ending decisively in the Battle of Trafalgar in 1805.

Meanwhile back in England any British victory was cause for celebration, often publicly. Parson Woodforde, for one, never needed any encouragement, as his diary entry showed after the Battle of the Nile (August 1798) in which Nelson defeated Napoleon's fleet off the coast of Egypt:

> **We breakfasted, dined, &c. again at home. Great Rejoicings at Norwich to day on Lord Nelsons late great & noble Victory over the French near Alexandria in Egypt. An Ox rosted whole in the Market-Place &c. This being a day of general Thanksgiving Mr Cotman read Prayers this Morning at Weston-Church, proper on the Occasion. Dinner today, Leg of Mutton rosted &c. I gave my Servants this Evening after supper some strong-Beer and some Punch to drink Admiral Lord Nelson's Health on his late grand victory and also all the other Officers with him and all the brave Sailors with them, and also all those brave Admirals, Officers and Sailors that have gained such great & noble Victories of late over the French.**

And the fashionable, just as alert to the news, were ready to adopt exotic costumery for their own swanky purposes. The Battle of the Nile had set the tone in ladies' dress for all things Egyptian: for example, fine red Mamalouc robes (named after the medieval Mamaluke rulers of Egypt), Mamalouc caps resembling fezzes, and hats adorned with a 'Nelson rose feather'. For a ball held in January 1799 at Kempshott Park, Lord Devonshire's Hampshire residence, Jane Austen wrote to Cassandra that she might indulge herself:

> **I am not to wear my white satin cap tonight after all; I am to wear a Mamalouc cap instead … It is all the fashion now, worn at the Opera, & … at Balls.**

Her frivolous side apart, Jane's perception of the war was provided by newspapers and letters, friends' hearsay, and letters from her two naval brothers, Charles and Frank, who were both heavily involved in active service in the Mediterranean. Her own letters were peppered with thoughts for their safety, their voyages, departures and later arrivals in Southampton or Portsmouth, and sometimes at the easterly ports of Dungeness and Deal. Tracking their whereabouts was difficult at the best of times. Despite this, the Austen sisters kept up with movements in the war. In the aftermath of the Battle of the Nile the Royal Navy was everywhere in the Mediterranean, as Jane described in her letter to Cassandra in November 1800:

> **We have at last heard from Frank; a letter from him to You came yesterday, & I mean to send it on as soon as I can get a ditto (*that means a frank*), which I hope to do in a day or two. En attendant, You must rest satisfied with knowing that on the 8th of July the Petterell [a sloop that Frank commanded] with the rest of the Egyptian Squadron was off the Isle of Cyprus, whither they went from Jaffa for Provisions &c., & whence they were to sail in a day or two for Alexandria, there to wait the result of the English proposals for the evacuation of Egypt … Of his Promotion he knows nothing, & of Prizes he is guiltless.**

The problems of communications in wartime resulted in the Austens at Steventon knowing of Frank's promotion to Post-Captain (awarded in May 1800) long before he did. The 'Prizes' refer to booty, to which naval officers and crews were entitled after capturing enemy vessels. At this time Frank's duty was to cruise the coastal waters intercepting any ships in his path. He captured nearly 40 vessels of various types between Marseilles and Genoa; one he came across was a fishing boat that turned out to be carrying enemy officers and $9,000 worth of coinage: the prize money for Frank from this seizure alone was $750. Every sailor dreamed of capturing a Spanish galleon returning from South America loaded to the gunnels with treasure. In October 1804 four such ships were intercepted on their way to Cadiz bearing a combined value of over a million pounds, destined to support Napoleon's war effort.

Prize money being an accepted part of naval officers' emolument, their pay was not high (Frank was paid an income of about £200 a year, depending on rank, in wartime), rather like a salesman's basic earnings, which are boosted by commission. In the case of Trafalgar, the victory had such significance in the war that Parliament voted to award £320,000 in prize money to be distributed to members of the fleet – alas, none of it went to Frank, as his ship, the *Canopus*, had been withdrawn at the last minute to fetch water supplies from Gibraltar.

Nelson's death at the Battle of Trafalgar had a profound effect on the nation. The public mood was caught between joy and relief on the one hand and deep mourning on the other. The grateful masses turned out in their many thousands to line the streets of London and catch a glimpse of their national hero's remains during the elaborate funeral procession on 9 January 1806. Robert Southey's *Life of Nelson* recorded the feelings expressed at the time:

> **The death of Nelson was felt in England as something more than a public calamity: men started at the intelligence, and turned pale, as if they had heard of the loss of a dear friend. An object of our admiration and affection, of our pride and of our hopes, was suddenly taken from us; and it seemed as if we had never, till then, known how deeply we loved and reverenced him. What the country had lost in its great naval hero was scarcely taken into the account of grief. So perfectly had he performed his part, that the maritime war, after the battle of Trafalgar, was considered at an end; the fleets of the enemy were not merely defeated, but destroyed ... The victory of Trafalgar was celebrated, indeed, with the usual forms of rejoicing, but they were without joy; for such already was the glory of the British navy, through Nelson's surpassing genius, that it scarcely seemed to receive any addition from the most signal victory that ever was achieved upon the seas.**

Trade and Empire

Even Napoleon's blockade of Europe did not prevent British ships slipping through the net to continue trading with their colonies and setting up new markets. No trade was more lucrative than the 'golden triangle' in which manufactured goods were carried to Africa, to be exchanged for slaves who were shipped to America and the West Indies, the empty ships returning to Europe with sugar, tobacco, rum and other raw commodities. Britain was one of the biggest trading nations in the business and it was the merchant navy who manned the slaving ships. Frank Austen made clear his feelings on the subject, condemning the colonial landowners for their 'harshness and desperatism'. On one occasion he reported in a letter on the obscenely overcrowded conditions aboard one ship he had stopped on the high seas.

Legislation of the time set a limit of 400 for a cargo of slaves but because the vessel was not British he had no authority to act:

> Chaced a ship which proved to be a Portuguese bound for Rio Janeiro. She had on board 714 slaves of both sexes, and all ages. She appeared to be about 300 tons!! And in those days the St Albans [Frank's ship] was compelled to let the craft proceed on her course.

Various opportunities to make financial gain presented themselves to ambitious naval officers when not preoccupied with the enemy. Unofficial trade was especially rife in the East India Company, based in Calcutta, Bombay and Madras. Via these ports Britain imported cotton, silk, ivory and spices, and many young employees made private business transactions on the side. The first Governor-general of India, Warren Hastings (appointed partly to sort out corruption), was, as has been said, a family friend of the Austens and he advised Frank Austen to contact his cronies in the East India Company if he wished to benefit from the unofficial trafficking of precious commodities.

Ironically, Hastings himself came under the scrutiny of the law when charged with corruption, and stood trial in Westminster Hall in 1788. At first his trial drew packed audiences, like a theatrical premiere. Philadelphia Hancock's letter to her brother at the time gives us a brief sketch of the proceedings, though she appears to treat it all with some flippancy:

> I have once been to the Trial which, because of an uncommon sight, we fancied worth going to, and sat from 10 till 4 o'clock, compleatly tired, but I had the satisfaction of hearing all the celebrated orators, Sheridan, Burke & Fox. The first was so low we c^d not hear him, & the 2nd so hot and hasty, we c^d not understand him, & the 3rd was highly superior to either as we c^d distinguish every word, but not to our satisfaction as he is so much against Mr Hastings whom we all here wish so well.

Seven years on, the trial came to an end with the acquittal of Warren Hastings when it emerged that the case rested largely on the enmity of a rival, Philip Francis, whom Hastings had once shot in a duel. Some, such as Horace Walpole, still thought the case served as a useful warning:

> The prosecution of Hastings, tho he shoud escape at all, must have good effect. It will alarm the Servant of the Company in India, that they may not always Plunder with Impunity, but that there may be a retrospect; & it will show them that Even bribes of Diamonds to the Crown, may not secure them from prosecution.

'Bribes of diamonds' alludes to a large diamond sent by the Nizam of Hyderabad to King George III through Hastings. Actually it was more likely that the diamond was really a bribe from Hastings, against whom legal proceedings had already begun in the House of Commons.

Meanwhile in South Africa in 1795 the British seized the Cape Colony settled by the Dutch East India Company, and took possession from 1814. The port served as a convenient stopping point en route to India in the days before the Suez Canal was built. At one point Henry Austen wished to join the newly raised 86th Regiment so that he could be stationed at the Cape of Good Hope, but later decided against it and signed up with the Oxford Militia instead.

Other commercial opportunism included the importing of exotic animals captured on colonial soil, again shipped by the swift merchant vessels owned by the East India Company. The following advertisement appeared in *The Times* in 1794:

> Lately arrived in the *Rose*, East Indiaman, a most wonderful living Male Elephant, and to be seen in a commodious room, over Exeter Change, in the Strand. Admittance 1 shilling each. Likewise is lately added to the Grand Menageries, as above, two very singular and most astonishing Kanguroos, male and female, from Botany Bay. Admittance 1 shilling.

It seems that Jane and Cassandra were aware of the these exhibits, as a letter between them refers to 'travelling into the Regions of Wit, Elegance, fashion, Elephants & Kangaroons'.

The Industrial Revolution

Colonial trade fuelled the Industrial Revolution. It was during Jane's lifetime that this momentous change for world civilization began in the small island of Britain, and it was exciting stuff for those who felt the tug of history in the making. The agricultural reformist Arthur Young wrote the following during his tour of southern England:

Get rid of that dronish, sleepy, and stupid indifference, that lazy negligence, which enchains men in the exact paths of their forefathers, without enquiry, without thought, and without ambition, and you are sure of doing good. What trains of thought, what a spirit of exertion, what a mass and power of effort have sprung in every path of life, from the works of such men as Brindley, Watt, Priestley, Harrison, Arkwright ... In what path of life can a man be found that will not animate his pursuit from seeing the steam-engine of Watt?

The groundswell of new ideas that had infused so many areas of life, in the arts and the sciences, translated into booming prosperity for industrialists everywhere. Adam Smith wrote his ground-breaking thesis, *The Wealth of Nations*, in 1776 and in so doing created the foundation for modern economics. His theory, that the less government interferes with business the more prosperous the nation will be, played the tune for the march of progress in every field of the economy. Louis Simond wrote at the beginning of the 19th century:

The English are great in practical mechanics. In no country in the world are there, perhaps, so many applications of that science. I might say, of that instinct of the human species.

The world's first iron bridge spanned a river at Coalbrookdale in the year after Jane Austen was born. When she was eight years old, engineer James Watt coined the word 'horse-power' while developing his unique steam engine with the help of Birmingham manufacturer Matthew Boulton, who felt the tide of history in his day, as he conveyed to Watt in a letter in 1769:

My idea was to settle a manufactury near my own, by the side of our canal, where I would erect all the conveniences necessary for the completion of engines, and from which manufactury we would serve all the world with engines of all sizes ... It would not be worth my while to make for three counties only; but I find it very well worth my while to make for all the world.

And to James Boswell, Boulton would brag:

I sell Sir what all the world desires: Power.

This was also the great age of canals, which by linking up with navigable rivers provided collieries and new factories with vital access to British ports. A nationwide system of waterways was envisaged whereby the four main estuaries of England – the Thames, Severn, Mersey and Humber – would be linked by canals in a scheme called 'The Grand Cross', an industrialists' dream that came true in 1790. Now 30 tons of coal could be drawn on a barge instead of one ton by horse and cart. The potential of this revolutionary mode of transport inspired a rash of building activity everywhere and during the1790s – the years of 'canal mania' – more than a hundred projects were approved for building. Factories went up as quickly they could be built along canal banks; the new face of industrial Britain was already taking shape. By the 1840s some 2,500 miles of canal had been constructed, but already in Regency Britain there were those who saw the future of transport differently. In 1813 the Irish inventor Richard Edgeworth (father of novelist Maria Edgeworth) wrote to James Watt:

> **I have always thought that steam would become the universal lord, and that we should in time scorn post-horses. An iron rail-road would be a cheaper thing than a road on the common construction.**

Richard Trevithick's first steam locomotive made its maiden run in 1804 and in the 1820s George and Robert Stephenson were pioneers of the railway age to come.

Some of the first successful attempts to send men flying were achieved late in the 18th century. While Eliza Comtesse de Feuillide was living in Paris in 1784 she described a balloon flight to her cousin Phylly:

> **I gave you some account of the globes or *ballons* in my last [letter]. The attention of the public has been once more awakened by an improvement attempted in this discovery by a Mr Blanchard who undertook by means of wings & a rudder to direct the course of the *Ballon*. On the day appointed for the experiment a most prodigious concourse assembled to witness it, but alas the obstinacy of one individual soon overset their expectations. It had been agreed that M. Blanchard & a Benedictine monk should ascend with the globe in order to regulate its motions, but at the instant they were seating themselves in the car fixed under the machine for the purpose of their conveyance, one of the young men belonging to the *Ecole militaire***

(or military academy) insisted on being of the party, nor could the strenuous opposition he met with prevail on him to relinquish his design; a violent scuffle ensued & the wings & rudder were soon demolished. M. Blanchard had however the courage notwithstanding the shattered condition of his vehicle to set out alone for the aerial regions; he ascended to the height of 1500 fathoms [9,000 feet] & returned from thence in perfect heath & safety to the astonishment of most of the spectators.

The following year Monsieur Blanchard made his maiden aerial crossing of the English Channel and with it delivered the first package of international airmail. Several pioneers in England were eager to follow his example. The first ascent was made in September 1785 by Vincent Lunardi, secretary to the Neapolitan embassy, accompanied by a dog, a cat and a pigeon, who went up in a balloon from the Artillery Ground in London, watched by a large crowd that included the Prince of Wales, Edmund Burke and Charles James Fox. The balloon descended in a field in Hertfordshire four hours later, to much applause and excitement. As Walpole said to Sir Horace Mann in May 1785:

> Of conversation the chief topic is air balloons. A French girl, daughter of a dancer, has made a voyage into the clouds and nobody has yet broken a neck; so neither good nor harm has hitherto been produced by these enterprises.

Alas, tragedy was not far off. In July of the same year the balloon of two Frenchmen, while high in the air over Boulogne, suddenly caught fire and the men dropped to their deaths. The news on reaching England dampened the spirit of adventure and the ballooning craze came down to earth as adventurers turned their attentions elsewhere.

On a higher note still, advances were being made in astronomy by an amateur enthusiast, William Herschel (1738–1822). In 1781 this eccentric German musician eschewed all the current telescopes on the market and, using his own superior home-made version, discovered the only planet hitherto unknown to the ancients: Uranus. He wanted to name the planet Georgium Sidus ('George's Star') after the English monarch but was persuaded to follow the tradition of naming planets after Greek gods. Nevertheless, in acknowledgement of his kind offer, King George made him court astronomer. A friend of William Herschel's described a visit to his house in Bath:

> After the play I went with Mr. Herschel, who plays at the playhouse on the harpsichord, to his house in New King street, where through his telescope, which magnifies 460 times, [I saw] the double star Castor, the treble one in Zeta Cancer, the new planet [Uranus] in Gemini. In his papers on Saturn I saw there were two belts on the body [of the planet].

Meanwhile in the textile industry, a barber from Bolton, Richard Arkwright (1732–92), invented the cotton-spinning machine and established a mill with water-powered spinning machines in Derbyshire, where he manufactured the first cloth made completely out of cotton. Following this triumph, Arkwright set up factories right across Britain, becoming a pioneer of mass production.

Such a frenzy of activity in this new industrial age was bound to produce its rivalries and jealousies. Patenting inventions was a big issue of the time and virtually every sector of industry had its squabbles. Arkwright, Watt, Josiah Wedgwood and Dr Erasmus Darwin were all involved in court cases about patents. On the subject of new ideas of the age, Erasmus Darwin published in 1794 a paper, Zoönomia, or The Laws of Organic Life, arguing that all life 'evolved' from a single source – an idea that foreshadowed the theory of evolution formulated by his eminent grandson, Charles Darwin. Erasmus concluded his paper with the following speculation:

> Would it be too bold to imagine that, in the great length of time since the earth began to exist, perhaps millions of ages before the commencement of the history of mankind, would it be too bold to imagine that all warm-blooded animals have arisen from one living filament, which the great First Cause endued with animality, with the power of acquiring new parts, attended with new propensities, directed by irritations, sensations, volitions and associations, and thus possessing the faculty of continuing to improve by its own inherent activity, and of delivering down these improvements by generation to its posterity, world without end!

As far as his views went about the Industrial Revolution, however, this physician shared the anxiety of many who could foresee its darker side. The following verse betrays a scientist trembling at the prospect of how new machines might be deployed:

Soon shall thy arm, UNCONQUERED STEAM! Afar
Drag the slow barge, or drive the rapid car;
Or on wide-waving wings expanded bear
The flying-chariot through the fields of air.

– Fair crews triumphant, leaning from above,
Shall wave their flattering kerchiefs as they move,
Or warrior-band alarm the gaping crowd,
And armies shrink beneath the shadowy cloud.

The mystic William Blake also questioned what he saw happening around him and famously set down his thoughts in a poem, later turned into the patriotic anthem *Jerusalem*. At the time he wrote it, in 1804, Blake was a poor engraver and, using Christian ideas, he contrasted the brilliance of divine redemption with the menacing reality of the times:

And did those feet in ancient times
Walk upon England's mountains green?
And was the holy Lamb of God
On England's pleasant pastures seen?

And did the Countenance Divine
Shine forth upon our clouded hills?
And was Jerusalem builded here
Among these dark Satanic mills?

Conditions of work were often scandalous in the factories and pits, with little regard for safety. Revd Skinner of Somerset regularly recorded local accidents, frequently in the nearby colliery. His entry for 9 January 1806 read:

William Britain, another collier, was killed in the coal pits by a shocking accident. He was riding in a small coal cart underground drawn by an ass, which vehicle is usually employed to convey the coal from different parts where it is dug to the large store below the mouth of the pit, but was then empty. As the ass was going along at a brisk pace he did not observe he was come to a spot where the roof of the passage was much lower than it was before, and, neglecting to stoop his head, his back was bent double by the sudden violence of the shock and his spine snapped. The poor fellow was drawn up and lived some hours, but his extremities were quite paralysed.

A further iniquity of the age involved child labour. During these early years of industrial boom, when factory workers had to work very long hours for a mean wage, families supplemented their income by sending their children to work too. Their cause was taken up by Robert Peel, MP and mill owner, who piloted legislation through Parliament to restrict child labour, but the law proved ineffectual and abuses continued. It took the efforts of a sustained campaign to stir the nation's conscience and the poet Samuel Taylor Coleridge championed the cause in his numerous letters and pamphlets. One article appeared in *The Courier* in October of 1816 supporting a parliamentary investigation into the matter:

Among the useful labours of the Select Committees of the House of Commons during the last Session, one of the most useful perhaps was the inquiry into the *state of the children employed in manufactories*. It did, we must confess, excite other feelings besides those of surprise to find children employed in manufactories 13 hours a-day. Which, we ask, ought most to excite our surprise, that any parents can consign, or any manufactories receive children to be so employed? [Such acts Coleridge elsewhere stated as committing 'Soul-murder and Infanticide'.] We were quite pleased with the answer of Dr. Baillie [physician to George III], who, upon being asked, 'At what age may children, without endangering their health, be admitted into factories, to be regularly employed 13 hours a-day, allowing them one hour and a half to go and return from meals, and one hour for instruction?' replied, 'I should say, that there was no age, no time of life whatever, where that kind of labour could be compatible, in most constitutions, with the full maintenance of health.' Certainly not: But for children to be employed so long! What time can they have for proper instruction – what for that which is necessary to health at that tender age, running about or playing in the open air? The confinement to one spot, to one position, cannot we should think but be injurious to faculties both [of] body and mind. But it is attempted in the examination before the Committee, to shew that such employment is not injurious. In one manufactory it is said, of 875 persons there were not more than two to five deaths: and in another of 289 persons, two only died in 1815. Be it so, and allowing the full weight to these facts, we then say, that the injury to health might not be then visible, that no disease might then have broken out. But we ask, whether the very privation at that early age ... does not lay the foundation of disorders, which may and must break out at a more advanced period of life?

Dr. Baillie thinks 'that seven years old is the earliest age at which children ought to be employed in factories, and then only four or five hours a day; at eight and nine years of age, six and seven hours; afterwards they might be employed ten hours, and beyond that there ought to be no increase of labour.'

A further Act of Parliament was passed in 1819 to curb these excesses, though it was not until 1833 that inspectors of factories were appointed to enforce its restrictions, namely that a child's working day should last no more than nine hours in the textile industry, one of the largest employers. Even then, teenagers and women still had to endure a working week of more than 60 hours.

The Agricultural Revolution

Before the Industrial Revolution, the wealth of the nation was built on agriculture. Wool had been the source of much of that wealth since the Middle Ages, providing employment to weavers and a settled life of comfort for graziers. The Austen family itself was once an ancestral clan living off the land of the Weald in Kent. According to Edward Hasted, the 18th-century Kentish historian, the Austens were one of a number of families who between them possessed most of the landed property in the Weald and ran clothing businesses. They were one of the ...

Antient families of these parts, now of large estate, and genteel rank in life, and some of them ennobled by titles, [who] are sprung from and owe their fortunes to ancestors who have used this great staple manufacture, now almost unknown here ... They were usually called, from their dress, The Grey Coats of Kent, and were a body so numerous and united, that at county elections, whoever had their votes and interest was almost certain of being elected.

They had been powerful in times gone by. Jane's father George Austen came from this stock, though the fortune had long since gone. Now farming had taken on a different hue. Through the 18th century a revolution every bit as important as its industrial counterpart for the lives of the British people was taking place in agriculture. Its most radical aspect – with a big impact on the landscape as well as the economy – was enclosure. With the rapid increase in population (around 30 per cent during the last quarter of the 18th century) caused chiefly by the emergence of new manufacturing towns, pressure mounted on farming to modernize its methods and expand. It was during this period that Jethro Tull invented his seed drill, and machines for threshing and chaff cutting were introduced. Agriculture had to be run like an industry, with efficient management.

To this end, common land was taken away from villagers – and with it their grazing rights – and granted instead to landowners to manage. Most of the Enclosure Acts were passed by Parliament in Jane Austen's lifetime, producing the sort of landscape familiar today: a patchwork of rectangular fields bordered by hedges, with clumps of trees for shelter. In 1803 farmer Thomas Rudge reported on the rural economy of Gloucestershire:

> **The hill district includes the Cotswolds. Within these last hundred years a total change has taken place on these hills. Furze and some dry and scanty blades of grass were all their produce, but now with few exceptions the downs are converted into arable enclosed fields.**

The enclosure process happened in two main phases: first, from 1750 to about 1780, the open-field system of the Midlands was enclosed and put to pasture; and second, from about 1780 onwards, vast tracts of common and former grazing land across the south and east of England were turned over to cereals to satisfy the greater demand for grain. Prices shot up, profits rose (especially during the Napoleonic Wars when French blockades hampered trade) and pressure grew to cultivate even more land.

The impact of all this upheaval felt by the common man was devastating. Amid booming prosperity for landowners there were those who once worked their modest parcel of common land now eking out an uncertain livelihood. Revd David Davies, the rector of Cookham in Berkshire, said in 1795:

> **An amazing number of people have been reduced from a comfortable state of partial independence to the precarious condition of mere**

hirelings, who when out of work immediately come on the parish.

Even the agriculturalist Arthur Young, who started out being enthusiastic about the enclosure system, had changed his mind by the turn of the century as the new phenomenon of rural poverty emerged in Georgian Britain:

Go to an ale-house of an old enclosed country, and there you will see the origin of poverty and poor-rates. For whom are they to be sober? For whom are they to save? (Such are their questions.) For the parish? If I am diligent, shall I leave to build a cottage? If I am sober, shall I have land for a cow? If I am frugal, shall I have half an acre for potatoes? You offer no motives: you have nothing but a parish officer and a work-house! – Bring me another pot!

Some diehards persevered, whatever the conditions, without complaint. Two farm workers from Surrey, James Strudwick and his wife Anne, worked all their lives on the same farm, as Frederick Eden reported:

He worked more than threescore years on one farm: and his wages, summer and winter, were regularly a shilling a day. He never asked more: nor was he ever offered less. Strudwick continued to work till within seven weeks of the day of his death; and at the age of fourscore, in 1787, he closed, in peace, a not inglorious life; for, to the day of his death, he never received a farthing in the way of parochial aid. His wife survived him about seven years; and though bent with age and infirmities, and little able to work, excepting as a weeder in a gentleman's garden, she also was too proud either to ask or receive any relief from her parish. For six or seven of the last years of her life, she received twenty shillings a year from the person who favoured me with this account, which he drew up from her own mouth. With all her virtue, and all her merit, she yet was not much liked in her neighbourhood; people in affluence thought her haughty, and the paupers of the parish, seeing, as they could not help seeing, that her life was a reproach to theirs, aggravated all her little failings.

By contrast, tenant farmers, who towards the end of the 18th century were put in charge of cultivating most of this farmland, were inching their way up the economic ladder to become reasonably well off. Jane Austen saw this trend and represents one such farmer in Robert Martin in *Emma*, as one who through his own ambition and application is rising in society, sufficiently indeed to win the hand of the middle-class Harriet Smith. The rural poor are not often mentioned in Jane Austen's novels but she knew of their hardships and the widening gap between them and their rich neighbours. In the character of Emma she depicts the sympathetic person who, if nothing else, offers the milk of human kindness and will meet them on their own terms:

> Emma was very compassionate; and the distresses of the poor were as sure of relief from her personal attention and kindness, her counsel and her patience, as from her purse. She understood their ways, could allow for their ignorance and their temptations, had no romantic expectations of extraordinary virtue from those, for whom education had done so little; entered into their troubles with ready sympathy, and always gave her assistance with as much intelligence as good-will.

The grim George Crabbe was scathing of attempts to romanticize the harsh reality of farm labourers' toil in his well known poem of 1783, *The Village*:

> I grant indeed that fields and flocks have charms
> For him that grazes or for him that farms;
> But when amid such pleasing scenes I trace
> The poor laborious natives of the place,
> And see the mid-day sun, with fervid ray,
> On their bare heads and dewy temples play;
> While some, with feebler heads and fainter hearts,
> Deplore their fortune, yet sustain their parts:
> Then shall I dare these real ills to hide
> In tinsel trappings of poetic pride?

Protest, Riot and Anarchy

There were many who were not prepared to accept the status quo, and they mounted their protest against government policy, war, poverty and capitalist greed, or simply joined ranks with bloody-minded mobs. Spontaneous flashpoints were not uncommon. In the autumn of 1795, after a poor harvest and two years of war, an angry mob attacked George III's carriage as he rode to the state opening of Parliament. Stones and clods of earth were hurled at the coach and one of the assailants fired a pistol at the king from close range, but missed. Windows of the prime minister's house in Downing Street were smashed and the crowd kept up a chant through most of the afternoon:

No war! No famine! No Pitt! No king!

One of the most sustained eruptions of political violence in the 18th century, known as the Gordon Riots, happened in 1780. In June, Lord George Gordon, MP, led an organization of hardline Protestants in an 'anti-Popery' rally that attracted up to 80,000 supporters. Lined across the streets, eight abreast, wearing blue cockades in their hats, singing hymns and waving banners, the lively crowd marched on the House of Commons to protest against an Act of Parliament passed two years earlier easing restrictions on Catholics owning property. By evening the mob had turned nasty and went on the rampage, burning Catholic property and terrorizing innocent citizens. The trouble spilled over into the following few days. An eye-witness report, given by Thomas Holcroft in A *Plain and Succinct Narrative of the Gordon Riots*, described:

> ... flames ascending and rolling in vast and voluminous clouds ... the conflagration was horrible beyond description ... Men, women, and children were running up and down with beds, glasses, bundles, or whatever they wished most to preserve. In streets where there were no fires numbers were removing their goods and effects at midnight. The tremendous roar of the insatiate and innumerable fiends who were the authors of these horrible scenes were heard at one instant, and at the next the dreadful report of soldiers' muskets, as if firing in platoons; in short, everything which could impress the mind with ideas of universal anarchy and approaching desolation seemed to be accumulating.

The trouble spread to other cities – including Bath, where the experience of one priest was recorded first hand:

> I am the unfortunate Roman Catholic clergyman, who was hunted from place to place and pursued through several streets the evening of the Bath riot: it was with great difficulty I escaped from falling a victim to the fury of the mob. Being here the public minister for

people of our persuasion I am well known and was openly attacked in the street that evening by one Butler, then servant to Mr Baldwin. ... After pursuing me at the head of the mob he led them to my house and chapel, both which, together with all the furniture and books, were entirely destroyed. The unhappy man was afterwards tried and hanged on the spot.

Fanny Burney, staying in the city at the time, gave her account of the scene in a letter to her father on the following day:

We did not leave Bath till eight o'clock [in the] evening, at which time it was filled with dragoons, militia, and armed constables, not armed with muskets, but with bludgeons: those latter were all chairmen, who were sworn by the mayor in the morning for petty constables. A popish private chapel, and the houses of all the Catholics, were guarded ... and the inhabitants ordered to keep house.

What threatened to turn into nationwide anarchy subsided after a week of mayhem, leaving 285 people dead and Lord Gordon incarcerated in Newgate Prison. Perhaps it was fear of repeat turbulence that prevented the Catholic Emancipation Act from being passed until 1829.

Riots were frequent occurrences in the late Georgian period; they were the common way for people to express their grievances. When the American scientist and statesman Benjamin Franklin stayed in Britain for a while he was appalled at the level of public violence he witnessed:

I have seen, within a year, riots in the country, about corn; riots about elections; riots about workhouses; riots of colliers, riots of weavers, riots of coal-heavers; riots of sawyers; riots of Wilkesites [followers of jailed radical politician John Wilkes]; riots of government chairmen; riots of smugglers, in which custom house officers and excise-men have been murdered, the King's armed vessels and troops fired at.

More organized forms of protest by industrial workers were also taking shape. One of the growing economic evils of the day was inflation. Caused chiefly by war, price rises diminished the buying power of already low wages (further eroded when William Pitt later introduced income tax to pay for

the French wars). Manual workers clubbed together to form Combinations
(trade unions) to press for wage rises. If these failed to materialize, workers
sometimes elected to take action, as illustrated by this notice appearing in
a 1776 edition of the *Bath Chronicle* penned by its leader:

> ... at a Meeting of Journeymen Carpenters Having Consider'd the
> many hardships we labour under with our wifes and familys in
> the City of Bath Owing to the masters Giving Low wages and the
> Exspence of tools and high Price of Provision &c. We hereby Gives
> Notise to all Masters that they Solicits their Wages to be Advanced
> According to their Merritt and unless their Masteres think fitt to raise
> Adequate to their Workmanship three Shillings pr week – Resolved
> all to Strik on Monday next.

Without the financial back-up that unions of today would be able to
provide for their members, the threats had no clout. Disruption was
sufficiently widespread by the end of the century to prompt the government
to outlaw the new movement through the Combination Acts and decree
three-month prison sentences for transgressors. Harsh though these
measures were, they would not stop the most determined of dissenters,
notably the Luddites of Nottinghamshire, who took matters into their own
hands in 1811. Faced with crippling unemployment, even starvation, these
textile workers smashed up factory machinery, which they deemed to be
the cause of their plight. The violence spread to neighbouring counties
and soon caused nationwide alarm. The *Leeds Mercury* declared in
December of that year:

> The Insurrectional state to which this country has been reduced for
> the last month has no parallel in history, since the troubled days of
> Charles the First [the English Civil War].

Luddites were tried and executed, but the problem did not go away. Some
feared that a revolution by the labouring masses might well become a reality
if the government did not do something to ameliorate the conditions of the
poor. Robert Southey uttered this warning early in the 19th century:

> A manufacturing poor is more easily instigated to revolt [than
> religious zealots]. They have no local attachments; the persons to

whom they look up for support they regard more with envy than respect, as men who grow rich by their labour; they know enough of what is passing in the political world to think themselves politicians; they feel the whole burthen of taxation, which is not the case with the peasant, because he raises a great part of his own food: they are aware of their own numbers. A manufacturing populace is always ripe for rioting, – the direction which this fury may take is accidental; in 1780 it was against the Catholics [the Gordon Riots], in 1790 against the Dissenters. Governments who found their prosperity upon manufactures sleep upon gun-powder.

Do I then think that England is in danger of revolution? If the manufacturing system continues to be extended, increasing as it necessarily does increase the number, the misery, and the depravity of the poor, I believe that revolution inevitably must come, and in its most fearful shape.

Although Luddites are mainly remembered for resisting technical progress, many also protested and rioted about food shortages in wartime Britain. So widespread was the problem that centres of emergency food relief were set up around the country after seven years of wartime deprivation. The *Bath Herald* ran a piece in September 1800 detailing the 'bounty' on offer:

After an unwearied attention of upwards of nine months to the relief of the poor of this city, the PROVISION COMMITTEE closed their laudable efforts, for the present, on Wednesday last. The liberality of the affluent has enabled them to render essential service, during a most trying period, to hundreds of distressed families, who have generally expressed their gratitude in the most fervent terms; whilst a few others, we are sorry to say, daily received the bounty, without being conscious of the benevolence extended to them. The provisions which have been disposed of, soup, potatoes, and rice, were of the very best quality that could be made or purchased –

> Above sixty thousand Quarts of Soup,
> Upwards of two hundred Barrels of Rice,
> An equal number of Sacks of Potatoes,
> And full 317 Tons weight of Coal.

Have been distributed at a price much under what those articles could be bought at, even in times of the greatest plenty.

Abolition of Slavery

Equally noteworthy for their efforts to achieve lasting change for the good
were those who expressed their dissent by peaceful means. Moral reformers
who campaigned inside and out of Parliament often worked together in
voluntary organizations. Their aim was to win the hearts and minds of the
people through reason, by petitioning, issuing pamphlets and adopting
the longer-term view of enlightened education. One of the biggest issues
of the day was slavery and its abolition.

A leader of the anti-slavery movement and its eventual champion was
the Evangelical reformer and MP William Wilberforce, despite the fact that
most of his fellow Tories were against any limits being imposed on the highly
profitable slave market. At the height of the trade some 70,000 slaves were
transported each year from Africa to the Americas; in the 1770s nearly 200
'slavers', as the vessels were called, sailed from Liverpool, London and Bristol.
During the War of American Independence, which included a number of
skirmishes with the French, George III was anxious about the threat to
Britain's lucrative colonies in the Caribbean. In a letter of 1779 the king left
his addressee, Lord Sandwich, in no doubt as to the gravity of the situation:

**Our islands must be defended even at the risk of an invasion of this
Island, if we lose our Sugar Islands it will be impossible to raise
Money to continue the War.**

This reflected the commonly held attitude of the time that slavery served
as an accepted means to an end, even if from time to time reports of
inhumanity seeped back to the British public. Generations of English
families owned investments in the West Indies. Jane Austen's father himself
was for many years a trustee of a plantation in Antigua and the owner, James
Nibbs, was made godfather to James Austen. Even the Austens regarded
plantation ownership as a normal part of everyday commerce. Horatio
Nelson was proud of the colonial possessions, though he of anyone should
have been aware of what the process involved. In a letter to a colleague,
Simon Taylor in Jamaica, he defended his position as late as 1804, when the
abolitionist campaign had exposed much of the evil trade:

**I ever have been, and shall die, a firm friend to our present Colonial
system. I was bred, as you know, in the good old school, and taught**

to appreciate the value of our West India possessions; and neither in the field, nor in the senate, shall their just rights be infringed, whilst I have an arm to fight in their defence, or a tongue to launch my voice.

In a similar vein, it was natural in England to buy and sell black slaves as chattels. The *London Advertiser* ran an advertisement in 1756:

To be sold, a Negro boy age about fourteen years old, warranted free from any distemper, and has had those [diseases] fatal to that colour; has been used two years to all kinds of household work, and to wait at table; his price is £25, and would not be sold but the person he belongs to is leaving off business.

The first significant stirrings of conscience about slavery can be traced to 1759 when a naval officer, Captain Charles Middleton, underwent a life-changing experience after witnessing a slave ship from Bristol in the grip of an epidemic. The impact was so profound that from that moment he devoted much of his life to bringing about abolition. On entering Parliament he became a driving force, alongside other evangelical reformers, including the historian of the slave trade, Thomas Clarkson (with whom Jane Austen once declared to Cassandra she was in love), and together they persuaded William Wilberforce, a close friend of Prime Minister Pitt, to lead the abolitionist campaign.

By 1788 the activities of Wilberforce and Clarkson had generated mass support in England. George Canning, an enlightened Tory reformer, campaigned for abolition and Josiah Wedgwood manufactured a jasper-ware cameo of a slave in chains with the motto, 'Am I not a man and a brother?' which he distributed freely by the hundreds. Explorers such as Captain Cook returning from the South Seas also helped the cause through their vivid descriptions of paradisal environments, and a new respect was found for their inhabitants in the cult of the noble savage. In a letter to Edmund Burke, staunch defender of capitalist interests in the Caribbean, the polemical writer Mary Wollstonecraft lambasted his traditionalist views:

Allowing his servile reverence for antiquity, and prudent attention to self-interest, to have the force which he insists on, the slave trade ought never to be abolished; and, because our ignorant forefathers, not understanding the native dignity of man, sanctioned a traffic that

outrages every suggestion of reason and religion, we are to submit
to the inhuman custom, and term an atrocious insult to our country
... security of property! Behold, in a few words, the definition of
English liberty. And to this selfish principle every nobler one is
sacrificed ... Our penal laws punish with death the thief who
steals a few pounds; but to take by violence a man is no such
heinous offence.

Matters came to a head in a momentous speech given to the House of
Commons by Wilberforce on 12 May 1789. Unlike today, there was no
official recorder of parliamentary speeches. Instead newspapers put out their
own versions and were known to alter the content to suit their own political
agendas. The version that follows was published by William Cobbett in his
Parliamentary Debates, bought in 1811 by the Hansard family who founded
the recording service used today in Parliament:

Mr. Wilberforce now rose and said '... I mean not to accuse any one,
but to take the shame upon myself, in common, indeed, with the
whole parliament of Great Britain, for having suffered this horrid
trade to be carried on under their authority. We are all guilty—we
ought all to plead guilty, and not to exculpate ourselves by throwing
the blame on others.

'... I must speak of the transit of the slaves in the West Indies.
This I confess, in my own opinion, is the most wretched part of the
whole subject. So much misery condensed in so little room, is more
than the human imagination had ever before conceived ... Let any
one imagine to himself 600 or 700 of these wretches chained two and
two, surrounded with every object that is nauseous and disgusting,
diseased, and struggling under every kind of wretchedness! How can
we bear to think of such a scene as this? One would think it had
been determined to heap upon them all the varieties of bodily pain,
for the purpose of blunting the feelings of the mind; and yet, in this
very point (to show the power of human prejudice) the situation of
the slaves has been described by Mr. Norris, one of the Liverpool
delegates, in a manner which, I am sure will convince the House how
interest can draw a film across the eyes, so thick, that total blindness
could do no more; and how it is our duty therefore to trust not to the
reasonings of interested men.'

Wilberforce went on to condemn the testimony of a slave-ship representative, Mr Norris of Liverpool, who had described the conditions as though befitting a pleasure cruiser:

'Their apartments,' says Mr. Norris, 'are fitted up as much for their advantage as circumstances will admit. The right ancle of one, indeed is connected with the left ancle of another by a small iron fetter, and if they are turbulent, by another on their wrists. They have several meals a day; some of their own country provisions, with the best sauces of African cookery; and by way of variety, another meal of pulse, &c. according to European taste. After breakfast they have water to wash themselves, while their apartments are perfumed with frankincense and lime-juice. Before dinner, they are amused after the manner of their country. The song and dance are promoted,' and, as if the whole was really a scene of pleasure and dissipation it is added, that games of chance are furnished. 'The men play and sing, while the women and girls make fanciful ornaments with beads, which they are plentifully supplied with.'

... What will the House think when, by the concurring testimony of other witnesses, the true history is laid open? The slaves who are sometimes described as rejoicing at their captivity, are so wrung with misery at leaving their country, that it is the constant practice to set sail at night, lest they should be sensible of their departure. The pulse which Mr. Norris talks of are horse beans; and the scantiness, both of water and provision, was suggested by the very [report] of Jamaica ... that called for the interference of parliament. Mr. Norris talks of frankincense and lime juice; when surgeons tell you the slaves are stowed so close, that there is not room to tread among them ... that even in a ship which wanted 200 of her complement, the stench was intolerable. The song and the dance, says Mr. Norris, are promoted ... The truth is, that for the sake of exercise, these miserable wretches, loaded with chains ... are forced to dance by the terror of the lash, and sometimes by the actual use of it. 'I,' says one of the other evidences, 'was employed to dance the men, while another person danced the women.' Such, then is the meaning of the word 'promoted'; and it may be observed too, with respect to food, that an instrument is sometimes carried out, in order to force them to eat.

Not wishing to depend entirely on witness statements and the Jamaican report to the Privy Council for his case, the arch-campaigner ended his speech with some hard facts:

> **Death, at least, is a sure ground of evidence … It will be found, upon an average of all the ships of which evidence has been given at the privy council, that exclusive of those who perish before they sail, not less than 12½ per cent perish in the passage. Besides these, the Jamaica report tells you, that not less than 4½ per cent die on shore before the day of sale, which is only a week or two from the time of landing. One third more die in the seasoning, and this in a country exactly like their own. The diseases, however, which they contract on shipboard, the astringent washes which are to hide their wounds, and the mischievous tricks used to make them up for sale, are, as the Jamaica report says, one principal cause of this mortality. Upon the whole, however, here is a mortality of about 50 per cent and this among negroes who are not bought unless (as the phrase is with cattle) they are sound in wind and limb.**

There was for Wilberforce, as indeed there should have been for all, one conclusion only:

> **The number of deaths speaks for itself. As soon as ever I had arrived thus far in my investigation of the slave trade, I confess to you sir, so enormous so dreadful, so irremediable did its wickedness appear that my own mind was completely made up for the abolition. A trade founded in iniquity, and carried on as this was, must be abolished, let the policy be what it might,—let the consequences be what they would, I from this time determined that I would never rest till I had effected its abolition.**

Sir Charles Middleton's appointment as First Lord of the Admiralty in 1805 gave him and his fellow abolitionists some leverage over Parliament and alliances were formed with William Pitt and various evangelical MPs. Finally, in 1807, after 20 years of campaigning and despite much resistance from those with vested interests, slavery was made illegal. Jane Austen makes very little comment on these issues. Antigua was the island she chose in *Mansfield Park* as the place where Sir Thomas Bertram owns a plantation.

On his return from visiting it, the topic of slavery is brought up in conversation by his niece Fanny Price. When she and Sir Thomas's son Edmund discuss this the next day, there is an apparent awkwardness which may betray the sensitivity of the subject at the time. Fanny begins:

'Did not you hear me ask him about the slave trade last night?'
'I did—and was in hopes the question would be followed up by others. It would have pleased your uncle to be inquired of farther.'
'And I longed to do it—but there was such a dead silence!' [from Sir Thomas and his daughters]

Duels of Honour

If the fray of politics should reach no satisfactory conclusion by dispute, a traditional way of settling the score was by duel. Even in these relatively enlightened times politicians were known to 'call out' each other. Viscount Castlereagh was once so angry with his political rival George Canning, who accused him of military incompetence in the French war, that he challenged Canning to a duel. In the event both survived. Duelling was largely a matter of honour and was conducted as a face-saving act. Today, in the Houses of Parliament any unseemly conduct, such as making a personal remark about a political opponent, demands an apology and, if this is not forthcoming, at worst would result in a member's dismissal from the house. In the Georgian period it would demand 'satisfaction': when Prime Minister Pitt used 'unparliamentary' language against George Tierney, MP, in 1798, his refusal to retract was followed up by a written challenge from the offended member. Pitt accepted and the two met on Wimbledon Common, accompanied by their two witnesses. Each fired his pistol and they were reconciled.

One notable duelling resort was Kensington Gardens, the scene of many famous encounters in the Georgian period. Henry Fielding, in *Amelia* (published in 1751), said that it:

... may properly be called the field of blood, being that place a little to the left of the Ring, which heroes have chosen for the scene of their exit from this world.

The Spectator condemned the practice, despite the rise in the number of incidents as the century neared its end. In the eyes of the law, duelling was regarded as murder or manslaughter and might be punished as such, though frequently survivors who were convicted got away with a fine. Happily for the Austens none of their family is recorded as having been called out. For all their spleen and bluster, most rural squires tended to have a bark bigger than their bite.

The New Press

For those who preferred the pen to the pistol as an instrument of combat there were increasing opportunities for journalists in Jane Austen's day, as new magazines and newspapers were being launched all the time. However, newspaper circulation, though growing steadily, was never high in the 18th century: 2,000 was a good print run. By 1795 *The Times* reached 4,800, but sales were kept down by high stamp duty and readers passing copies to each other, for example in coffee houses and libraries. Most of those who read them were interested in parliamentary proceedings, which took up at least half the space and allowed the intelligent public to keep abreast of political developments. One of the four pages that made up a newspaper carried advertisements, job vacancies, and details of forthcoming cultural events. Provincial newspapers were also popular.

A new type of publication in the 18th century was the periodical. As now, it tended to specialize in topics of interest tailored to particular sectors of society. The Austen family read some of the popular titles: the *Tatler*, started by Richard Steele in 1709; *The Spectator*, published by Steele and Addison in 1711; *The Rambler* by Samuel Johnson. By far the most successful of the general periodicals was the *Gentleman's Magazine*, published from 1731, with a circulation of about 10,000. It contained a miscellany of information, from news summaries and political reports to literary reviews, poems, obituaries, recipes and sundry essays. Its female counterpart from 1770 was the *Lady's Magazine*, which also carried essays and was especially strong on fiction, poetry and readers' letters. Voices in favour of political emancipation for women had yet to gain momentum in society, but education was a constant theme and views were usually expressed in characteristically strident tones, such as appear in this letter printed in an issue of the *Lady's Magazine* in 1808:

I should be very glad to be informed why those females who endeavour to improve their minds by reading, and take some little care

to qualify themselves for companions to men of sense, should by those means become objects of ridicule. The gentlemen are very liberal in bestowing the epithets of triflers and silly women on those who have a mere female education; if any of us have resolution enough to soar beyond narrow limits, and dare to read anything of more importance than a play or a novel, we are called critics, wits, female pedants, &c.

Like the press today, newspapers tended to have a political bias. In times of war and political tension some journalists would dare to speak out against the establishment and risk the consequences. A 'hot potato' of the time was abuse of military power within the army. One editor, John Drakard of *The Stamford News*, was imprisoned for running a campaign evidencing cases of extreme military punishment, or 'torture' as he called it. The influential William Cobbett himself overstepped the mark in 1809 when he ran an article, published two days before a royal fête attended by foreign dignitaries, in which he condemned the brutal flogging of militiamen by German troops in Ely. The royal house, having a strong German background, was not pleased. To rub salt into the wound Cobbett parodied a reactionary opinion supporting the German actions in the weekly *Political Register* that he published at the time:

Five hundred lashes each! Aye, that is right! Flog them; flog them; flog them! They deserve it, and a great deal more. They deserve a flogging at every meal-time. 'Lash them daily, lash them duly'. What, shall the rascals dare to *mutiny*, and that, too, when the German legion is so near at hand! Lash them, lash them, lash them! They *deserve* it. O, yes; they merit a double-tailed cat [cat-o'-nine-tails]. Base dogs! What, mutiny for the sake of *the price of a knapsack*! Lash them! Flog them! Base Rascals!

Cobbett's punishment was a fine and two years' imprisonment.

An almost universal subject exciting political comment was whether the Prince Regent should accede to the wishes expressed in some newspapers that the political system be reformed. The Whiggish *Morning Chronicle* was taken to court for suggesting that the Prince Regent was neglecting his duty by not doing so. The *Examiner* went further and conducted a sustained polemic against the Regent in 1812, risking prosecution with every issue. When the *Morning Post*, a newspaper affecting to be the organ of the court, released a horribly sycophantic defence of the Prince, the *Examiner's* leader writer and 'man of letters', Leigh Hunt, could contain himself no longer:

What person, unacquainted with the true state of the case, would imagine, in reading these astounding eulogies, that this 'glory of the people' was the subject of millions of shrugs and reproaches? – that this 'Adonis in loveliness' was a corpulent man of fifty? In short, this delightful, blissful, wise, pleasurable, honourable, virtuous, true, and immortal PRINCE, was a violator of his word, a libertine over head and ears in disgrace, a despiser of domestic ties, the companion of gamblers and demireps [people of doubtful reputation], a man who has just closed half a century without one single claim on the gratitude of his country or the respect of posterity.

For his trouble, Hunt was convicted of libel and jailed for two years in 1813. Though kept in confinement, the times were not so harsh for him as one might suppose. He was allowed to dine with his family in private every day and receive visitors, of which there were many, including the poets Lord Byron, Thomas Moore and Charles Lamb, the essayist William Hazlitt and the philosopher Jeremy Bentham.

Regency Horror

One of the most extraordinary periods in the history of English royalty was the era known as the Regency, when the Prince Regent held power in the king's absence due to prolonged illness from 1811 to 1820. This was also the period in which all six of Jane Austen's novels were published. Three of them were wholly composed then and bear its influence; indeed *Emma* was dedicated to the Regent. Famous for his extravagant lifestyle, the Prince of Wales started out as a popular man whom even Leigh Hunt supported in his early days. Tall, handsome, witty and intelligent he became known as 'the first gentleman of Europe'.

That was before the excesses of his lifestyle, which horrified his father George III, began to work against him. Flamboyance coupled with obesity were meat and drink to the new phenomenon of political lampooning by such cartoonists as Thomas Rowlandson and George Cruickshank, who referred to him as the 'Prince of Whales'; James Gillray entitled one cartoon 'A Voluptuary under the Horrors of Digestion'. Meanwhile the king became ill, probably with a rare hereditary disease of the metabolism known as porphyria, whose symptoms included strange bouts of derangement and chronic pain. A major attack in 1788 prompted ministers to discuss the possibility of a regency, by which the king's eldest son George Augustus Frederick would stand in until he recovered. But the king recovered quickly, apparently, and all was well again.

The Prince of Wales brought no comfort to his aides in his choice of marriage partners and certainly he knew how to rub up his father the wrong way. In 1785 he secretly married Mrs Maria Fitzherbert, who was older than him, twice widowed, a commoner and Roman Catholic to boot. The Hanoverian dynasty had come to the British throne earlier in the century precisely because they were Protestants and, to reinforce the point, the king had passed the Royal Marriages Act in 1772, stipulating that all wives must be Protestant. So the prince's marriage was illegal too.

But of equal concern was the prince's great extravagance. So much from the state's coffers had been frittered away – his racing activities alone were costing £30,000 a year – that the matter had become a most serious embarrassment to king and minister alike. The Prince, however, hatched a plan to secure himself more advances, as Cobbett described in his history of the Regency period (published in 1830):

> **The Prince of Wales (later George IV), who had attained the age of thirty three years, was *greatly embarrassed with debts,* which the nation was by no means *disposed to pay.* The country was at this time involved in a most expensive and wasteful war against the people of France ... The taxes, on account of the war, pressed heavily upon the nation; the government armed itself at all points ...**
>
> **Under such circumstances, an enormous sum, granted to pay the *debts* of a prince who had always received a large annual stipend out of the taxes, was what even Pitt, daring as he was, had not the confidence to propose without being furnished with some plausible pretence for the proposition. The marriage *furnished this pretence.***

Marriage to his German cousin, Princess Caroline of Brunswick, was the strategy by which the Prince could be granted a larger spending allowance. His choice of partner this time was a good-looking, fashionable young woman of impeccable pedigree – on paper just what the Prince needed to swing fortune back into his favour. Frank Austen manned one of the ships escorting her to England, and was able to describe to Jane her elegant apparel of a fine muslin dress and beaver hat sporting blue and black feathers. Cobbett continued:

> The marriage took place on the 8th April 1795. The Prince, notwithstanding his extravagance, was, at the time, by no means *unpopular*. The Princess, who was of a most frank and kind disposition, extremely affable and gracious in her deportment, by no means suffered in a comparison with the Queen; and the nation seemed delighted with the prospect ... In a few days after the celebration of the marriage, the king communicated to the parliament his request that a *settlement* should be made on the Prince. Upon this message from the king, Pitt founded his proposition to the House.

What was hoped to be an amicable solution was deemed far from satisfactory in some quarters, as Cobbett explained:

> ... there were men, on both sides of the House, to oppose any grant of money with a view of paying the *debts* of the Prince. Amongst these was Earl Grey; his speech was well calculated to produce upon the country an impression very little favourable to the Prince, who had had *his debts paid by parliament once before*.
>
> This former payment of the Prince's debts took place in 1787. The amount was very large; and certainly, with a clear annual allowance of *sixty thousand pounds*, money enough to maintain 3,000 labourers' families, the nation had a right to complain, when a new clearing off of debts was called for. Nevertheless, the new debt, which had arisen in little more than seven years, amounted to the enormous sum of £639,890 sterling. He had been spending at the rate of £140,000 a year instead of £60,000!

A compromise was reached by which commissioners were appointed in 1795 to superintend the payment of the debts. But, said Cobbett, this was hardly to the Prince's liking:

> The commissioners were to have complete power to inquire into the *origin* and *nature* of every debt; to watch over the *future expenditure*; the prince was placed under a guardianship and control as severe as

if he had still been an infant, or something even lower in the scale of intellectual capacity. Thus his marriage, instead of affording the prince that relief from embarrassment, was, to him, a season of the *deepest humiliation.*

Furthermore, the figure of loveliness he had married turned out to be a profligate hoyden, and the cost of maintaining the marriage was much more than he had bargained for. The ploy had backfired. The couple separated after a short time together. However, the parties continued unabated, it seems as much to bate his poor father as for his own amusement. When finally the prince was made Regent in 1811, he celebrated in style at his residence at Carlton House. The poet Thomas Moore described the fête to his mother:

I ought to have written yesterday, but I was in bed all day after the fête, which I did not leave till past six in the morning. Nothing was ever half so magnificent; it was in *reality* all that they try to imitate in the gorgeous scenery of the theatre; and I really sat for three quarters of an hour in the Prince's room after supper, silently looking at the spectacle, and feeding my eyes with the assemblage of beauty, splendour, and profuse magnificence which it presented.

As for the Princess of Wales, she was deeply hurt by the whole affair, but the decision to wash her dirty linen in public did not win as much sympathy with the populace as she hoped, though they were always happy to read whatever private correspondence she released to the newspapers. Dishing the dirt on your royal partner has a long precedence!

A letter composed by Princess Caroline's advisers to her estranged husband expressing her grievances was published in the Whig newspaper, the *Morning Chronicle*, in January 1813. Jane Austen enjoyed a good royal scandal and she expressed her feelings to her close friend Martha Lloyd:

I suppose all the World is sitting in Judgement upon the Princess of Wales's Letter. Poor Woman, I shall support her as long as I can, because she *is* a Woman, & because I hate her Husband—but I can hardly forgive her for calling herself 'attached & affectionate' to a Man whom she must detest ... I do not know what to do about it;—but if I must give up the Princess, I am resolved at least always to think that she would have been respectable, if the Prince had behaved only tolerably by her at first.

Jane's loathing of the prince did cause her conscience to be tested once when she was given an opportunity to breathe his royal air. Her niece Caroline tells the story of Jane's stay in London in 1815:

> One of [two physicians attending my uncle] had very intimate access to the Prince Regent, and ... he told my Aunt one day, that the Prince was a great admirer of her novels: that he often read them, and had a set in each of his residences—That *he*, the physician had told his Royal Highness that Miss Austen was now in London, and that by the Prince's desire, Mr Clarke, the Librarian of Carlton House, would speedily wait upon her ... three [novels] had then been published—the invitation could not be declined—and my Aunt went at the appointed time, to Carlton House ...
>
> She saw the Library, and I believe, some other apartments ... I do well recollect that Mr. Clarke, speaking again of the Regent's admiration of her writing, declared himself charged to say, that if Miss Austen had any other novel forthcoming, she was quite at liberty to dedicate it to the Prince.
>
> My Aunt made all the proper acknowledgements at the moment, but had no intention of accepting the honor offered—until she was avised [*sic*] by some of her friends that she must consider the permission as a command—
>
> Emma was then in the Publisher's hands—so a few lines of dedication were affixed to the 1st volume, and following still the instructions of the well informed, she sent a copy, handsomely bound, to Carlton House.

That was not the only royal approval Jane received for her novels. The 16-year-old Charlotte, only child of the Prince Regent and Princess Caroline, expressed her appreciation of *Sense and Sensibility*:

> Sence and Sencibility I have *just finished* reading; it certainly is interesting, & you feel quite one of the company. I think Maryanne & me are very like in *disposition*, that certainly I am not so good, the same imprudence, &c, however remain very like. I must say it interested me much.

Health

and Illness

The Georgians generally liked exercise and believed it kept them healthy. Country walks and riding were popular; in *Mansfield Park*, for example, Fanny Price rides regularly to keep fit. But the most fashionable thing to do for health, both to cure illness and to prevent it, was to spend time at the natural springs in Bath, or various other inland spas that emerged in the 18th century, such as Cheltenham and Tunbridge Wells.

The spa was to Georgians what the sickroom became in the 19th century and the health farm is today. It was the original purpose, after all, of visiting Bath. The elderly and sick from all over the country came to benefit from the purported medicinal properties of its mineral waters, and memorial stones on the Abbey walls testify to the wonders of these curatives. Jane's uncle, James Leigh-Perrot, drank the Pump Room waters twice a day for six months of the year, and Tobias Smollett had this to say about his early experience there:

I can feel a very sensible Effect from the waters. I have no sooner drank a large Glass of them hot from the Pump than my Face my Hands, and feet begin to glow; and this Sensation is succeeded by an itching and tingling all over the Surface of my Body, resembling what is called the prickly Heat in the west indies. I think I can plainly perceive these mineral waters opening up the obstructed Capillaries, and restoring the Perspiration which in the Extremities had been in great measure lost. I intend in a few days to bathe with a View to open still more effectually the Strainer of the skin.

The place became a commercial hive for the medical profession. Over 40 doctors and surgeons resided in Bath to be on hand to offer advice and regulate treatments, all at a price. The Revd John Penrose, a Cornish clergyman, went there to find relief for his gout and thought the waters beneficial but was dismayed by all the instructions he received:

> The Doctor has altered my Regimen: I am now to take Water from the Cross Bath at 7 and 8 o'clock mornings, and from the King's Bath at 12, quarter a Pint each time. Every one, who comes in, tells me this exactness as to Time and Quantity is a mere Farce, notwithstanding the Doctors so gravely prescribe. It may be so for ought I know; but as it may not be so, I'll try strictly adhere to Rule.

Some visitors were less charitable. Smollett, especially, spent a good many years assessing whether this hot water really did heal, and finally wrote to a doctor friend with his conclusion:

> There are mysteries in physick, as well as in religion ... Between friends, I think, every man of tolerable parts ought, at my time of day, to be both physician and lawyer, as far as his own constitution and property are concerned. For my own part I have had an hospital these fourteen years within myself, and studied my own case with painful attention ... I have for some time been of the opinion, (no offence, dear doctor) that the sum of all your medical discoveries amounts to this, that the more you study the less you know – I have read all that has been written on the Hot Wells, and what I can collect from the whole is that the water contains nothing but a little salt, and calcarious earth, mixed in such inconsiderable proportion as can have very little effect ... For such a paltry advantage as this spring affords ... [a man] exposes himself to the dirt, the stench, the chilling blasts, and perpetual rains, that render this place to me intolerable. If these waters, from a small degree of astringency, are of some service in the *diabetes, diarrheoa,* and *night sweats*, when the secretions are too much encreased, must not they do harm in the same proportion, where the humours are obstructed, as in the *asthma, scurvy, gout,* and *dropsy*?

As for the sedan chairs, which acted like wheelchairs to carry invalids as well as those in perfect health to the baths, Smollett doubted their value too:

> The chairs stand soaking in the open street, from morning to night, till they become so many boxes of wet leather, for the benefit of the gouty

and rheumatic ... the close chairs contrived for the sick have their frize linings impregnated, like so many spunges, with the moisture of the atmosphere, and those cases of cold vapour must give a charming check to the perspiration of a patient, piping hot from the Bath, with all his pores wide open.

Gradually people came to believe that better results than those to be had from inland spas were achieved from sea air and bathing in salt water. Seaside resorts such as Lyme Regis and Weymouth had been popular ever since George III, acting on advice from his doctors after suffering his first fit of insanity in 1789, recommended sea bathing at Weymouth as a means to restoring full health. One physician of the time, Dr Augustus Granville, explained:

Sea-water is in fact a *mineral water* to all intents and purposes. We may, therefore, look with as much confidence for beneficial results from its employment as from the employment of other mineral waters.

Jane Austen's cousin Eliza took the advice of her doctor and spent January and February in Margate, daily immersing her six-year-old son Hastings in the sea in the belief that at this time of year the salt water was more efficacious. Jane satirizes the vogue for these excursions to seaside resorts in her uncompleted novel of 1817, *Sanditon*, in which Arthur Parker is portrayed as an avid promoter of the new (fictitious) little resort of Sanditon on the Sussex coast. Speaking to the Heywood family, he expounds on his pet subject:

... healthy as they all undeniably were—[he] foresaw that every one of [the visitors] would be benefited by the sea.—He held it indeed as certain, that no person could be really well, no person (however upheld for the present by fortuitous aids of exercise & spirits in a semblance of health) could be really in a state of secure & permanent Health without spending at least 6 weeks by the Sea every year.—The Sea air & Sea Bathing together were nearly infallible, one or other of them being a match for every Disorder, of the Stomach, the Lungs, or the Blood. They were anti-spasmodic, anti-pulmonary, anti-sceptic, anti-bilious and anti-rheumatic. Nobody could catch cold by the Sea,

Nobody wanted appetite by the Sea, Nobody wanted Spirits, Nobody wanted Strength.—They were healing, softing, relaxing—fortifying & bracing—seemingly just as was wanted—sometimes one, sometimes the other.—If the Sea breeze failed, the Sea-Bath was the certain corrective;—& where Bathing disagreed, the Sea Breeze alone was evidently designed by Nature for the cure.—His eloquence however could not prevail. Mr & Mrs H never left home.

Complaints and their Cures

In 1796, William Buchan declared in his *Observations Concerning the Prevention and Cure of Venereal Disease*:

> For a long while air, water and even the light of the sun were dealt out by physicians to their patients with a sparing hand. They possessed for several centuries the same monopoly over many artificial remedies. But a new order of things is rising in medicine, as well as in government. Air, water, and light, are taken without the advice of a physician, and Bark and Laudanum are now prescribed every where by nurses and mistresses of families, with safety and advantage.

Medicine began at home. Before anyone sought advice from a doctor, home-produced remedies would be tried. It was the duty of every housekeeper, with the help of her cook, to prepare suitable remedies to treat illness. A knowledge of nature for growing medicinal herbs, together with a good manual, would see a family through many of its common complaints. The main source of authority was Nicholas Culpeper's *Complete Herbal and English Physician*, a book first published in 1653 and still in print in Jane Austen's time. Compiled for people who could not afford doctors and wished to treat themselves, it was filled with 'such things as only grow in England'.

Jane's friend Martha Lloyd, who lived with her at Chawton before marrying Frank Austen, made her own collection of remedies over the years and bound them together in her *Household Book*. It contains all sorts of weird and wonderful prescriptions, from relieving a headache to treating Mad Dog Bite. Jane was very proud of her friend, as is clear from a letter to Martha in 1812:

> We shall be glad to hear, whenever you can write, & can well imagine that time for writing must be wanting in such an arduous, busy, useful

office as you fill at present. You are made for doing good, & have quite as great a turn for it I think as for physicking little Children. The mental Physick which you have lately been applying bears a stamp beyond common Charity, & I hope a Blessing will continue to attend it.

The most common complaints of the day were colds, fevers, stomach upsets, gout, consumption, rheumatism and 'nerves'. Martha prescribed for these and other ailments, including toothache, worms, bodily aches and pains, salves for sore eyes and lips, and a condition she called 'the staggers' (probably giddiness). Many of her treatments were aimed at childhood illnesses, such as mumps and whooping cough, the recipe for the latter being:

Cut the hair from the top of the head as large as a crown piece. Take a piece of brown paper of the same size: dip it in rectified oyl of amber, and apply it to the part for nine mornings, dipping the paper fresh every morning. If the cough is not remov'd try it again after three or four days – this medicine is sometimes used by rubbing it along the backbone.

In 1804 Fanny Burney was confident of knowing how she could treat her sick son, aged six, and communicated the details to her husband:

I have not mentioned, I believe, that on Saturday, finding he had no more fever, I omitted the saline draughts, & gave him sulphur, cream de Tartre, & Honey, for his worms, as the most cooling medicine I dared administer, for I fear rhubarb with his Cough, & Bark & Garlick & Wine are hors de question.

'Rhubarb' mentioned here would not have been the edible stem we are familiar with but the rootstock of a related species imported from China and bought from the local apothecary. Unspecific (that is, unknown) fevers were commonplace. Jane nursed her brother Henry through a severe fever in 1815 and she portrays many of the characters in her novels as suffering from undiagnosed illnesses. Some, of course, proved lethal, as the Austens were to experience at Steventon when Warren Hastings' child, placed under their care for several years, died at the age of six from what was described as 'putrid sore throat'.

Jane's mother suffered quite a bit from ill health, especially colds. Jane always relayed news of her health to Cassandra during her frequent stays at Godmersham:

> My mother continues hearty, her appetite & nights are very good, but her Bowles are still not entirely settled, & she sometimes complains of an asthma, a Dropsy, Water in her Chest and a Liver disorder.

Plasters were made to apply to various maladies, not just cuts. Parson Woodforde, who drank a pint of port a day, regularly had recourse to the plaster to dress his gout:

> My ankle having given me so much Pain last Night, I having applied nothing to it but our Family Plaster, sent soon after breakfast to John Reeves at the Heart who practises something in the doctoring way.

If home treatment failed, it was down to the apothecary, physician or surgeon to find a solution.

Doctor or Quack?

In the 18th century there was a curious ambivalence towards doctors, or physicians, as they were known. On the one hand there was an increased demand for doctors as more money in society was available to pay them, and on the other hand people were sceptical about their usefulness, especially as their increased number also brought about a proliferation of unlicensed so-called quacks, who took advantage of society's ignorance and readiness to pay. Mrs Leigh-Perrot was in a quandary once about calling a local man to look at her poor husband, who was in great pain. She relayed her anxiety to her cousin in January 1800:

> I thank God he is now better but for one whole Night, and all the Next day, did he lie in such an Agony of Pain, that my distress was cutting indeed. I was desirous of having the Medical Man of Ilchester, though my Heart ached at the Alternative, (as his *trades* are *Apothecary, Surgeon, Coal dealer, Brick and Tile Maker, &c.* which seemed to bespeak his being good at None) but the dread of his mistaking the Constitution, so naturally full of Gout and the

Assurance from my poor Sufferer that he knew it was a severe fit of Gravel, or something like it (I hope not Gall Stones by the acuteness of pain) made us give this Assistance up, and as he has been better for the last two or three days my mind is a little easier on his Account.

The healer's art was not always given much credence. What mattered most for patients was his character and temperament. No one expected a doctor to perform miracles but in times of distress they needed someone with sound judgment, a good bedside manner and the sense to allow ultimate control to rest with the patient. Samuel Johnson's close friend Mrs Hester Thrale (who had encouraged the budding young author Fanny Burney) summed up Georgian attitudes to doctors thus:

A physician can sometimes parry the scythe of death, but has no power over the sand in the hourglass.

Nevertheless the medical profession prided itself on the precision of its diagnoses, regarding its mission as 'going to war against a fever', as the prominent Midlands physician Erasmus Darwin put it. Doctors commandeered the 'pharmaceutical artillery' of 'bleeding, blisters … boluses and draughts'. The main thrust of their strategy was to expel toxic substances from the body – by purging, sweating, vomiting and blood-letting – and thereby restore its right balance. Many of these processes could be administered by the household nurse but doctors liked to concoct a course of therapy consisting of many different elements spread over a long time. Parson Woodforde was an assiduous follower of his general practitioner's lengthy and most unpleasant-sounding directions:

Dr Thorne's Method of treating the Ague and Fever is thus—To take a Vomit in the Evening not to drink more than 3 half Pints of Warm Water after it as it operates. The Morn' following a Rhubarb Draught—and then as soon as the Fever had left the Patient about an Hour or more, begin with the Bark taking it every two Hours till you have taken 12 Papers which contains one Ounce. The next oz. etc you take it 6 Powders the ensuing Day, 5 Powders the Day after, 4 Ditto the Day after, then 3 Powders the Day after that till the 3ʳᵈ oz. is all taken, then 2 Powders the Day till the 4ᵗʰ oz. is all taken and then leave of. If at the beginning of taking the Bark it should happen to purge, put ten **Dropps of Laudanum** into the **Bark** you take next, then 4, then 3, then 2, then 1 and so leave of by degrees.

No wonder that many patients didn't bother about remedies. It was sometimes in the doctor's interest to keep the prescription brief and practical. When Fanny Knight got married, her husband Sir Edward Knatchbull, MP, had to obtain advice from his doctor on combating the treacherous November weather during his trips up to Parliament. He told Fanny:

I am to wear an additional piece of Flannel on my chest—to pay proper attention to my diet and habit of Body—to take regular exercise and particularly to ride on Horseback—to avoid all risk of catching cold, and not to expose myself to the night air ... have I not got a full Guinea's worth of advice? ... at breakfast I am (unless you will do it for me) to put four Cloves and eight Cinnamon Flowers into hot water—to let it stand and drink it an hour before dinner—I dare say it will be nasty and very beneficial.

Georgian doctors dished out this sort of advice particularly frequently in bad weather. Their diaries are filled with visiting appointments – Erasmus Darwin claimed to travel about 10,000 miles on calls in a year (no clinics yet existed for patients to visit). A doctor could therefore notch up reasonable earnings over the year: a provincial one could make £1,000 quite comfortably. This attracted many young men to medicine as a career, and as the century wore on the profession expanded and needed regulation. By 1779 the first national register was published, listing 3,000 official practitioners across three grades of the medical hierarchy: doctors, surgeons and apothecaries.

The more ambitious began to develop expertise in particular areas of medicine, for example, in combating certain diseases. Obstetrics, or man-midwifery, was one growth area and through the 18th century the traditional female midwife was gradually replaced by the man-midwife in towns, though in many rural areas a nurse was usually hired. She would help with delivering the baby and keep an eye open for symptoms of illness or infection, both in the newborn and the mother. Childbirth was a precarious event; three wives of Jane Austen's brothers died giving birth. An additional fear was developing puerperal fever, with probably fatal results a week or so later.

The increased use of doctors meant a greater dependency on them, a trend deplored by the old order who reckoned that most cases were the product of the imagination. People were thought to be more sensitive to pain and less prepared to put up with it than in the past. The result was a marked rise in hypochondria, particularly among the well off who had nothing better to do than dwell on their constitutions. Jane must have come across a fair few in her time, as she portrays the condition in some of her characters. Mr Woodhouse in *Emma* is forever complaining about the sickly London air, but perhaps the best example appears in her uncompleted novel *Sanditon*, begun in 1817 when hypochondria was more evident than ever: the young Arthur Parker suffers from most of the popular complaints of the time. His conversation with the newly introduced Charlotte Heywood runs as follows:

… he began even to make a sort of apology for having a fire.

'We should not have one at home,' said he, 'but the sea air is always damp, I am not afraid of anything so much as damp.'

'I am so fortunate,' said Charlotte, 'as never to know whether the air is damp or dry. It has always some property that is wholesome and invigorating to me.'

'I like the air too, as well as anybody can;' replied Arthur, 'I am very fond of standing at an open window when there is no wind—but unluckily a damp air does not like *me*. It gives me the rheumatism. You are not rheumatic I suppose?'

'Not at all.'

'That's a great blessing. But perhaps you are nervous.'

'No—I beleive not. I have no idea that I am.'

'I am very nervous. To say the truth nerves are the worst part of my complaints in *my* opinion. My sisters think me bilious, but I doubt it.'

'You are quite in the right to doubt it as long as you possibly can, I am sure.'

'If I were bilious,' he continued, 'you know wine would disagree with me, but it always does me good. The more wine I drink (in moderation) the better I am. I am always best of an evening. If you had seen me today before dinner, you would have thought me a very poor creature.' Charlotte could believe it.

By the 19th century there was so much doctoring that a new phenomenon emerged, namely the fashionable illness, which was claimed to be the result of the stresses that the new commercial society was bringing on its people. In his *Lectures on Diet*, Dr A Willich identified one very common complaint:

> The greater number of our fashionable complaints and affections
> are nearly related to each other. The gout, formerly a regular but
> uncommon disease, which attacked only the external parts of persons
> advanced in years, has now become a constitutional indisposition, a
> juvenile complaint, torturing the patient in a thousand different forms
> … Instead of the gout in the feet or hands, we hear every day of the
> nervous gout, the gout in the *head,* and even the fatal gout in the
> *stomach.* No rank, age, or mode of life seems to be exempt from this
> fashionable enemy.—The next and still more general malady of the
> times, is an extreme sensibility to every change of the atmosphere;
> or rather, constantly sensible relation to its influence.

As today, the tendency of 200 years ago was to reach for stimulants and
sedatives. Tea, alcohol, tobacco and drugs were consumed in ever greater
quantities. One drug in particular became widely available and was prescribed
as a highly effective pain-killer, despite reservations about its addictiveness.
The physician George Cheyne thought it nothing less than a divine gift:

> When our patience can hold out no longer, and Our Pains are at least
> come to be *insupportable,* we have always ready at Hand a Medicine,
> which is not only a present Relief, but, I may say, a standing and
> *constant Miracle.* Those only who have wanted it most, and have felt
> its friendly and kind Help in their Tortures, can best tell its *wonderful
> Effects,* and the great *Goodness* of Him who has bestowed it on us.
> I mean *Opium,* and its solution *Laudanum;* which when properly
> prescribed, and prudently managed, is a most *certain* and *sudden*
> Relief in all *exquisite* and *intense* Pain.

In the absence of anaesthetics or modern pain-killing agents, opium was
prescribed on a massive scale to reduce the agony inflicted by some diseases.
The sale of powerful narcotics on the open market facilitated their use for
recreational purposes too. The poets Samuel Taylor Coleridge and William
de Quincey discovered that opium could fire the Romantic imagination, and
their writings lauded its influence in plumbing new depths of the soul.

People were intrigued by the new developments in the world of medicine
and scientists in turn were encouraged to experiment more. One of the
most prominent of the day was Thomas Beddoes, who risked his reputation
by dabbling in gas experiments at the end of the 18th century. Using his

assistant Humphrey Davy as a guinea pig, the doctor commenced a trial with nitrous oxide that was to have momentous results. By ingesting increasingly large quantities, Davy became heavily intoxicated but not in any way known hitherto. He described what he felt:

> By degrees as the pleasurable sensations increased, I lost all connection with external things; trains of vivid visible images rapidly passed through my mind and were connected with words in such a manner, as to produce perceptions perfectly novel. I existed in a world of newly connected and newly modified ideas. I theorized; I imagined that I made discoveries … 'Nothing exists but thoughts!—the universe is composed of impressions, ideas, pleasures and pains!'

Thus was discovered the first anaesthetic, known as 'laughing gas'. It quickly became a source of curiosity to all society – Robert Southey declared that 'the air in heaven must be this wonder-working gas of delight!' Davy went on to become a renowned chemist in his own right (in 1815 he designed the safety lamp named after him for use in mines). He was also famous for his choice of laboratory assistant in Michael Faraday, who began to devise ways of harnessing electricity in the 1820s. But well before then electricity was being employed as a means of healing various ills. In the summer of 1799 Edward Austen decided to rent an apartment in Bath in order to take advantage of the treatments there to address his troublesome gout, as Jane related to her sister:

> What must I tell you of Edward? … He was better yesterday than he had been for two or three days before, about as well as while he was at Steventon—He drinks at the Hetling Pump, is to bathe tomorrow, & try Electricity on Tuesday;—he proposed the latter himself to Dr Fellowes, who made no objection to it, but I fancy we are all unanimous in expecting no advantage from it.

The emergence of this rather violent shock treatment was not received with universal approval. Many held their suspicions of these speculative medical ventures, and stories circulated about their failures, of experiments going disastrously wrong. This was the period when the novelist Mary Shelley, who was fascinated by anatomy and dissection, dreamed up her tale of Dr Frankenstein, whose creature composed of dead body parts was frighteningly brought to life by lightning electricity during a storm. That the creature turned into a dreadful monster was perceived as an indictment of the irresponsible experimentation of the time.

Lumped in with this condemnation were those unlicensed peddlers of pills and potions, the quacks, who sold their substances to anybody gullible enough to buy. Some bizarre examples were identified by Robert Southey:

> **The most eminent quack of the last generation was a Doctor Graham. ... His latest method of practice was something violent; it was to bury his patients up to the chin in fresh mould. J— saw half a score of them exhibited in this manner for a shilling ... The operation lasted four hours; they suffered, as might be seen in their countenances, intensely from cold for the first two, during the third they grew warmer, and in the last perspired profusely, so that when they were taken out the mould reeked like a new dunghill. Sailors are said to have practised this mode of cure successfully for the scurvy.**
>
> **... Another gentleman quacks with oxygen, and recommends what he calls vital wine as a cure for all diseases. Vital wine must be admitted to be something extraordinary; but what is that to a people for whom solar and lunar tinctures have been prepared! Another has risen from a travelling cart to the luxuries of a chariot by selling magnetic girdles; his theory is that the magnetic virtue attracts the iron in the blood, and makes the little red globules revolve faster, each upon its own axis, in the rapidity and regularity of which revolutions health consists, – and this he proves to the people by showing them how a needle is set in motion by his girdles.**

Medical practice could be so outrageous that one surgeon in the profession, Thomas Wakley, launched a periodical specifically for the purpose of exposing the worst excesses. Thus was founded the *Lancet* in 1823, which became one of the world's leading independent journals in its field.

Surgeons and Apothecaries

Those who wielded the scalpel and the knife formed the second tier in the medical pyramid, below doctors and above apothecaries. George Austen's father was a surgeon in Tonbridge. Contrary to the prestige of surgeons today, their counterparts in Jane Austen's time commanded little confidence in the public's mind (until the middle of the 18th century they had been classified as barber-surgeons because they combined the two occupations). To be fair, they had none of the resources available to the modern practitioner. There were no anaesthetics, no antiseptics, and surgical instruments were crude. The most basic incisions and fractures could turn septic or gangrenous. Wartime brought plentiful opportunities to practise, dressing gun wounds and amputating limbs, many of which procedures resulted in further complications. In peacetime surgeons performed various minor operations at patients' homes, such as lancing boils and dressing wounds.

Those sufferers who could not afford to pay for their treatment might be admitted to one of the new Georgian hospitals, which had developed out of the traditional hospices that cared for the sick poor. Many hospitals had been founded up and down the country in the 18th century in the light of the new optimism about being able to treat disease. Some of the great London hospitals were built in this period, as were those in the provinces, at Bristol, Exeter, Winchester and Bath. One of the largest in Europe was the Royal Naval Hospital at Gosport, the overflow town to Portsmouth, which could accommodate up to 1,000 war-wounded patients.

How much the hospitals could do for the sick was questionable. No highly infectious cases were admitted and most patients left in no better shape than when they entered. What the hospitals did develop of use to the public was their out-patients' dispensary of drugs. These formed part of a wider network of druggists, or apothecaries, who ran shops, like pharmacies or drugstores today, supplying medicines and other chemical compounds such as toiletries and cosmetics. Most small towns had an apothecary, who might be the only local source of knowledge on a medical subject, as Jane describes in *Emma*:

He had been at the pains of consulting Mr. Perry, the apothecary, on the subject. Mr. Perry was an intelligent, gentlemanlike man, whose frequent visits were one of the comforts of Mr. Woodhouse's life; and upon being applied to, he could not but acknowledge (though it seemed rather against the bias of inclination) that wedding-cake might certainly disagree with many – perhaps with most people, unless taken moderately.

Until the 18th century the role of the apothecary had been to dispense physicians' prescriptions only, but in 1704 licensed apothecaries won the right to prescribe their own medication. The following article, taken from

The Book of Trades, or Library of Useful Arts, published in 1807, outlines the pride of the profession:

> The office of the apothecary is to attend on sick persons, and to prepare and give them medicines, either on his own judgement or according to the prescription of the physician ... In many places, and particularly in opulent cities, the first apothecaries' shops were established at the public expense, and belonged, in fact, to the magistrates. A particular garden also was often appropriated to the use of the apothecary, in order that he might rear in the necessary plants, and which was therefore called the apothecaries' garden. In conformity to this principle, Sir Hans Sloane, in the year 1721 presented the apothecaries' company with a spacious piece of ground at Chelsea, for a physic garden, on condition of their ... presenting to the Royal Society fifty samples of different sorts of plants grown there, till they amounted to two thousand. The pine-tree, coffee-tree, tea-shrub, and sugar-cane, are among the curiosities which may be seen at this place.
>
> ... This is a very genteel business and a youth intended to be an apothecary should be a good scholar, at least he should know as much of Latin as to be able to read the best writers in the various sciences connected with medicine. All persons apprenticed to an apothecary are bound for eight years. An assistant, or journeyman, to an apothecary will have from forty to fourscore pounds per annum, exclusive of his board.

Pulling Teeth

Dentists were found only in the larger cities. Hence Jane took her nephews and nieces to London when they needed treatment. Her mother had lost most of her front teeth by the time she was 50, probably as much due to poor diet in the winter months as anything else. There were home remedies, such as opium prescribed by Martha Lloyd, to combat toothache. But for emergency extractions it was usually a matter of asking someone local who could turn his hand to such an operation. Parson Woodforde recorded one instance in 1776 when he asked the local farrier to help him out:

> My tooth pained me all night, got up a little after 5 this morning, & sent for one Reeves a man who draws teeth in this parish and about

7 he came and drew my tooth, but shockingly bad indeed, he broke away a great piece of my gum and broke one of the fangs of the tooth, it gave me exquisite pain all the day after, and my face was swelled prodigiously in the evening and much pain … Gave the old man that drew it however 0-2-6. He is too old, I think to draw teeth, can't see very well.

Killer Diseases

One of the medical breakthroughs of the Georgian period was the discovery in 1796 of vaccination against smallpox, the most common child-killer of the time. Dr Edward Jenner noticed that people such as dairymaids who had had the milder cattle disease cowpox did not catch smallpox. In an experiment on a small boy, whose arm he scratched with a little fluid of cowpox, he tested out his theory that by so doing he would encourage the body to build up an immunity to the disease. The boy immediately displayed symptoms of cowpox but recovered, and despite later exposure to sufferers of smallpox did not contract the disease himself. Doctors were so impressed that some made it their mission to carry out mass vaccinations of entire parishes.

Tuberculosis and appendicitis were constant fears. Cholera was a blight of the Victorian era but other tropical diseases brought in by traders and seamen were a constant fear in the ports. There was an outbreak of typhoid fever while Jane and her sister were attending school in Southampton, and Cassandra Austen's fiancé, Revd Tom Fowle, was sent to West Indies with the British Expeditionary Force in 1795 and died there of yellow fever. 'New diseases', including rickets and whooping cough, could be severe enough to claim lives, as could other unknown 'fevers' of the time such as diphtheria (described as 'putrid sore throat'), measles and scarlet fever. In 1803 a 'flu epidemic devastated Europe, for which, like another killer disease syphilis, the French were blamed.

The cause of Jane's own early death is thought to have been a rare progessive disorder of the adrenal gland, now known as Addison's Disease. On 23 March 1817 Jane described a little of her condition to her favourite niece, Fanny Knight:

Many thanks for your kind care for my health; I certainly have not been well for many weeks, & about a week ago I was very poorly, I have had a good deal of fever at times & indifferent nights, but am considerably better now, & recovering my Looks a little, which have been bad enough, black and white & every wrong colour. I must not depend upon being ever very blooming again. Sickness is a dangerous Indulgence at my time of Life.

The following day she was well enough to ride a donkey but days later she relapsed, then recovered, and so her health alternated in fits and starts until the end of April, when she must have realized she might never recover and so made out her will:

I Jane Austen of the Parish of Chawton do by this my last Will & Testament give and bequeath to my dearest Sister Cassandra Elizth. Every thing of which I may die possessed, or which may be hereafter due to me, subject to the payment of my Funeral Expenses, & to a Legacy of £50 to my Brother Henry, & £50 to Mde. Bigion [Madame Bigeon, Eliza's faithful French servant] – which I request may be paid as soon as convenient. And I appoint my said dear Sister Executrix.

With worsening symptoms in May she took the advice of those around her who thought medical help was needed closer at hand than was available at her home in Chawton. As ever, Jane was appreciative of all the affection and help given to her. One of the last letters she wrote was to her former governess and friend Anne Sharp on 22 May:

How to do justice to the kindness of all my family during this illness, is quite beyond me!—Every dear Brother so affectionate and anxious!—And as to my Sister!—Words must fail me in any attempt to describe what a Nurse she has been to me. Thank God! she does not seem the worse for it *yet*, & as there was never any Sitting-up necessary, I am willing to hope she has no after-fatigues to suffer from. I have so many alleviations & comforts to bless the Almighty for!—My head was always clear, & I had scarcely any pain; my chief sufferings were from feverish nights, weakness & Languor.—This Discharge was on me for above a week, & as our Alton Apoth^y did not pretend to be able to cope with it, better advice was called in. Our nearest *very good*, is at Winchester, where there is a Hospital & capital Surgeons, & one of them attended me, & *his* applications gradually removed the Evil.—The consequence is, that instead of going to Town to put myself into the hands of some Physician as I sh^d otherwise have done, I am going to Winchester ... to see what Mr Lyford [surgeon] can do farther towards re-establishing me in tolerable health.—On Sat^y next, I am actually going thither—my dearest Cassandra with me I need hardly say—and as this is only two days off you will be convinced that I am now really a very genteel, portable sort of an Invalid.—The Journey is only 16 miles, we have comfortable Lodgings engaged for us by our kind friend Mrs Heathcote who resides in W. & are to have the accommodation of my elder Brother's Carriage which will be sent over from Steventon on purpose. Now, that's a sort of thing which Mrs J. Austen [James's second wife Mary] does in the kindest manner!

Jane's condition puzzled her doctors; all they could really do was administer sedatives. Mary joined Cassandra to help with the nursing, after the duty nurse was discovered asleep at Jane's bedside. Despite worsening health she staggered on to live another two months in her Winchester lodgings before dying peacefully on 18 July 1817 with Cassandra at her bedside.

Even up to the last few days before her death Jane's sense of humour did not desert her. It was St Swithin's Day on 15 July, when everyone in and around Winchester followed the custom of going to the races. This day, of course, has passed into folklore as being cursed by the saint ever since his relics, buried as he wished outside the cathedral, were exhumed by monks and moved to a shrine inside. A violent storm is said to have been followed by 40 days of rain as a sign of his displeasure. As all the pleasure-seekers of Winchester trundled off to the race course bemoaning the wet weather, Jane could not resist composing one final poem, *Venta* (after the Roman name for the city), in a wry celebration of immortality:

When Winchester races first took their beginning
It is said the good people forgot their old Saint
Not applying at all for the leave of Saint Swithin
And that William of Wykeham's approval was faint.

The races however were fixed and determined
The company came and the Weather was charming
The Lords and the Ladies were satine'd and ermined
And nobody saw any future alarming.—

But when the old Saint was informed of these doings
He made but one Spring from his Shrine to the Roof
Of the Palace which now lies so sadly in ruins
And then he addressed them all standing aloof.

'Oh! subjects rebellious! Oh Venta depraved
When once we are buried you think we are gone
But behold me immortal! By vice you're enslaved
You have sinned and must suffer, ten farther he said

These races and revels and dissolute measures
With which you're debasing a neighbouring Plain
Let them stand—You shall meet with your curse in your pleasures
Set off for your course, I'll pursue with my rain.

Ye cannot but know my command o'er July
Henceforward I'll triumph in shewing my powers
Shift your race as you will it shall never be dry
The curse upon Venta is July in showers—' .

Like St Swithin, Jane Austen was buried in Winchester Cathedral and now
draws her own brand of devotees. Rather in the same way that medieval
pilgrims would have venerated the relics of saints, members of the Austen
family followed a funerary custom of their time by which locks of the
deceased's hair were kept as mementoes. Before the lid of the coffin was
closed Cassandra cut off several of Jane's locks and distributed them to loved
ones. Her brothers would have had one each, her governess was sent one,
Fanny had hers set in a specially made brooch and Cassandra commissioned
a ring to be made with a dear curl laid among pearls, a piece of jewellery she
treasured for the rest of her life.

Select Bibliography

Austen, Caroline, *Reminiscences of Caroline Austen* (Jane Austen Society, Chawton, 1986)

Austen, James, *The Loiterer* (Oxford, 1789–90)

Austen-Leigh, JE, *A Memoir of Jane Austen* (Richard Bentley, London, 1871, enlarged edition; Clarendon Press, Oxford, 1926)

Austen-Leigh, RA, *Austen Papers 1704–1856* (privately printed for the London Library by Spottiswoode, Ballantyne & Co., London, 1942)

Burney, F, *Selected Letters & Journals* (ed. J Hemlow, Clarendon Press, Oxford, 1986)

Chapman, RW, *The Works of Jane Austen, Vol. VI, 'Minor Works'* (OUP, 1954)

Chesterfield, PDS, *Letters of Lord Chesterfield to His Son* (Dutton, London, 1929)

Cobbett, W, *Cottage Economy* (C Clement, London, 1822)

Cobbett, W, *History of the Regency & Reign of George IV* (W Cobbett, London, 1830)

Cobbett, W, *Rural Rides* (A Cobbett, London, 1853)

Collins, I, *Jane Austen and the Clergy* (Hambledon Press, London, 1993)

Davidson, C, *A Woman's Work Is Never Done: A History of Housework in the British Isles, 1650–1950* (Chatto & Windus, London, 1982)

Hickman, P, *A Jane Austen Household Book (with Martha Lloyd's recipes)* (David & Charles, Newton Abbot, 1977)

Hubback, JH and EC, *Jane Austen's Sailor Brothers* (Jonathan Lane, London, 1906)

Le Faye, D, *Jane Austen's Letters* (OUP, Oxford, 1995)

Locke, J, *Some Thoughts Concerning Education* (1705; 12th edn printed for J Brown, Edinburgh, 1752)

Porter, R, *English Society in the 18th Century* (Allen Lane, London, 1982)

Porter, R and D, *Patient's Progress* (Polity Press, Cambridge, 1989)

Sales, R, *Jane Austen and Representations of Regency England* (Routledge, London, 1994)

Simond, L, *An American in Regency England: Journal of a Tour 1810–1811* (History Book Club, London, 1968)

Skinner, J, *Journal of a Somerset Rector 1803–1834* (Oxford University Press, Oxford, 1984)

Southey, R, *Letters from England* (Cresset Press, London, 1951)

Stone, L, *The Family, Sex and Marriage in England, 1500–1800* (Weidenfeld & Nicolson, London, 1977)

Strutt, J, *Sports and Pastimes of the People of England* (printed by T Bensley for White & Co., London, 1801)

Sydney, WC, *England and the English in the Eighteenth Century*, 2 vols (John Grant, Edinburgh, 1891)

Wollstonecraft, M, *A Vindication of the Rights of Man and A Vindication of the Rights of Woman* (Cambridge University Press, Cambridge, 1995)

Woodforde, J, *The Diary of a Country Parson, 1758–1802* (Oxford University Press, Oxford, 1949)

Chronology Of Events

1775	**Jane Austen born on 16 December**
1776	America declares independence from Britain on 4 July
	First Classic horse race, St Leger, held at Doncaster
1778	Britain and France go to war over colonies
1779	World's first iron bridge built, across River Severn
1780	Gordon Riots break out in protest against Catholic easement
1781	Astronomer William Herschel discovers planet Uranus
1782	**Jane and Cassandra Austen sent to boarding school in Oxford**
1783	William Pitt becomes prime minister, aged 24
1784	Mail-coach system introduced in England
1785	Hot air balloon makes first air crossing of English Channel
1787	**Jane Austen finishes formal education and begins writing**
1788	Trial of Warren Hastings begins in Westminster Hall
	King George III shows first signs of madness
	First convicts shipped to Australia
1789	French Revolution begins with storming of Bastille in Paris on 14 July
	Mutineers on HMS *Bounty* set Captain Bligh adrift in South Seas
1790	'Canal mania' begins with completion of Grand Cross linking four major English rivers
	Josiah Wedgwood produces his finest porcelain in Staffordshire
1791	Radical journalist Thomas Paine publishes *The Rights of Man*
1792	Feminist writer Mary Wollstonecraft publishes *A Vindication of the Rights of Woman*
1793	Revolutionary France declares war on Britain after executing Louis XVI
1794	Erasmus Darwin publishes *Zoönomia or The Laws of Organic Life*
1795	Prince of Wales marries Princess Caroline
1796	Dr Jenner discovers smallpox vaccination
	JMW Turner exhibits first oil painting, *Fishermen at Sea*, at Royal Academy
1798	Samuel Taylor Coleridge writes *The Rime of the Ancient Mariner*
1799	William Pitt introduces income tax

1800	Chemist Humphry Davy discovers anaesthetic
1801	**The Austens move to Bath**
1802	Treaty of Amiens ends nine years of war with France
	Robert Peel, MP, pilots new legislation to regulate child labour
1803	War with France resumed after Napoleon Bonaparte violates Treaty of Amiens
1804	Martello towers built on Britain's coast to defend against expected invasion from France
	Engineer Richard Trevithick builds first steam locomotive
	William Blake writes poem 'Jerusalem'
1805	Lord Nelson dies victorious at the Battle of Trafalgar
	George Austen dies
1806	**The Austens move to Southampton**
	Prime Minister William Pitt dies
1807	Britain abolishes slave-trading
1809	**The Austens move to Chawton**
	Iberian Peninsular War begins
1811	Prince of Wales becomes Regent
	***Sense and Sensibility* published**
1812	Duke of Wellington liberates Madrid from Joseph Bonaparte, while Joseph's brother Napoleon retreats from Moscow
1813	Iberian Peninsular War ends
	Journalist Leigh Hunt jailed for two years for libelling Prince Regent
	Reformer Elizabeth Fry visits Newgate Prison in London
	***Pride and Prejudice* published**
1814	Napoleon exiled to Elba; escapes
	***Mansfield Park* published**
1815	Wellington victorious at Battle of Waterloo and Napoleon exiled for final time
1816	Percy Bysshe Shelley expelled from Oxford University for writing pamphlet on atheism
	***Emma* published**
1817	**Jane Austen dies 18 July**
1818	***Persuasion* and *Northanger Abbey* published posthumously**

Gazetteer (Population figures based on the 1801 census)

Adlestrop, Gloucestershire. Adlestrop House (now Park) has been home to one branch of the Leigh family since 1553.

Alton, Hampshire. Henry Austen's banking firm, Austen, Gray & Vincent, was located at 10 High Street, and the local apothecary a few doors further down. The town is now almost one with the village of Chawton.

Ashe, Hampshire. Village 2 miles from Steventon. Ashe Rectory was home to the Lefroy family.

Basingstoke, Hampshire. Market town 9 miles from Steventon. Jane Austen came to dance at the Assembly Rooms situated in the Market Place on the upper floor of the town hall.

Bath, Somerset. Provincial town and famous Georgian spa with population of 32,000. The Austens lived here from 1801 until 1806. Among the many landmarks are Queen Square, The Circus, Pulteney Bridge, Royal Crescent and the Pump Room. The Assembly Rooms were destroyed in World War II but reconstruction has enabled them to reopen as a museum housing costumes of Jane Austen's period. The Austens lived in turn at 4 Sydney Place, 3 Green Park Buildings East, 25 Gay Street, and Trim Street.

Birmingham, Warwickshire. Provincial town with population of 74,000. Developing centre of industry.

Brighton, Sussex. Fashionable seaside resort (formerly Brighthelmstone) frequented by the Prince Regent, whose Pavilion (now a museum) was built in the 1780s. Henry Austen came here with the Oxford Militia at the outbreak of hostilities with Revolutionary France.

Bristol, Somerset. Main seaport for the west of England with population of 64,000. Famous for its role in the slave trade and the import of rum, tobacco and sugar from America and the West Indies.

Cambridge, Cambridgeshire. County town, 60 miles from London, with one of England's two universities at the time of Jane Austen.

Canterbury, Kent. County town 60 miles from London and familiar to Jane Austen on her trips to visit her brother Edward at Godmersham Park. She shopped here and once visited the jail.

Charmouth, Dorset. Fishing village 3 miles from Lyme Regis.

Chawton, Hampshire. 17 miles from Steventon. Jane Austen lived with her mother, sister, and Martha Lloyd at Chawton Cottage, which her brother Edward inherited from the Knights as part of the estate of Chawton Great House. The cottage is now a museum of Jane Austen memorabilia.

Cheltenham, Gloucestershire. Spa town fashionable from the late 18th century.

Colyton, Devon. Pretty village between Sidmouth and Lyme Regis, with much Georgian architecture remaining.

Dawlish, Devon. Fishing village and seaside resort. The Austens spent a holiday here in 1802; Jane complained the library was 'pitiful and wretched'.

Deane, Hampshire. Village 2 miles from Steventon. Jane's father was rector from 1773 until his death in 1805, but the church has since been demolished. He lived at the parsonage in his early married life and his first three children were born here. After the Austens moved to Steventon the vacant parsonage was let to a clergyman's widow, Mrs Lloyd and her three daughters, whom the Austen sisters visited regularly. When James Austen took over the parsonage as his father's curate, the Lloyds moved out.

Godmersham Park, Kent. Georgian mansion 8 miles from Canterbury. Jane Austen's brother Edward lived here from 1783 and inherited the estate from his adoptive father, Thomas Knight. Cassandra Austen stayed here frequently.

Kempshott Park, Hampshire. Great country estate 4 miles from Basingstoke let to the Prince of Wales from 1788 to 1795, and then to Lord Dorchester. Little has survived. James Austen frequently went hunting with the Prince here and Jane attended a ball during the Dorchesters' occupation.

London. Capital of England and largest city in the world with over a million inhabitants. Jane Austen was familiar with the West End. Places that she visited include: the **British Gallery** in Pall Mall, holding exhibitions of paintings; **Carlton House**, palace home of the Prince Regent in Pall Mall facing St James's Park, demolished in 1827; **Drury Lane Theatre**, Covent Garden, rebuilt in 1811 after a fire; **Henrietta Street**, also in Covent Garden, where Henry Austen lived at number 10; **Hyde Park**, a royal park at the western limit of London, enclosing Kensington Gardens and the Serpentine lake; **Liverpool Museum**, Piccadilly, also known as Bullock's Museum of Natural & Artificial Curiosities, forerunner of the Natural History Museum, now demolished; **Theatre Royal**, Covent Garden, now the Opera House, burnt down in 1808.

Lyme Regis, Dorset. Seaside resort where the Austens stayed in 1803, probably in the cottage now named Pyne House in Broad Street. The Assembly Room was situated at the foot of Broad Street overlooking the sea but has since been demolished. Jane was particularly fond of Lyme and set scenes from *Persuasion* here, on the promenade and the Cobb.

Manydown Park, Wootton St Lawrence, Hampshire. Large manor house, dating back to the 14th century, and home to the Bigg-Wither family until its demolition in 1965. Jane often stayed overnight here after attending Basingstoke balls. It was here that Harris Bigg-Wither proposed to her.

Oxford, Oxfordshire. County town with England's oldest university, dating back to at least the 12th century. Jane's father attended St John's College as a student and, briefly, a don. James and Henry followed in their father's footsteps; James

staying for 11 years and founding the weekly journal *The Loiterer*. Jane and Cassandra went to school in the city. Mrs Austen's father, Thomas Leigh, was a Fellow of All Souls College.

Portsmouth, Hampshire. Seaport with population of 32,000. Famous naval dockyard now with outdoor museum exhibits, including HMS *Victory*, the flagship of Lord Nelson in the Battle of Trafalgar in 1805. Francis and Charles Austen attended the Royal Naval Academy in the dockyard and its buildings still stand. Jane Austen set some of *Mansfield Park* in Portsmouth, where the fictional Lieutenant Price of the Royal Marines is based.

Sidmouth, Devon. Resort where Jane spent her first holiday in Devon in 1801.

Southampton, Hampshire. Quiet, elegant seaport. The Austens lived at a house in Castle Square from 1807 to 1809. Jane briefly went to school here earlier but was forced by illness to leave.

Steventon, Hampshire. Village where George Austen was rector from 1761 until his death in 1805; in 1768 he moved into Steventon Rectory (owned by Thomas Knight of Godmersham Park) where five of his children (including Jane) were born. Steventon Manor was let to tenants, the Digweeds. The rectory was demolished in 1824.

Stoneleigh Abbey, Warwickshire. Ancestral home to one branch of the Leigh Family, originally a Cistercian abbey, and inherited by Mrs Austen's cousins in 1806.

Tonbridge, Kent. Provincial town 35 miles from London. George Austen's father worked as a surgeon here, and many Austen forebears lived in this area.

Weymouth, Dorset. Seaside resort made famous by George III, who stayed at Gloucester House in 1789.

Winchester, Hampshire. County town, 16 miles from Chawton. Jane Austen died at 8 College Street and is buried in the north aisle of the cathedral. Winchester College, founded in 1382, was Britain's first public school.

Ashe Rectory
Deane House
Overton
Manydown House
Basingstoke
Kempshott Park
Steventon Rectory
Alton
Chawton

0   1   2 miles

The
Liverpool

ST

WOF

HEREFORD-
SHIRE

Chel

GLOU

WALES

Bristol   Ba

SOMERSET

Taunton

DEVON

Exeter
Colyton
Charmouth
Lyme Regis
Sidmouth
We
Teignmouth
Exmouth
Dawlish

CORNWALL

Plymouth

Falmouth

E N G L I S

Chatsworth

LINCOLNSHIRE

DERBY-
SHIRE

NOTTINGHAM-
SHIRE

Cromer

LEICESTERSHIRE

RUT-
LAND

NORFOLK

Norwich

ningham

heleigh

NORTHAMPTON-
SHIRE

HUNTING-
DON-
SHIRE

Newmarket

RWICK-
HIRE

Northampton

Cambridge

SUFFOLK

CAMBRIDGE-
SHIRE

E N G L A N D

BEDFORD-
SHIRE

rop

OXFORD-
SHIRE

BUCKING-
HAM-
SHIRE

Oxford

HERTFORDSHIRE

ESSEX

BERKSHIRE

MIDDLESEX

London

Southend

Harpsden

orough

Reading

Windsor

Dartford

Gravesend

Margate

RE

Ibthorpe

Basingstoke

Epsom

Sittingbourne

Sevenoaks

Canterbury

Steventon
(see inset)

Alton

Guildford

▲ Box Hill

Tonbridge

Godmersham

Chawton

SURREY

Tunbridge Wells

bury

Winchester

KENT

HAMPSHIRE

SUSSEX

Hastings

Southampton

Worthing

Brighton

Eastbourne

Portsmouth

Isle of Wight

H A N N E L

0   25   50 miles

Sources

Aspinall, A, ed., *Letters of the Princess Charlotte 1811–1817*, p.26, Home & Van Thal, 1949 253

Austen, Caroline, *My Aunt Jane Austen*, Jane Austen Society 92–3, 93, 93–4, 94, 98, 100, 103, 253

Austen, Caroline, *Reminiscences of Caroline Austen*, Jane Austen Society, 1986 52, 56–7, 203–4

Austen Papers 1704–1856, ed. RA Austen-Leigh, Spottiswoode, Ballantyne, 1942 14, 15, 66, 97, 104, 111–12, 141, 141–2, 142, 176–7, 181, 186, 198, 228–9, 260–1, 270

Austen-Leigh, JE, *A Memoir of Jane Austen*, 1871, OUP, 2002, by permission of Oxford University Press 19, 56, 65, 70, 71, 91, 106, 113, 117, 134, 188, 192, 197

[quoted in] Bence-Jones, M, *Clive of India*, Constable, 1974 32

[quoted in] Brown, Francis, *A History of the English Clergy, 1800–1900*, p.18, Faith Press, 1953 44

Canning, Elizabeth, letter, Bath Central Library 167–8, 168

'CMCA to Amy Austen-Leigh', taken from *Jane Austen, A Family Record*, p.122, eds Austen-Leigh & Le Faye, 1989, pub. British Library, by permission of the British Library 30, 31

Davies, Revd David, quoted in Roy Porter, *English Society in the Eighteenth Century*, p.228, Allen Lane, 1982 234–5

Defoe, Daniel, quoted in Roy Porter, *English Society in the Eighteenth Century*, Allen Lane, 1982 55

Diaries of Fanny Knight (later Lady Knatchbull), 1804–72, The, Centre for Kentish Studies 159

Early Journals and Letters of Fanney

Burney, ed. Lars E Troide, vol. 1, Clarendon, 1988 102

Eden, Frederick, quoted in Roy Porter, *English Society in the Eighteenth Century*, p.318, Allen Lane, 1982 235

Fry, Katherine, *Memoir of the Life of Elizabeth Fry*, Patterson Smith, 1974 144

Gentleman's Magazine, 1797, Hartley Library, Southampton University 83

Gentleman's Magazine, 1833, vol. 103, part 2, pp.42–3, by permission of the British Library 151

Gibbon, E, *Autobiography*, ed. MM Reese, Routledge & Kegan Paul, 1970 73

Giddy, Davies, from Roy Porter, *English Society in the Eighteenth Century*, Allen Lane, 1982 87

Gilpin, W, *Observations on the Western Parts of England Relative Chiefly to Picturesque Beauty*, Cadell, 1798, republished by Richmond Press, 1973 91

Hampshire Chronicle, 23 May 1798, Hampshire Record Office (HRO 3A00W/A3/9) 221

Hampshire Chronicle, 29 July 1776, Hampshire Record Office (HRO 3A00W/A3/2) 140

Hampshire Chronicle, 13 October 1806, Hampshire Record Office (HRO 3A00W/A3/11) 135–6

[quoted in] Hibbert, C, *The English A Social History 1066–1945*, Grafton, 1987 73

Higgins, Matthew, *A Letter on Administrative Reform* (1855), quoted in WL Burn *The Age of Equipoise*, George Allen & Unwin, 1964 46

Holcroft, T, *A Plain and Succinct Narrative of the Gordon Riots, London, 1780*, pp.32-3, Emory University, Atlanta, 1944 237

Howard, C, 'Reminiscences for my Children', 1831, quoted in Laurance Stone, *Family, Sex and Marriage*, Weidenfeld & Nicolson, 1977 61

Hubback, JH & EC, *Jane Austen's Sailor Brothers*, Jonathan Lane, 1906; reprinted Ian Hodgkins, 1986 53, 53–4, 225

JA's Letters, quoted in *Jane Austen's Letters*, ed. Deirdre Le Faye, OUP, 1995, by permission of Oxford University Press 24, 24–5, 25, 26, 31–2, 33, 34, 46, 49, 56, 74, 98, 99, 102, 104, 108, 110, 122, 155, 156, 157, 168–9, 173, 175, 176,   179, 183, 185, 186, 196, 206–7, 222, 223, 252–3, 258–9, 260, 265, 269–70, 270–1

James Austen's *Occasional Writings*, Hampshire Record Office (HRO 23M93/60/3/2) 92

Journal of John Wesley, The, ed. Percy Livingstone Parker, Moddy Press, 1951 121, 123

Journals of Agnes Porter, The, 1797, quoted in J Martin, *A Governess in the Age of Jane Austen*, Hambledon, 1998 62–3, 80–1

Knatchbull, Lady (Fanny Knight), Diaries and Letters of, Centre for Kentish Studies 172

Knatchbull-Hugesson, Sir Hughe, *Kentish Family*, Methuen, 1960 203

Knight, D, *Humphry Davy: Science & Power*, p.30, Blackwell, 1992 265

Knight, Fanny, quoted in Maria Hubert, *Jane Austen's Christmas*, Sutton, 2003, by permission of Maria Hubert von Staufer 173–4

La Rochefoucauld, F De, *A Frenchman in England*, 1784 (1933), trans. S Roberts, Cambridge University Press 197

Lackington, James, in Roy Porter, *English Society in the Eighteenth Century*, Allen Lane, 1982 101

Lady's Magazine, The, 1773, pp. 183–4, by permission of The British Library

28–9, 34

Lady's Magazine, The, 1774, by permission of The British Library (SM 5143.624600) 83–4, 84

Lady's Magazine, The, March 1808, by permission of The British Library 247–8

Lady's Monthly Museum, The, by permission of the British Library (SM 5143.62600F) 16–17, 17–18

Lady's Monthly Museum, The, 1799, vol. 2, pp.218–19, by permission of the British Library (SM 5143.62000F) 22–3, 208–9

Lamb, Charles, 'The Superannuated Man', quoted in *The Hutchinson Book of Essays*, ed. Frank Delaney, The Folio Society, 1990 58–9

Le Faye, Deirdre, *Jane Austen, The World of Her Novels*, Francis Lincoln, 2002 167

Letter from Henry Thomas Austen to Bishop of Winchester, 5 November 1816, Winchester diocese ordination papers, Hampshire Record Office (HRO 21M65/E1/4/2601) 49

'Letters from Sir Edward Knatchbull to Fanny, 1820–49', Knatchbull family papers, Centre for Kentish Studies 262

Letters and Prose Writings of William Cowper, The, eds King & Ryskamp, Clarendon, 1979–86 118, 119, 119–20, 121–2, 180

Letters of Tobias Smollett, ed. Lewis Knapp, Clarendon, 1970 255

Life of a Licensed Victualler's Daughter. Written by Herself, 1844, quoted in Caroline Davidson, *A Woman's Work is Never Done, A History of Housework in the British Isles 1650–1950*, Chatto & Windus, 1982 109

Locke, J, eds JW Yalton & S Jean, *Some Thoughts Concerning Education*, 1705, OUP, 1989, by permission of Oxford University Press 71–2, 74, 75, 75–6

Loiterer, The, 7 February 1789, by permission of the British Library (SM 5292.480000N) 42–3

Loiterer, The, 28 March 1789, by

permission of the British Library
(SM 5292.480000N) 82
Loiterer, The, 20 June 1789, by
permission of the British Library
(SM 5292.480000N) 43
Lunar Society of Birmingham, The,
Clarendon, 1963 227, 228

Moritz, Pastor, quoted in Roy Porter,
English Society in the Eighteenth Century,
Allen Lane, 1982 97
[from] Mr Rowlandson's England, ed. John
Steele, Antique Collectors' Club, 1985
123–4, 125–6, 126, 129, 130, 132, 145,
180

Nelson, Lord, letter, in The Nelson
Touch, ed. C Dane, Heinemann, 1942
241–2

Parreaux, André, Daily Life in England in
the Reign of George III, Allen & Unwin,
1969 96
'Poor Robin's Almanac', in Washington
Irving, The Sketch Book of Geoffrey
Crayon, Gent 124–5
[quoted in] Porter, Roy, English Society
in the Eighteenth Century, Allen Lane,
1982 86–7, 143, 146, 146–7, 160, 256

Rogers, Nicholas, Crowds, Culture and
Politics in Georgian Britain, Clarendon,
1998 238
Rudge, Thomas, quoted in Roy Porter,
English Society in the Eighteenth Century,
Allen Lane, 1982 234

Selwyn, David, ed., Jane Austen:
Collected Poems and verse of the Austen
family, p.25, Jane Austen Society, 1996
70–1
Skinner, John, Journal of a Somerset
Rector 1803–1834, eds H & P Coombs,
OUP, 1984 45, 127, 127–8, 128, 231–2
Southey, Robert (Don Manuel Alvarez
Espriella), Letters from England, in
Mr Rowlandson's England, Antique
Collectors' Club, 1985 51

Spas of England and Principal Sea-Bathing
Places, p.9, Henry Colburn, 1841,
quoted from Manning-Sanders, Seaside
England, Batsford, 1951 257
Spectator, by permission of the British
Library 150

Times, The, May 1794, by permission of
the British Library 226
Torrington Diaries: Containing the tours
through England and Wales of the
Hon. John Byng (later fifth Viscount
Torrington) between the years 1781 and
1794, ed. C Bruyn Andrews, Eyre and
Spottiswoode, reprinted Barnes and
Noble, Methuen, 1970, by permission
of Taylor & Francis 155
[from] Trevelyan, GM, English Social
History, Longmans, Green, 1944 101

Vick, Robin, 'Rural Crime', Jane Austen
Society Report, 1996, pp. 41–5, in vol.
V Collected Reports 136
[quoted in] Virgin, Peter, The Church
in an Age of Negligence, James Clarke,
1989 44

Weeton, Ellen, Miss Weeton's Journal as
a Governess, ed. JJ Bagley, David &
Charles 1969 61, 78
Williams, JA, Post-Reformation
Catholicism in Bath, vol. 1, pp.198–9,
Catholic Record Society, 1975–6
237–8
Woodforde, James, The Diary of a
Country Parson, 1758–1802, ed. John
Beresford, OUP, 1949; by permission
of AP Watt Ltd on behalf of Benedict
Beresford 40, 95, 105, 109, 112, 118,
120, 133, 214–15, 222, 260, 261–2,
268–9
Works of Jane Austen Vol VI: Minor
Works, ed. RW Chapman, OUP, 1963,
by permission of Oxford University
Press 22, 97–8, 107, 116, 257–8, 263,
271–2

Index

Acknowledgments

I would like to express my gratitude to the individuals and institutions who have assisted in bringing this book to publication. Special thanks go to Ruth Binney, my editor, for her guidance and enthusiasm, and to my wife Miranda whose knowledge of Jane Austen's literature and practical support were of great help. Librarians, archivists and sundry individuals have made valuable contributions in providing and tracking down important sources, especially unpublished manuscripts; my thanks to them: Bath Reference Library, *Bath Chronicle*, The British Library, Centre for Kentish Studies, David Selwyn, English Faculty Library of Oxford University, Hampshire Record Office, Hartley Library of Southampton University, The Jane Austen Society, London Library, Somerset County libraries.

The publisher would like to thank Val Porter, Beverley Jollands and Anne Plume for editorial work; Tony Hirst for indexing and Tehmina Boman for picture research.

Picture Credits

Cover background © Mary Evans Picture Library; foreground © Musee de la Ville de Paris, Musee Carnavalet, Paris, France/Lauros/Giraudon/The Bridgeman Art Library. **Chapter Openers** all taken from *Pride and Prejudice* by Jane Austen, illustrated by Hugh Thomson, reproduced courtesy of Dover Publications Inc., 31 East 2nd Street, Mineola, NY 11501 USA. **Plates** 1 Private Collection/The Bridgeman Art Library; 2 © 2003 Topham Picturepoint; 3 Private Collection/The Bridgeman Art Library; 4, 5, 6, 7, 8 © 2003 Topham Picturepoint; 9 Private Collection/The Bridgeman Art Library; 10 © Lebrecht Music & Arts; 11 Private Collection/The Stapleton Collection/The Bridgeman Art Library; 12 © 2003 Topham Picturepoint; 13 Abbot Hall Art Gallery, Kendal, Cumbria, UK/The Bridgeman Art Library; 14 Victoria & Albert Museum, London, UK/The Bridgeman Art Library; 15 By permission of the Warden and Scholars of Winchester College; 16 Private Collection/The Bridgeman Art Library; 17 Yale Center for British Art, Paul Mellon Collection, USA/The Bridgeman Art Library; 18 Victoria Art Gallery, Bath and North East Somerset Council/The Bridgeman Art Library; 19 © 2003 Topham Picturepoint; 20 Private Collection/The Bridgeman Art Library; 21 Yale Center for British Art/Paul Mellon Collection, USA/The Bridgeman Art Library; 22 The Art Archive/Bath Museum; 23 Private Collection/The Stapleton Collection/The Bridgeman Art Library; 24 Bibliotheque des Arts Decoratifs, Paris, France/Archives Charmet/The Bridgeman Art Library; 25 Private Collection/The Bridgeman Art Library; 26 © 2003 Topham Picturepoint; 27 Private Collection/The Stapleton Collection/The Bridgeman Art Library; 28 Sarah Jackson/Edifice/CORBIS; 29 Private Collection © Charles Plante Fine Arts/The Bridgeman Art Library; 30 The Art Archive; 31 The British Library/Heritage-Images; 32 British Library, London, UK/The Bridgeman Art Library; 33, 34 Courtesy of the Warden and Scholars of New College, Oxford/The Bridgeman Art Library; 35 British Library, London, UK/The Bridgeman Art Library.

3 1143 00773 6961